THE LOVES OF RICHARD WAGNER

THE LOVES OF
RICHARD WAGNER

BY

JULIUS KAPP

AUTHORISED TRANSLATION

W. H. ALLEN
LONDON
1951

2.97 2.

MADE AND PRINTED IN GREAT BRITAIN BY
THE GARDEN CITY PRESS LIMITED, LETCHWORTH, HERTS

CONTENTS

Permission has been granted to make extracts from the
Burrell Collection of Wagner's letters, edited by John N. Burk,
and published by the Macmillan Co. in America, and by
Victor Gollancz Ltd. in England.

ILLUSTRATIONS

TYPOGRAPHICAL NOTE

*A major portion of this work consists of extracts from letters
written by Wagner.
In order to make for readability, and to differentiate them from
the rest of the text, these extracts are printed throughout the
book in smaller type.
The general text is set in 11 point Garamond, the extracts in
10 point.*

PREFACE

EROS is the fundamental force in all creative art and no more valid proof of this thesis can be found in the whole cultural history of mankind than the life of Richard Wagner. Each and every one of his works, from the first chaotic fragment (" Die Hochzeit ") down to the sublimated swan-song, " Parsifal," was either directly inspired, or its development decisively affected, by an emotional experience. A biography of Wagner centring round Eros therefore becomes automatically a history of his creative achievement. The motley train of women who swirled through his life, the never-ending love song in which the harshest discords invariably melted into a Furioso of intoxicating beauty, lift for us some of the veils concealing the ever inexplicable mystery that is creative genius.

Wagner's turbulent life, which sounded the depths and shoals of human experience, ran the full gamut of the passions. Its broad arc extended from ordinary sensual episodes and trifling entanglements—some tragic, some ludicrous—through a romantic and disastrous marriage and the hopeless frustration of a profound passion (to which we owe the febrile ardours of "Tristan," his most imperishable masterpiece) down to a belated domestic happiness.

In the present work it has been my aim to trace this emotional trajectory (parts of which read like a thrilling romance) and then to show the deeper significance of the love story, thus unfolded, on his creative work. In so doing, I have kept strictly to facts, avoiding all idle rumour and cheap sensationalism, and have based my simple chronicle exclusively on available source material, which includes a large quantity of hitherto inaccessible documents. Any attempt of this kind is open in principle to the quite justifiable objection that the private life of a great man does not concern the public ; that the biographer should call a halt before those things that touch the purely personal life of the individual. But this point of view is only valid if, and so long as, the individual himself preserves the proper discretion.

9

In Wagner's case, however, the very reverse is true. He himself was the first to give publicity—from tendentious motives—to unfortunate episodes in his life and the lives of those most intimately associated with him. Was it necessary, for instance, to expose his first wife's antecedents and early career, disclose certain illicit affairs after her marriage, reveal the secret of her illegitimate child, which she had guarded so carefully all her life, discuss the Laussot episode, depict his relations with the Wesendoncks in such a false light ? The moment that Wagner himself publicized a distorted version of these various incidents, and " semi-official " Wagner literature created further legends based on those Wagner himself had started, serious Wagner research not only had the right but the obligation to verify the prosaic facts for itself.

From a purely human point of view it is quite understandable that the relatives and descendants of a great man should try to suppress as far as possible all his weaknesses and errors, as well as all those facts that conflict with views he sponsored later on ; in other words, to free him of the earth-earthy and let him stand forth in all his ideal greatness. But independent research has nothing in common with this pietistic attitude. For it, the hero under investigation (in this case Wagner) is not a family idol. As a historical personality he has become common property ; a biased interpretation of facts at the cost of those concerned, as Wagner endeavoured to give in his autobiography, cannot be permitted. Justice must also be done those persons with whom he came in contact ; and in so far as authoritative sources are available, tendentiousness of any kind must be replaced by an objective and exact portrayal of the facts.

When this book first appeared in Germany in 1912 I was able, on the basis of the material assembled for my edition of the *Collected Correspondence of Richard Wagner* (over 6,400 letters in all), to rectify a number of facts that had hitherto been incorrectly presented or interpreted through lack of data. Among the most important of these were details touching Wagner's first marriage (based on a number of previously unpublished letters of Minna Wagner), the catastrophe on the Green Hill, *first publication* of the pertinent parts of the famous letter to Mathilde Wesendonck which was intercepted by Minna and now forms part of the Burrell Collection (Exhibit 306), Wagner's liaison with Frederike

Meyer, the Penzing Idyll (letter to Marie), and the romantic episode with his first Isolde, Malwine Schnorr, with then unpublished letters of Wagner treating of this affair. After six successive German editions, followed by translations into French, English, and Swedish, the book was amplified in 1921 and again in 1929 through a quantity of new material that had recently come to light.

The present edition now represents an entirely new work. The text has been greatly expanded and supplemented, a large portion of it has been entirely rewritten, references given in detail to the related documents in the Burrell Collection and letters quoted wholly or in part which have never before appeared in English translation. This material has been derived from several hitherto unpublished letters of Richard and Minna Wagner and the following works :

Jachmann-Kapp : Richard Wagner und seine erste Elizabeth.
Hans von Buelow : Newly published letters.
du Moulin Eckart : Cosima Wagner, ein Lebens- und Charakterbild. Die Herrin von Bayreuth.
Koenig Ludwig II und Richard Wagner : Briefwechsel.
Richard Wagner Briefe an Hans Richter.
Richard Wagner Briefe an Mathilde Maier.
Richard Wagner Briefe an Judith Gautier.
Letters of Richard Wagner—The Burrell Collection, edited by John N. Burk.

With this new material at hand an attempt could be made to clarify the Wagner-Buelow matrimonial tragedy from its beginnings to the disastrous climax, which marked the end of the long friendship between these two men, and to explain its interrelationships and causes. Now, only, was it possible to do full and proper justice to Cosima's rôle in Wagner's life. So here also for the first time the three feminine stars in Wagner's constellation, Minna, Mathilde, Cosima, stand forth, one alongside the other, in full equality of right. Disputation and criticism have been deliberately avoided. The facts speak most clearly and eloquently for themselves.

JULIUS KAPP.

Berlin, January 1951.

CHAPTER I

ADOLESCENT LOVE

" Love gilds the scene, and woman guides the plot."
Richard Brinsley Sheridan.

SIX months after Richard Wagner's birth his father died,[1] and scarcely eight years later a malign fate robbed him of his stepfather, to whom he was sincerely attached. So for the second time the large family was deprived of its head and breadwinner. Ludwig Geyer, who married Richard's mother nine months after her husband's death,[2] passed away just at a time when the unruly young madcap needed the guiding touch of a firm masculine hand. " Every day (wrote a contemporary) Richard leaves the seat of his trousers on the fence ! " So the lad was now left to be brought up by his mother and Rosalie, the eldest of his five sisters, but his real favourite in the family, and his playmate and accomplice in all his boyish escapades, pranks and quarrels was his step-sister Cæcilie, who was nearly two years his junior. In later years Wagner, in his letters to her, repeatedly recalled some amusing or tragi-comic lark of their childhood

" when we two were the ones who were really most closely attached to each other. I have no memories of those days (he wrote on 30th December 1852) in which you do not figure in some way."

Richard also loved his mother devotedly and in after years, when he got into trouble of any kind, he always turned to her and found the way to her heart. His intensely moving tributes to maternal love in " Siegfried " and " Parsifal," which sprang from the innermost depths of his being, furnish eloquent proof of this. A letter written to his mother in 1835, when he was twenty-two, manifests a similar feeling.

[1] Exhibit 14, Burrell Collection. Death certificate of Wagner's father, 23rd November 1813.
[2] Exhibit 13, Burrell Collection. Marriage certificate of Ludwig Geyer and Johanna Wagner, 28th August 1814.

" When I think of the past, it is you alone, dearest mother, whom I recall with the deepest love and most profound emotion. I know quite well that brothers and sisters go their own ways. Each is thinking of himself and his own future and the things concerned therewith. So it is, and I feel it myself; there comes a time when the ways separate of themselves—when external considerations alone govern our relationships to one another. We become friendly diplomats, one towards the other. We keep silence when it seems politic to us to do so, and we speak out when we consider it necessary. And when we are absent from one another, then we talk the most.

" But ah! how far above all this is a mother's love! I'm also one of those persons who can't always express his feelings at the moment. Otherwise you would often have seen me from a far softer side. But the feelings are just the same. And see, mother, now that I'm away from you, I'm so overwhelmed with gratitude for your wonderful love towards your child (of which you have again recently given such warm sincere proof) that I would like to write and tell you of it in the tenderest accents of a lover to his mistress. But oh! far more so—for isn't a mother's love far greater, far purer than any other?

" No! now I'm not going to philosophize. I only want to thank you over and over again—and I should like so much to enumerate all the individual proofs of your love for which I have to thank you—if there weren't so many of them. But I still know that there is certainly no other heart that beats so warmly, so solicitously for me, as yours; that it is perhaps the only one in fact that watches over me at every turn, not with intent to criticize coldly. No, but to remember me in your prayers. Weren't you always the only person who remained absolutely loyal to me when others, judging solely by externals, turned from me with a philosophic shrug? I would indeed be terribly presumptuous if I demanded the same affection from everybody. In fact I know that such a thing is impossible. I realize it myself. With you, everything springs from the heart, from that dear, kind heart which, God grant, may always be inclined towards me; for I know that should all else forsake me, it would always be my last fond refuge.

" O mother, if you should die too soon, before I've proved to you that you have bestowed your love on an honourable and ineffably grateful human being! No, that can never be! You must live on to enjoy many fine rewards. Ah! when I think of this last week with you! It's a perfect boon, a refreshment, to recall to my soul each single aspect of your loving kindness! Dear, dear mother, what a miserable wretch I should be if I were ever to grow cold towards you!"

Even though demonstrations of affection were not common in their family circle, and their dealings (as Wagner said) were marked " by a certain impetuous, almost passionate and boisterous manner," nevertheless the fact that he was brought up entirely among feminine surroundings did not fail to leave a lasting impress on the emotional life of the growing boy. This constant association with women was bound to arouse erotic feelings prematurely, which however first took the form of sentimental moods and daydreams. For instance, the mere touch of his sisters' dresses made his " heart beat so violently " that " it frightened him " and led to his casting languishing glances at other girls. But the feminine world outside his own home first made a powerful impression on him when his mother moved to Prague in 1826 and he was sent to Dresden to lodge with the family of a school friend.

" Grown-up daughters of the family and their girl friends often filled the shabby little rooms (he tells us in *Mein Leben*). I recall that a very lovely well-behaved young girl—whose name was Amalia Hoffmann if I am not mistaken—astonished me so when she entered the room one Sunday in all her best finery (which she was only rarely able to do) that I was bereft of speech for a long time. Other times I remember pretending that I was overcome by sleepiness so that the girls would have to carry me off to bed with all the exertions that my condition seemed to necessitate, because I once found to my excited surprise that such a condition brought me into direct and titillating contact with womankind."

In the winter of that same year Richard's mother took him back with her to Prague for a week, when he made an acquaintance that completely turned his head. Two sisters, Jenny and Auguste Pachta, friends of his sister Ottilie and celebrated beauties later on, altogether bewitched him. He found it very hard to part from them, and the lure proved so great that during the Easter holidays in 1827 he and his schoolmate, Rudolf Boehme, set out for Prague on foot. After numerous adventures on the way they finally reached their destination, thoroughly bedraggled and exhausted. And Richard was not a little grieved and mortified to encounter the real authors of his suffering, these adored friends, on the highway when he was in such a disreputable state before he had had an opportunity to freshen up properly at his mother's. Only after he had rid his face of the sunburn with applications of parsley poultices for two days, and had transformed himself again into the outward semblance of a lover, did he venture to present himself to the idols of his heart. The holidays passed away very quickly. Once more the parting almost broke his heart.

" When on the way home I looked back at Prague (he wrote in *Mein Leben*) from a little hill, I burst into tears, threw myself on the ground, and it was a long time before my astonished friend could persuade me to continue the journey."

But this was the end of the little affair for the time being.

After his return to Dresden this very precocious youth began to lead a rather dissipated life, which was all the easier as he now no longer lived with the Boehmes but had taken a little attic room of his own where he spent his time writing verses instead of doing his lessons.

His mother gladly gave him her consent to go to Leipzig, all the more so as she was moving there herself. The student life in that city had great attraction for him and besides, he had also lost his heart to his sister Louise, whom he had just seen again after an interim of several years. " For the first time (he wrote) a sister treated me with tenderness." One day he saw a wonderful big dog at her house belonging to her friend, Leah David, a lovely Jewish girl of fifteen. Having been a great lover of animals ever since he was a child, he took an immediate fancy to the dog and lost no time in transferring his affection to its owner. Leah was the only daughter of a wealthy banker, and as her mother had died very early she now kept house for her father, who entertained a great deal. So Richard was soon a frequent guest and the affair, especially as far as he was concerned, grew more and more ardent until one day Leah's prospective husband came to call on her, and Richard's beautiful dream vanished into thin air. Whereupon he turned his back on his " friend," richer by a bitter disappointment.

In the meantime he had become more and more irregular in his attendance at school, and to the horror of his family spent all his time in verse making and composing. This latter activity, which had no theoretical foundation and followed this way or that, as the freak took him, came to an abrupt end as the result of an overwhelming impression made on him by Wilhelmine Schroeder-Devrient, when she acted as guest star in Leipzig as Fidelio.

" When I think back on my life as a whole (he wrote later in *Mein Leben*) I can find no event that compares with this in the way it affected me. Anyone who remembers this marvellous woman at this period of her life will be able to testify in one way or another to the almost

RICHARD AND COSIMA WAGNER IN 1872

From a drawing by C. L'Allemand

JOHANNA WAGNER IN 1855

dæmonic ardour which emanated perforce from the ecstatic performance of this incomparable artist. When the performance was over, I rushed off to the house of an acquaintance of mine to write a short note in which I briefly informed the great artist that from that moment my life had acquired its true significance, and if she should ever hear my name mentioned in a praiseworthy way in the world of art, she should remember that on this evening she had made me what I then and there vowed I was going to become. I left this letter at her hotel and ran out into the night like one possessed. . . .

"I did not know how to set to work, how to start, in order to create something myself in direct proportion to the impression I had received. And everything that had no bearing on this seemed so shallow and worthless to me that I was unable to occupy myself with it. I wanted to write a work that would be worthy of Schroeder-Devrient; but as this was absolutely impossible, I dropped all artistic endeavours in my headlong despair, and since academic subjects also failed to interest me I turned directly to life, drifting aimlessly into all kinds of youthful excesses in company with a strange assortment of companions. The really dissolute period of adolescence now began for me."

After overcoming family opposition through his passive resistance to school, Richard became a *Studiosus musicæ* in earnest and thoroughly enjoyed all the pleasures of student life. Homage was paid to Venus no less than to Bacchus, while a third and far more dangerous tempter, the Demon of Gambling, was soon added to these two.

"Despair over my losses (he continued) heightened the passion to the point of madness. . . . I was even completely indifferent to the contempt of my sister Rosalie, who with my mother scarcely deigned to look at the incomprehensible young profligate who, pale and distraught, rarely put in an appearance at home. In my growing desperation I finally had recourse to the radical expedient of boldly defying my bad luck. I felt that I could only win by hazarding larger amounts, and I therefore decided to use for this purpose a fairly large sum that had been entrusted to me, namely, my mother's pension which I had collected for her. That night I lost every penny that I had, except one *thaler*. . . . On this I staked my life. For a return to my family was now out of the question. I saw myself fleeing at dawn across the fields and through the woods into the unknown, like the Prodigal Son. I was so desperate that when my card won, I immediately staked my gain again and repeated the procedure a number of times until my winnings amounted to a fairly substantial sum.

"I now had a run of luck. I grew so confident that I took the wildest risks. Then it suddenly struck me in a flash that I was playing that day for the last time. My luck was so conspicuous that the croupiers decided it would be just as well to close shop. I had actually not only won back all the money I had lost but also the sum total of all my debts. The glow that filled me more and more during the proceedings had something solemn about it. As my luck increased I had the distinct feeling that God or His angel was standing beside me whispering warning and consolation.

" Once again I had to climb over the gate at dawn to reach my room. There I fell into a deep and invigorating sleep from which I awoke late, physically refreshed and mentally purified. No feeling of shame kept me from voluntarily making a clean breast to my mother (when I gave her back her money) of the events of this fateful night and also of my misuse of her property. She folded her hands and thanked God for His mercy towards me and expressed her firm belief that I was saved and that it would be impossible for me to succumb to similar temptations in the future. As a matter of fact that temptation had lost its power over me forever. . . .The passion for gambling had already made me completely indifferent to all other student follies. Freed from this passion, I found myself confronted all at once by an entirely new world to which I belonged from then on, filled with hitherto unknown zeal for my musical education, which now entered a new phase for me."

Richard now gave himself up in earnest to his studies with Theodor Weinlig, Cantor at St. Thomas's Church, and soon had the satisfaction of seeing several of the compositions written under his teacher's supervision meet with public acclaim. Just at this time he became seriously attached to the young singer, Marie Löw,[1] but the feeling was not reciprocated, owing chiefly to the restless, eccentric manner of the young *Musikus*. But the two always remained good friends from then on. In the midsummer of 1832 Richard took a trip to Vienna and returned by way of Bohemia as he was anxious to see the Pachta sisters again. He stayed five weeks on the Count's estate in Provonin.

" O what heavenly days ! (he wrote his friend Theodor Apel on 16th December 1832). For not only Nature but also Love ennobles me ! And to what an extent ! Imagine Jenny as an ideal of beauty— and with my glowing imagination, you have the whole story. My passion fancied it saw in her beauty everything that could make her a glorious apparition. My idealizing eye saw in her all it wanted to see ; and this was the misfortune ! I fancied my feeling was reciprocated and all that was needed was a bold advance on my part to ensure her response ! But what a response ! An uneasy presentiment deterred me. And yet what a struggle I had with my tempestuous passions ! At

---

[1] Mother of Lilli Lehmann.

night my dreams were disturbed. I often awoke dreaming I had avowed my love, and sensed nothing but the night that crushed me with painful foreboding."

The old youthful flame had suddenly blazed up anew. Wild passions raged through him and moments when he was ardent, dreamy, and lovelorn alternated with hours of blind jealousy and insufferable priggishness.

"Evening was coming on (he wrote his friend Apel on 12th December). I sat alongside Jenny at the piano when suddenly my emotion overflowed. To conceal my tears from her, I rushed outdoors to the castle. Ach! there in front of me glowed the evening star! I fixed my gaze on it—it absorbed my tears. I became calmer, yet I still could not define my feelings. Then the evening bells rang out. This cleared up everything for me. It was without doubt the same feeling that possessed you when you wrote your ' Abendglocken.' I hurried to my room, took the poem from my portfolio, and improvised on it at the piano.[1]

"I soon remarked to my disgust (he confessed in *Mein Leben*) a very superficial knowledge of æsthetics ; yet on the other hand a very pronounced facility in everything touching externals. None of my enthusiastic pronouncements on the finer issues of life, that now in particular appealed to me, met with any response whatsoever on the part of the girls. I inveighed passionately against the trashy novels of the lending library which formed their sole reading; against the Italian arias that Auguste sang ; and finally against the horsy, brainless cavaliers who now and then put in an appearance to pay court to the two in an indelicate way that revolted me. In fact it was my zeal on this latter score that soon caused a great rumpus. I became rough and offensive, pontificated at length on the spirit of the French Revolution and went so far as to advise the girls in a fatherly manner to stick, for heaven's sake, to the educated middle class and to have done with the presumptuous aristocracy, an association that could only ruin their reputations.

"I often had to resort to sharp retorts in an effort to rebuff the indignation aroused by these expostulations of mine. However, I never apologized but tried through the feigned or the real jealousy that possessed me to give, in the long run, a more bearable and flattering turn to the annoying element in my angry outbursts. So, undecided whether I was in love or was angry with them, but nevertheless on the best of terms, I took leave of the pretty youngsters on a cold November day, to meet the family again in Prague a little later on."

It is easy to understand the unexpected turn which the affair took shortly afterwards if one takes into consideration the

[1] Both Apel's poem and Wagner's setting of it are now lost.

peculiar family circumstances of the two girls. They were the illegitimate daughters of Count Pachta through an affair with a beautiful but rather ordinary Frau Raymann. Since it was impossible for Count Pachta to marry their mother since he and she were both married, though separated from their spouses, the two girls were torn between the hope of making an aristocratic marriage and the necessity of accepting a wealthy commoner. At the time of Wagner's visit there was no lack of aristocratic suitors (for the girls were considered great beauties), so poor Richard, who was penniless into the bargain, was in a fair way to meet with a rebuff. Fate also stepped in quickly to settle the matter. He continued to pay court to Jenny until one evening when he went to call and found that Frau Raymann kept him out in the anteroom while the young ladies, arrayed in their very best for the occasion, entertained the detested cavaliers in the drawing-room, which brought home the situation to him in its full import.

" Everything which up till then I had failed to understand in certain love intrigues, namely, in some of the Tales of Hoffmann, now become horribly vivid to me, and I left Prague with an evidently exaggerated and unjust idea of things and persons."

A contemporary letter to his friend Apel explains this rather cryptic remark in *Mein Leben* : " I was in Prague again (he wrote) and spoke there to the mistresses of Count Baer and Baron Bethmann, the girls we knew formerly as Jenny and Auguste."

" Listen to this, and give me your sympathy ! (he wrote Apel on 16th December under the shock of his bitter disappointment). She was unworthy of my love ! The chill of death descended upon my spirit. Oh ! if I could only have renounced at once all my fond hopes ; if I could have turned to ice, I should have counted myself happy ! But to feel every spark of the once so brilliant flame die out one by one ; to see each atom of a glowing hope fade away little by little ; to see the nimbus of spiritual beauty melt away hour by hour ! O, that wrings tears from one, the bitterness of which can be felt but never expressed ! When I wanted to warm myself with the last remnant of my fire and felt it die out more and more under the breath of death, I looked back as though paralyzed into the fiery stream of the past, into the icy caverns of the future ! Enough—enough ! and already far too much ! For in spite of the aching void in my breast, I still feel a craving for love. . . .It was under such conditions that I began to write the poem for my opera."

In this opera (" Die Hochzeit "), his first dramatic attempt, he took a gruesome romantic episode that had made a great impression on him when he first read it, and blended it in true Hoffmannesque style with his own tragic love affair to form a " Gloomy Tale of the Deepest Hue." But his sister Rosalie, who, as shown by one of his later letters to her, was probably the only member of the family who knew of his thwarted wooing, saw nothing attractive in this grisly tale. So in order to show her how greatly he valued her opinion, he at once consigned to the flames the lovely work in which he had taken such pride. Only one brief fragment, which he had already set to music, survived the holocaust. Richard really adored this sister, whose charming manner, motherly character and financial solicitude and provision for the large family made her a sort of guardian angel.

" It had become a major ambition with me (he wrote in retrospect) to bring this sister (who was just about to give me up as lost) round at last to follow my work with respect and keen expectation. Under such circumstances I at last developed a tender, in fact an almost effusive, affection for Rosalie ; which in purity of sentiment and genuine warmth can only be compared with the noblest relationship between man and woman. . . .Though her histrionic talent was nothing to speak of, her imagination, her appreciation of art and the finer things of life, however, were all the keener. It was from her that I first heard the gushing enthusiasm for all those things that later moved me so greatly myself."

As Wagner had meanwhile completed his apprenticeship with Weinlig, he was anxious to secure a minor engagement where he could acquire the practical experience that he lacked and at the same time earn his living. Therefore in January 1833 he accepted an invitation from his eldest brother Alfred to go to Würzburg, where the latter, as singer and actor, held an influential position. In view of this it was a simple matter for him to secure a post for Richard as chorus director at a salary of 10 *gulden* a month.[1] Wagner threw himself into the duties of his new office with the characteristic zeal and impetuosity of a newcomer, and tasted all the joys and sorrows afforded by such a little provincial theatre with its gay and irresponsible stage people. A pretty pile of debts at the end of the year was the regrettable outcome. History is silent regarding his amorous exploits during this glorious

---

[1] One *gulden* was approximately 2s. ; 1 *thaler*=3s. ; 1 *Louisdor*=16s. ; 1 *Friedrichsdor*= 16s. 9d. ; and 1 *ducat*=9s. 4d.

period as chorus director except for his own account in his autobiography, which is far too naïve a tale to lay much claim to completeness.

" It was quite natural (he writes there) that one of the young singers in the chorus, whom I had to coach every day, understood how to attract my attention. The lovely soprano voice of Therese Ringelmann, a gravedigger's daughter, led me to believe that I must train her to become a great singer. After I made the suggestion to her, she took particular pains to dress herself for the chorus rehearsals, and by winding a string of pearls in her hair, knew how to fire my imagination.

" In the summer when I remained behind alone, I gave Therese regular singing lessons according to a method which remains a mystery to me to this day. I also went frequently to her house, where I always met her mother and sister, though I never saw her gruesome father. We also met in the public park ; but a feeling of shame, that was not very creditable, kept me from admitting my liaison to my friends. I really cannot say whether this was due to the modest circumstances of the family, to Therese's real lack of education, or my own doubts as to the sincerity of my affection. I only know that when a more express declaration was demanded of me and I also began to be jealously suspicious in the bargain, the liaison soon vanished into thin air.

" I had a more ardent liaison with Friederike Galvani, the daughter of a mechanic of very definite Italian origin. As she was very musical with a charming and extremely flexible voice, my brother had taken her under his wing and helped her make her début at the theatre, which proved a great success. Very slight in figure, but with big black eyes and an affectionate disposition, she had already captured the capable first oboeist of the orchestra, a thoroughly good musician who was deeply in love with her. He was considered her fiancé, but was not permitted to enter her parents' house before the wedding (which was still sometime in the future) because of some shady incident in his past.

" As autumn approached, I was invited by several friends, including our oboeist and his fiancée, to a country wedding a few hours from Würzburg. Everything was very gay in typical country fashion. There was drinking and dancing, and I myself tried to recover my one-time facility on the violin without, however, being able to manage the second violin part even to the tolerable satisfaction of my fellow musicians. However, I had all the greater personal success with the good Friederike with whom I danced madly up and down several times between the rows of peasants until the time came when the general excitement banished all personal discretion, even for us, and we actually kissed and fondled each other while the official lover played for the dancing. The fact that the fiancé, on noting the tender nonchalance and ingenuousness of Friederike's behaviour towards me, accepted his lot sadly, without actually raising any objections, awakened in me for the first time in my life a flattering self-assurance. . . .

" The Frankish wine contributed its share to an ever-increasing confusion, under cover of which Friederike and I at length behaved quite openly as lovers. Late in the night, in fact as dawn was breaking, we all drove back to Würzburg on a rackwagon. This was the snug triumph of my charming adventure. While all the rest, including in the end the worried oboeist, slept off their debauch in the early morning hours, I, reclining with my cheek against Friederike's, watched the sun come up amid the songs of the larks.

" During the days that followed we had scarcely any consciousness of what had happened. A not unbecoming shame kept us away from each other. However, I easily won access to her family and from then on was a welcome daily visitor and spent several hours in undisguised love-making in the very circle from which the unfortunate fiancé was barred. This last liaison was never mentioned in any way and Friederike never had even the slightest notion of making any change. It never occurred to anyone that I perhaps should take the fiancé's place. The confidence with which I was accepted by everybody, and most of all by Friederike, had altogether the character of a natural phenomenon, pretty much as when spring comes and winter is done. Logical middle-class conclusions never occurred to anyone, and this is what made this first love affair so pleasant and flattering. For it never degenerated in any way into a relationship giving rise to scruples or worry. This liaison only ended with my departure from Würzburg, when we bade one another the most tender and tearful farewell."

This innocent idyll, which is sung so warmly by Wagner, was not without its amusing side when we find him writing to Apel a year and a half later : " Oh, by the way ! I was in Würzburg again. In the meantime my girl had had a baby—a country bumpkin was my fortunate rival." He also gave an account of this latter incident in *Mein Leben*, in which he treated Friederike with due gentleness, though tending to delude the reader regarding the parentage of the child. " Her oboeist (he wrote) remained faithful to her. But although marriage between them was impossible she became a mother. Then I never heard anything more of her."

He returned to Leipzig early in January 1834 with the complete score of his opera, " Die Feen." But in spite of the most zealous efforts on his part he was unable to get the director to produce the work, which his sister Rosalie had already persuaded the theatre management to accept. It was continually postponed on one pretext or another. Finally Wagner consoled himself by looking forward to the winter. The middle of June he left on a holiday trip to Teplitz with his friend Theodor Apel,[1] where he worked out the plot of his " Liebesverbot." The proximity of Prague, the scene of his unfortunate love affair with Jenny (which still rankled inwardly), now lured him anew. First of all he wanted his friend to " experience the same impressions as those which had once touched him there so deeply " and at the same time he longed to have his revenge. So with this in mind he introduced Apel to the Pachta-Raymann family who had been living in Prague since the death of the old Count.

" My friend was well received. The change in the family circumstances forced the charming girls more and more to come to a decision regarding their future, and a rich commoner (provided he was not actually in trade but had inherited property) seemed nevertheless a satisfactory expedient to the worried mother."

Wagner himself played the rôle of the gay libertine and revelled in the great impression made by his very well-to-do friend, particularly on the match-making mother. That such hopes on her part were vain gave him a cheap satisfaction for his own unfortunate experiences.

" Only once did it come to a more serious approach (he wrote in his autobiographical recollections). I was sitting at the piano and heard my friend telling the ladies that in the course of a conversation in a hotel I had found occasion to praise the domestic qualities and efficiency of my friends in the warmest manner to one who seemed surprised at this information. It now touched me deeply to see from the effect of this announcement what painful experiences the poor dears must have had, since this gesture on my part (which seemed so natural to me) moved them like some wholly unexpected happiness. Jenny came over to me, flung her arms round me and kissed me very heartily. From now on my right to conduct myself in the most ill-bred manner was unanimously conceded, and even jests and tomfoolery were my only response to Jenny's demonstrative outburst."

" I was very delighted to see the Raymanns (he wrote his sister Rosalie from Prague in July 1834). They are getting on well. Jenny has gone off very little in looks, while Auguste has grown even prettier than ever. Apel has left. The legacy matter has turned out most advantageously for the girls. It is estimated they will each get 30,000 Austrian florins. I could thrash that beast, the old lady, every time I

[1] Theodor Apel, who was two years younger than Wagner, was a fellow student at the St. Nicholas School. His father, the famous poet, who was a good friend of Adolf Wagner, left his son very well off at his death.

see her. Now is a fortunate turning point for the girls. If they take advantage of it and break loose, they can come out of the business quite well. If not, they can still go with the talented crowd and enjoy life—also not so bad ! "

They did both. First they enjoyed life and then married into the Austrian aristocracy.

When Wagner got back to Leipzig he was greeted by the news that he had been offered the post of musical director in Magdeburg. He naturally accepted it, but this marked the end of the carefree years of youth. He was now faced by the realities of life ; a position and the necessity of earning his own living were now his first consideration.

Chapter II

MINNA

" Du wilder Mann, so nimm mich hin ! "
                                        Liebesverbot.

THE Magdeburg dramatic and operatic troupe headed by Heinrich Edward Bethmann, a perfect specimen of the idle, chronically bankrupt provincial director, toured the smaller Thuringian watering-places during the summer months, and at the time of Wagner's appointment happened to be playing in Lauchstadt. When the new conductor arrived on the scene he was so disgusted with the management and found not only the members of the Bethmann troupe but the condition of things in general so lamentable that he at once firmly made up his mind to renounce the doubtful honour of being a member of the company. But Eros had other plans in store for him. The wily god chose the most seductive arrow in Lauchstadt's quiver, drew his bow, and hit the bull's eye. By chance the leading lady of the company (Minna Planer) sailed into the orbit of the young music director.

" Her looks and bearing (he wrote long afterwards) were in striking contrast to all the unpleasant impressions of the theatre that I had just received. Very charming and fresh in outward appearance, the young actress was distinguished by great poise and a grave assurance of manner and behaviour, which lent an agreeable, captivating dignity to the friendly expression of her face. Her scrupulously neat and modest dress completed the startling effect of the wholly unexpected encounter. After I had been introduced to her in the vestibule as the new music director, and she had taken stock, with amazement, of the very youthful candidate for this title, she kindly recommended me to her landlady as a lodger, and walked with quiet dignity across the street to the rehearsal. I took the room on the spot, agreed to conduct " Don Giovanni " on the following Sunday,[1] regretted not having

---

[1] Wagner, on arrival, learned that the Merseburg town band had refused to come to Lauchstadt for rehearsal, so he announced to Bethmann that he would have to find another conductor for " Don Giovanni." The unexpected encounter with Minna made him view the situation differently.

brought my luggage with me from Leipzig, and hurried back there as
fast as possible in order to return all the sooner to Lauchstadt."

He and his fellow lodger soon became the best of friends. He
thought of her as a " fairy caught in a dust-cloud of frivolity and
vulgarity who had been swept (one did not know how) into this
maelstrom. It never carried her away, however ; in fact it scarcely
touched her, for she stood out completely from her surroundings
by virtue of her unadorned solidity and exquisite neatness as well
as by the absence of all theatrical affectation and stagey airs."
And Minna accepted the impetuous wooing of her young adorer
with amiable astonishment, and responded with a quiet friendliness and composure that had something almost maternal in it.

After a few weeks the company moved on to Rudolstadt, and
here, to Wagner's great chagrin, a change came over Minna. It
seems that gossip had come to her ears that people were beginning
to couple her name with that of the music director. And Minna
was exceedingly careful of her reputation. In fact every night
she had the landlady lock the door of her room so as to quash
any theatre gossip of that kind right at the outset. At that time
she was generally regarded in her own circle as the fiancée of a
young nobleman who, however, being entirely without means,
was finally obliged, in consideration for his family and career, to
give up Minna and marry for money. This painful turn in her
affairs occurred while the troupe was playing in Rudolstadt, and
in her deep grief she remained cool to Wagner's impetuous
wooing, the sincerity of which she had every reason to doubt.
He was in despair.

" I am completely out of sorts (he wrote his friend Apel in September
1834) and my soul wallows in emptiness and inanity. In addition I
have let all my love affairs fizzle out."

Two days later, however, this despair was already a little modified.

" For the moment I am pretty free of love affairs (he wrote in his
next letter). I have no time for them, but I am keeping on with Toni
a bit. *Ach, du lieber Gott !* but that's the extent of it ! "

Yet not even Toni (who is not mentioned in his autobiography)
seems to have been able to soothe his despair and his jealous anger
over Minna's behaviour. He began to lead a reckless life with
frivolous companions, succumbed again to the vice of gambling,
and, as he confessed to Apel, got himself into such a mess of

debts that his hair fairly stood on end. " Excesses of all kinds have involved me still further (he wrote), but disappointed hopes have also played their part in my fate." Apel came to his rescue with 200 *thalers*.

Even after moving to Magdeburg at the beginning of October 1834 there was at first little change in his relations with Minna and his thoughtless dissipation as the result of the situation. In fact his jealousy took still more dangerous forms as Minna was very popular with all the gay young blades of Magdeburg.

" So we spent three unhappy months in ever-increasing estrangement from each other (he wrote) during which time, in sheer desperation, I pretended to take pleasure in the most promiscuous company and behaved in every way in such a shockingly reckless manner that Minna—as she told me afterwards—felt the deepest and most sympathetic anxiety for me. Furthermore, since the female personnel of the troupe showed the young conductor not altogether innocent attentions, and one young lady in particular, whose reputation was none of the best, appeared to set her cap at me, Minna's anxiety seemed to have moved her to take decisive action.

" The notion struck me to treat the wonderful élite of our opera personnel to oysters and punch in my room on New Year's Eve. The men were invited with their wives, and now the question was whether I could also persuade the unmarried Fräulein Planer to come to my party. She accepted without any embarrassment and arrived, neatly and modestly dressed as always, at my bachelor's apartment, where the party soon got into full swing. I had already warned the landlord of the storm that would break over his house and pacified him by assuming responsibility for any damage to the furniture. What the champagne failed to accomplish was finally achieved by the punch. All the bounds of that limited propriety that my guests usually sought to observe were broken, and gave way to general affability, no one raising any objections. It could now be seen how Minna stood out from all her companions through her really queenly composure. She never lost her dignity. No one attempted to take any liberties with her and the effect was all the greater (in the end, completely sobering in fact) when Minna, without any embarrassment, responded to my friendly and really affectionate caresses. This made clear to the entire company the exact nature of our relations, which could not be compared with that of any of the others. We had the strange satisfaction of seeing the young lady of easy virtue, who apparently had designs on me, go into convulsions over this discovery. From then on I remained on terms of intimate friendship with Minna."

Whenever Wagner called, an older colleague of Minna's (Frau Haas) was always present, apparently in the rôle of chaperone.

But she soon proved herself unfitted for the task, as she had not been altogether impervious to the attentions which the young Don Juan had previously shown her, and now became jealous of her favoured rival. In order to remove this last obstacle Wagner hatched up a dark plot. He himself tells how he engineered it and attained the goal of his wishes in a far from usual way; finding himself thereby in the bed of his mistress.

" One evening (reads the account in *Mein Leben*) I had promised to take tea with Minna and her older friend. I had inadvertently arranged a whist game, and bored though I was, kept on playing nevertheless, as I intended to go on to Minna's later when her troublesome colleague had left. I only succeeded in holding out with the aid of alcoholic beverages and I therefore had the odd experience of leaving a sober whist party in a completely intoxicated state, which had come upon me so imperceptibly that I really could not believe it. This incredulity induced me to keep my late tea engagement. To my terrific annoyance, I found the older friend still there, which immediately brought my intoxication to a head. When the lady, in a would-be joking way, expressed her surprise over my strangely violent and offensive behaviour towards her, I jeered at her in such a rude manner that, highly indignant, she at once got up and left !

" By that time I was only sober enough to take in Minna's hearty and astonished laughter over my unheard-of behaviour. Then calmly and good-naturedly she came to a nevertheless difficult decision. For my condition was soon so serious that there was no question of my leaving or of her getting me home without attracting considerable attention. Then, too, she was very sorry for me. She made me comfortable, and since I soon fell into a deep sleep, she gave up her bed to me without hesitation, and there I slept on into the wonderful dawn.

" Without frivolous joking, without wantonness or levity of any kind, we breakfasted decorously and soberly together, and then went for a long walk outside the fortifications at an hour in the morning when this could be done under such ticklish circumstances without attracting attention. We then parted, and from that time on gave ourselves up freely and without any embarrassment to our tender interests as openly acknowledged lovers."

From an artistic point of view the climax of the first Magdeburg winter was a guest engagement of Schroeder-Devrient, whose mature art thrilled Wagner anew. This time he made the acquaintance of the artist and she offered of her own volition to sing at his benefit concert. She arrived punctually on the appointed day, but the canny Magdeburgers had taken the announcement of her appearance as a publicity stunt of the beneficiary and were conspicuous by their absence. Devrient accepted the unusual situation very good naturedly and bore Wagner no grudge as a result of it. But the fiasco banished the last hope of paying his debts and being able to leave Magdeburg in a fairly decent manner. After he had put off the more pressing of his creditors with some difficulty he returned to Leipzig at the beginning of May in order to raise some money. Minna had to remain in Magdeburg for the time being, as the theatre was not yet closed, but she promised to visit him shortly when she went to Dresden to see her parents so they could work out their plans together for the coming season. Wagner wrote her glowing love-letters during their short separation, the earliest of which is dated from Leipzig on 6th May 1835.[1]

" Minna was here (he wrote Apel on the 6th June) and for my sake stayed three days, in the vilest weather, without going anywhere—just to be with me. That sort of thing is touching ; it's remarkable what an influence I have acquired over the girl ! You should read her letters— they are burning with passion, and as both of us know, that is not her nature at all. She sends you her kind regards."

Minna was staying with her family in Dresden, and Wagner naturally longed to join her there. Finally a music festival in Dessau provided the longed-for excuse of leaving Leipzig and his family without causing comment. He found Minna all ready to return to Magdeburg, but he nevertheless prevailed on her to join him in an excursion to the Saxon Alps, and the memory of the carefree happy hours of love when they lay awake in the romantic summer nights remained with them vividly for many years.

Wagner had also signed another contract with Bethmann for the winter on Minna's account, and arrived in Magdeburg in the autumn of 1835 after his friend Apel had rescued him from his tormentors there with 400 *thalers*. This season the company was on a much higher artistic plane, thanks to some artists whom Wagner had fortunately engaged during the summer on behalf of the director. Among these was his first Leipzig flame, Marie Löw, who was not only an excellent singer but also played the harp like a master. In Rossini's " Othello," for instance, she

[1] This letter is missing from Minna's published correspondence. The original is in the Burrell Collection (49).

always sang Desdemona's Willow Song to her own harp accompaniment.[1] Among Wagner's new singers was Minna's younger sister Amalie, whom he had engaged

" because (as he wrote Apel) of her beautiful contralto voice ; and I have now coached her in Romeo.[2] Few beginners have made such a sensation as she ; the public went absolutely mad over her. The opera had to be repeated straight away before a packed house, and the applause was as great as that for Devrient."

Wagner's relationship with Minna was unchanged. The only slightly disturbing element was her mother's protracted visit. The latter looked a little askance on the liaison, which moved them to take a more serious arrangement into consideration. Wagner's letters to Apel furnish a far more reliable and correct picture of his feelings for Minna at that time than his account in *Mein Leben*.

" Love gives me more strength than all the concepts of morality (he wrote his friend). A high flown, sentimental love affair would enervate me now ; but mine makes me happy and gay."

" Don't worry about Minna ! (he wrote on another occasion). I'm leaving it all to fate. She loves me and her love means a great deal to me now. She is now the focal point of my life, and gives me consistency and warmth. I can't give her up. I only know this much, dear Theodor, that you still haven't any idea of the sweetness of such a relationship. There is nothing vulgar, unworthy, or enervating in it. Our epicureanism is pure and strong—not a miserable illicit liaison. We love each other and believe in each other. The rest we leave to fate. You, of course, know nothing about this and one can only live in this way with an actress. This indifference to convention can only be found where the whole soil is whimsical caprice and poetic licence."

Outer events were soon to bind the lovers still more closely. Minna felt herself slighted at the Magdeburg Theatre because a rival, the wife of the leading stage manager, was always given preference when the rôles were assigned. So she accepted a guest engagement at the Königstädttische Theatre in Berlin. Wagner was in despair.

---

[1] This once led to a rather serious contretemps. Wagner was conducting, and when Marie Löw noticed him turning back the pages of the score she called down from the stage to " go on " (*Weiter! Weiter!*). The audience understood " *Feuer!* " (fire), and a panic broke out, though the error was quickly explained so that the performance could continue.
[2] In Bellini's opera " Montecchi e Capuletti."

" Minna left for Berlin early yesterday (he reported to Apel) and I can't tell you how I feel ! This isn't being in love ; this *is love itself* ! She is guesting there. Perhaps she will also stay there altogether as she has had numerous collisions here with a Mme Grabowsky. What a state I'm in ! *Mein Gott! Mein Gott!* If I wanted to be up to date, now would be the proper time for me to break things off. But there it is ! My heart is broken—in regular bourgeois fashion—broken ! "

In the most ardent of love letters, he daily implored his " sweet love " to come back to him.

" We must be married at Easter (he wrote) come what may. . . . No woman has ever been loved so much. I suspect you left Magdeburg surreptitiously with the fixed intention of not coming back to me any more. . . . But I'll carry you off by force. . . . I have brains and talent, and when I once have you, I'll have an incentive to make something of them."

He complained of Minna's cool reserve[1] and threatened if she continued to refuse to marry him that " he would take to drink and go to the devil as soon as possible."[2]

" You should have seen me during that fortnight when Minna was away from me ! (he wrote Apel again). Good God ! how that girl has bewitched me, without her having really meant to do so ! My brother-in-law Wolfram was in Berlin when she was there, stayed at the same hotel and was her constant escort and protector ; and he, who was dreadfully prejudiced against her by my family in the beginning, has altered his opinion so completely through her love for me and her exemplary behaviour that he writes me : ' Be true to her ! If any woman deserves it, she does ! ' She made a sensation in Berlin and turned down more than four offers that were made her on the spot. The devil ! That touches a man ! "

After Wagner had settled Minna's dispute with the director she declined for his sake a brilliant engagement offered her in Berlin, and returned to Magdeburg. On a very stormy winter's night he left by special post-chaise to meet his beloved, and, weeping for joy, brought her back in triumph to the Magdeburg home that had become so dear to them both.

" Let anyone come now and turn up his nose at my love for Minna (he wrote) and I'll bash it in for him ! God knows how and what I should now be without her ! "

---

[1] She only sent two evasive replies to his six tempestuous avowals, which he called " an infidelity." Burrell Collection, 9th November 1834.

[2] Letters of the 4th and 11th November 1834, now in the Burrell Collection.

MATHILDE WESENDONCK'S FAVOURITE PICTURE OF WAGNER,
TAKEN IN BRUSSELS IN 1860

MINNA WAGNER

But the Magdeburg joys soon came to a catastrophic end. The theatre went bankrupt, and all hopes of wiping out his burden of debts (which had again mounted to an alarming figure) through the promised benefit performance of his " Liebesverbot " were dashed in a tragi-comic manner through a fracas that broke out among the cast before the performance, in the course of which the leading singer was injured and was unable to appear. Minna helped her lover in his difficulties as best she could and also succeeded in diverting the threatened arrest for debt ; but there was no satisfying the creditors. In the meantime she and her colleague Marie Löw had taken the clever precaution to sign a contract with the Koenigsberg Theatre[1] as the director there had promised to keep the post of conductor (which was expected to be vacant shortly) open for Wagner. The two lovers bade each other a woeful farewell, and Minna then set out on her arduous eastward journey, hoping soon to be able to send for her friend.

But the conditions in Koenigsberg were not very promising for Wagner. The former music director (Louis Schuberth), who had already been engaged at Riga but was unable to take up his duties owing to a delay in the construction work on the theatre, showed no signs of leaving. He also was in love with the prima donna of the company, and now naturally intrigued with all his might and main against his designated successor. In spite of this far from happy prospect, Wagner, who was tortured by baseless jealousy of Minna, set off for Koenigsberg on 7th July 1836. In his letters to Minna from Berlin dated 5th to 21st and 22nd to 26th June 1835,[2] he had already pressed her urgently to marry him. But she felt that his material circumstances did not justify marriage.

Since she was very popular at the theatre in Koenigsberg, Wagner (as her official fiancé) was also well received. But the discouraging plight in which he found himself, the miserable rôle that he played as Minna's lover waiting for his position, the intrigues initiated against him, and the cheerless surroundings drove him to despair. The only thing that kept him going and helped him bear the undignified situation was his love for Minna.

---

[1] This contract is contained in the Burrell Collection (dated 28th March 1836), Exhibit 65.

[2] Exhibits 71 and 72, Burrell Collection.

C

But here, too, he suffered foolish torments, and through his jealousy (which naturally always found fresh fuel with such a popular actress) embittered for both of them the hours they spent together, especially since his rôle of lover gave him no claim over Minna in the eyes of the world. In fact it jeopardized her position. The situation became more and more untenable as time went on, so he decided to put an end to it by legalizing their relation.

" In order to give ourselves a right to be jealous, that is, to keep everybody else away from the object of our desire (he wrote Minna many years later) we enter into alliances and arrangements which are solely intended to assure us legal ownership, without ever stopping to think, and without considering whether other circumstances justify it ; in fact, we even fail to consider whether we are going to ensure the happiness of the object of our selfish desire thereby, or on the contrary, to endanger it seriously. This is the basis of all so-called love matches. Here no attention is paid to material circumstances. A simple survey of the situation, calm deliberation, would show us that perhaps just at this time (given existing circumstances and the precariousness of our material situation and everything connected therewith) the consequences cannot help but be confusing, depressing, distressing and worrisome. But blind craving for the exclusive possession of the loved one destroys all reason. Obstinacy wins out and—the results : anxiety, misery, and a hard life, stemming from an immature, socially wholly unsound, and materially highly precarious situation, are unavoidable and all the more acute and grievous, the more mercurial and hot-headed the individuals that draw them down on themselves."

Abraham Moeller, an older friend of the two, who was a great patron of the theatre, interceded in the matter and helped Wagner to carry out his plans. On the basis of an offer the two of them had received from Danzig, Moeller persuaded the manager of the theatre to give Wagner a definite promise of the post of musical director from Easter 1837 and authorize a wedding benefit performance for the pair under Wagner's direction. For this performance Wagner chose Auber's " Masaniello," in which Minna took the part of the dumb girl Fenella. They had a great deal of trouble to obtain the necessary documents for the marriage as Wagner was not yet of age according to Prussian law. But Moeller again proved a friend in need and knew how to get round the difficulties. As these official documents are fairly unknown they are quoted in full herewith exactly as they appear in the Register of the little church in Tragheim.

Entry No. 22—1836, dated Dresden 27th October 1836

Dear Herr Music Director :

We duly received your esteemed communication of the 9th instant and reply to same without delay. Of course, your news came as a great surprise, but our joy was only all the greater and more comforting to our hearts. It is with sincere pleasure that we hereby give our full consent to your marriage with our beloved daughter Minna, and at the same time send you our parental blessings from afar. We feel confident that your true and faithful love will certainly make our good daughter happy, even as we also earnestly beg and exhort her always, in all circumstances of life, to fulfil those obligations which she will assume before God, the Omnipotent, in the hour of her nuptial benediction.

You may be assured that our warmest and sincerest wishes will accompany you both at this important turning point in your lives, and nothing would give us greater pleasure than to welcome you and our daughter very soon in our midst as a happy and contented married couple.

So good-bye, with greetings and kisses for our dear Minna from ourselves and all the family, who also send you their best wishes. Begging you to hold us always in affectionate remembrance, we remain

With all our blessings,

Your parents-in-law,

GOTTHELF PLANER

CHRISTIANA PLANER.

I hereby certify *sub fide pastorali* that Herr Planer and his wife personally appeared before me and gave their consent to the marriage of their daughter Minna with Herr Music Director Wagner of Koenigsberg, and have duly certified to same in the aforesaid document under their own hand.

GUSTAV WILHELM STEINERT,

Pastor of the Orphanage.

(Seal).

Dresden, 27th October 1836.

The following banns were posted in Magdeburg, the official residence of Wagner and Minna during the twelve months immediately preceding :

It is hereby certified that the banns of marriage between Herr Wilhelm Richard Wagner, music director of the Koenigsberg Theatre, and his affianced bride, the virgin Christine Wilhelmine Planer, were posted in their presence without objection at the

Parish Church of St. Ulrich on the Sundays : 23rd and 30th
October and 6th November.

Magdeburg, 6th November 1836.

J. N. JUETZ,

Pastor of the Church of St. Ulrich.

The marriage certificate read as follows :

Juram. cölibatis

I, Wilhelm Richard Wagner

I, Christine Wilhelmine Planer

desiring to marry

the demoiselle Christi. Wilhelmine Planer

Herr Wilhelm Richard Wagner

hereby swear before God the Almighty that I have not been
married elsewhere, nor have I promised myself in marriage to any
other person publicly in the presence of a clergyman, so help me
God. Through Jesus Christ. Amen.

WILHELM RICHARD WAGNER, Music Director.

CHRISTINE WILHELMINE PLANER.

175
WILHELM
RICHARD
WAGNER.

On the 24th November Wilhelm Richard Wagner,
music director at the local theatre, twenty-four years
of age, was married to Demoiselle Christine Wilhelmine Planer, aged twenty-three, third daughter of the
Mechanikus, Herr Gotthelf Planer, residing till now in
Dresden. The bridegroom still has a mother residing
in Dresden and states that he was born on 22nd May
1812. The bride received the consent of her parents,
dated 27th October, Dresden ; which document has
been attested by Pastor Steinert of the Orphanage,
and duly deposited. The Notice of Banns, dated
Magdeburg 6th November, has been produced and
likewise deposited.

It will be seen that all the dates are incorrect. The bridegroom
represented himself as a year older, the bride as four years younger
than they actually were. His motive was undoubtedly to make him
appear of age ; hers, merely characteristic feminine vanity.

The wedding finally took place in the church at Tragheim on
24th November 1836 after the benefit performance the evening
before had passed off to everyone's satisfaction, both artistically
and financially. The eventful day closed with a bounteous feast
in the new home of the young couple. In commemoration each
guest received a pink satin handkerchief[1] on which was printed
the following effusion by an anonymous poet.

[1] Exhibits 76 and 79, Burrell Collection.

TO MINNA PLANER AT HER WEDDING BANQUET TO CELEBRATE
HER MARRIAGE TO MUSIC DIRECTOR RICHARD WAGNER

Though art may wind for you a wreath of flowers
So amiably to crown your lovely head,
When recognition of your golden powers
In unmixed praise and high applause is spread;
The laurel fades, beauty like fame deflowers,
Love only to eternal joy has led.
 But if the laurel with the rose be blended,
 You by true happiness will be attended.

Blessed are you that faithful friend in finding,
Who shares with you all sorrow as all joy,
And in dark hours when grief your life is grinding,
When thanklessness and envy would destroy,
Stands ready to protect, your wounds upbinding,
All love in grateful healing to employ.
 But friendship, too, good wishes still expressing
 Seeks to that covenant to add its blessing.

Thus, while both love and art sweet flowers scatter
Upon your path through life, so filled with light,
Long years may you, whom still the Graces flatter,
All Koenigsberg continue to delight.
You can give life to high poetic matter,
We, voiceless, owe you thanks that are your right.
 So may your lovely spirit still engender
 Full many a blossom, beautiful and tender.

Then, while your husband in high music winging,
Leads us into the land of harmony;
You represent the poet's beauty, bringing
To life his sacred dream for us to see,
Full many a poet's golden laurels springing
From out his brother's perfect artistry.
 What Schiller, Goethe, Lessing sang, so glorious,
 Through you may now in truth become victorious.[1]

[1] Translation of Olga Erbsloh Muller.

Here two young people had linked their lives together under the most unfavourable conditions conceivable. He : an intrepid Hotspur who abandoned himself to every passing mood and passion and was helpless to combat the sober realities of life—all temperament and ecstasy. She : a worldly wise, quieter nature who from her earliest youth had been forced by fate and circumstance to view the struggle for her daily bread as the all-powerful factor in life.

Minna's youth had been a difficult one. She was born in Oederau near Chemnitz on 5th September 1809,[1] the third daughter of Gotthelf Planer, who a short time before her birth had returned to his native town with the defeated troops after the Battle of Wagram, in which he had taken part as sergeant trumpeter. At first the family lived by working in their own home, and then before long moved to Dresden where Planer tried to earn a living as a craftsman. But bad luck in business plunged the family into misery, and the children had to turn to at a very early age and do their part to help support the family. The daughters, while still young and inexperienced, had come into close contact with the darker side of life.

Minna, who developed very early and had great charm, found it hard to defend herself against her ardent suitors, and finally one day succumbed to the wiles of Ernst Rudolph von Einsiedel, captain in the Royal Saxon Guards. When she told him that she was pregnant he promptly vanished from the scene. As Minna, not yet sixteen, could not take the law into her own hands and obtain redress from her faithless seducer, she had to throw herself on her mother's mercy. Her principal concern was to prevent the affair coming to her father's ears, since with his strict moral code he would have turned a dishonoured daughter out of doors without pity. Her mother therefore assumed full responsibility and persuaded her husband that she was going to have a fifth child on her silver wedding anniversary, Father Planer readily believing the comedy in the masculine pride and vanity of his fifty-six years.

When the time drew near for Minna's confinement her mother —to avoid gossip—went to her relatives in the country. But Minna's child—a girl christened Nathalie—was born in Dresden

---

[1] Exhibit 31, Burrell Collection.

on 22nd February 1826,[1] where Minna was in hiding. The secret was so carefully guarded in the family that Planer, up to the very day of his death, looked on the child as his own, and Nathalie also never learned that she was Minna's child and not her younger sister, as the world considered her and as she was also designated in Minna's will. It is not astonishing that Nathalie, who almost always lived with Minna after the latter's marriage, had difficulties with her mother later on when she grew up as a result of this anomalous relationship. For she naturally was not disposed to allow a sister to regulate her conduct for her, whereas she would certainly have accorded this right to a mother. After Nathalie's birth, Minna was faced with the necessity of making herself independent as soon as possible in order to support herself and her child. Through the good offices of a friend she was presented to the Dresden actor Emil Devrient, who taught her and prophesied a successful career for her as an actress, owing to her good looks and more than average ability. She also soon secured an engagement at the theatre, and although she was by no means stagestruck she viewed a theatrical career as the quickest way to earn an adequate income. Her behaviour to her brother shows how courageously and consistently she carried out her plans.

" He was to study in Leipzig (she wrote Apel from Paris), but my parents couldn't help him so I undertook to do so at a time when the finances of the company were in such a bad way that I often lacked four *groschen* to buy my lunch. I then pawned my earrings and other things of the kind, which were often indispensable to me at the theatre, and sent the money to my brother to pay for his lessons, keeping back only three *pfennigs* to buy myself a roll that I ate for my lunch while I walked about the town, having told the people with whom I lodged that I was invited out for lunch."

Minna held herself aloof from the tinsel of theatrical life and the frivolous ways of her colleagues and always knew how to uphold her dignity in every situation without being a killjoy. She only relaxed her dignified reserve in the case of persons important for her professional advancement, in a spirit of cool calculation, but in her effort to make no enemies she sometimes permitted them liberties and intimacies that could only be considered harmless when viewed as she viewed them, that is, as

[1] Exhibit 6, Burrell Collection. Copy of baptismal certificate from the parish register of the Kreuzkirche (Church of the Holy Cross), Dresden.

business exigencies, a means to an end. If before their marriage this behaviour on her part was the cause of numerous stormy scenes owing to Wagner's boundless jealousy, it was even worse after their marriage.

" Her strange tolerance towards certain intimacies and importunities, even against her person (he wrote in *Mein Leben*) on the part of those whom she took for patrons of the theatre wounded me very greatly, and it brought me to the point of desperation to see her assume an injured air when I reproached her on the subject. To make me completely wild Minna only needed to point out that she had turned down really advantageous offers in the bourgeois sense while she had succumbed with friendly sympathy and devotion to the ardour of the penniless, badly off young man whose talent had not passed any of the world's recognized tests. But the most damaging thing for me was the blustering violence of my words and speech which so offended the poor girl that on realizing my excess I had no other recourse than to propitiate her offended feelings. Thus all these scenes invariably ended to the outward advantage of the lady."

The hopelessness of the situation[1] and an increasing burden of debts all contributed to intensify the domestic dissension. The less he succeeded in making ends meet in the course of the winter the more Minna felt called upon to contribute her share through the exercise of her personal charms. The result was constant outbursts of jealousy that reached such a degree that Minna had repeated attacks of convulsions. Their life together became more and more of a torture, one irritating the other to no purpose. The crisis was then finally precipitated by an outward event.

" At all events, in those critical days (wrote Minna to a friend in after years) I had lost all love for Richard, but I don't believe things would have gone so far if a well-to-do man had not approached me just at this time with such marked evidence of sympathetic and touching understanding of the difficulties of my situation, and exhibited this sympathy in such a seductive way that under all these conflicting impressions, I began to waver for a time and could hardly consider Richard's love (which only manifested itself in such insulting excesses towards me as to be almost unrecognizable) as adequate compensation for all the misery this unhappy, headstrong, untimely marriage had brought upon us both."

With the help of this new friend, a rich local merchant named Dietrich, Minna slipped off one morning while Wagner was

---

[1] When he entered on his engagement the Koenigsberg Theatre was on the verge of bankruptcy.

rehearsing in the theatre, and took refuge with her parents in Dresden. Wagner tried in vain to go and fetch the runaway ; but owing to the many extra post-chaises *en route*, his money gave out and he had to return to Koenigsberg without having accomplished anything. But he could no longer remain there. With great difficulty and in all secrecy he managed to scrape enough money together with Moeller's aid to escape the pursuit of his creditors, and on 3rd June left the city where he had suffered so much bad luck. The news that Dietrich had accompanied Minna only part of the way and that she had gone on to her parents allowed Wagner to see things in a rosier light, and he finally arrived in Dresden, tortured by violent self-reproaches. At first everything seemed to turn out for the best. Minna allowed him to persuade her to go with him to Blasewitz to wait till it was time to take up his new engagement in Riga, for which he had just signed the contract. Then Dietrich turned up in Dresden and the poor woman, who was physically run down by her unfortunate experiences in Koenigsberg and no longer knew what to make of herself and Wagner, and saw no hope for the future in view of Wagner's disposition and their hopeless financial situation, let herself be persuaded, believed Dietrich's protestations, and fled from her husband for the second time. Wagner, who soon learned that she had stayed for some time at a Hamburg hotel with her seducer, had no other alternative than to authorize Moeller to take the necessary legal steps to procure a divorce at the Tribunal in Koenigsberg.

The middle of August 1837 he arrived in Riga to take up his post at the new theatre under Holtei's direction, of whom great things were expected. But the defection of the prima donna (Mme. Ernst) caused great difficulties in the repertory, whereupon Wagner suggested that the director engage his sister-in-law, Amalie Planer, with whom he had been friendly since the Magdeburg days and whom he had recently met in Berlin while on his way to Riga. Through her he received news of Minna who (she reported) " had returned to her parents in a pitiable condition and was now very ill," which Wagner " took very coolly."[1] Minna then wrote him " a most moving letter in which she frankly confessed her infidelity."

[1] Exhibits 84, 85 and 87, Burrell Collection.

" Just as she had been driven to this by despair (he wrote in *Mein Leben*) so now despair over the ill fortune into which she had fallen had caused her to retrace her steps. It appeared that she had been deceived in the character of her seducer and realization of her horrible situation had reduced her to an extremely wretched state, morally as well as physically, in which (ill and miserable) she now turned to me again, and confessing her fault, implored my forgiveness and assured me under all circumstances that only now did she really realize how much she loved me."

But the confident feeling with which Wagner had entered on his duties in Riga gave way to deep depression through disappointments of an artistic nature and the difficulties that soon began to mount up. The miserable little provincial theatre disgusted him. He was now firmly convinced that there was no scope for his talents here, and his thoughts therefore turned to Paris which at that time was the acknowledged threshold to every artistic career. In intrepid faith and confidence in his own abilities and his half-finished opera " Rienzi," he therefore decided to go to Paris. Four guest appearances of Minna at the Riga Theatre[1] and the proceeds of a benefit concert provided the necessary funds for the venture.

They set off in the middle of July 1839 on the flight that was by no means without danger. They had to leave town and cross the frontier in all secrecy on account of Richard's creditors, and after a stormy voyage of three and a half weeks on board the tiny Prussian-owned *Thetis* they finally arrived at Gravesend on the 12th August 1839. They stopped a week in London in order to rest, and then crossed to Boulogne. On the boat Wagner made the acquaintance of two Jewish ladies, a Mrs. Manson and her daughter, which proved very fortunate as they knew Meyerbeer, who happened to be staying at Boulogne at the time. After receiving a letter of introduction to the maestro from his new friends, Wagner decided to stop off in Boulogne in order to gain Meyerbeer's support, which would be of incalculable assistance to him and would have been difficult for this wholly unknown

---

[1] Theatre programmes are found in the Burrell Collection, Exhibit 91.
April 8th as Katharina in *Die Schauspielerin von Venedig*, by Harris.
April 11th as Preciosa in the Weber-Wolff romantic play of that name.
April 14th as Maria Stuart in Schiller's play.
April 18th as Christine in Theodor Hell's *Christinen's Liebe und Entsagung* and Julie in Wilhelm Marsano's *Die Heldin*.

young German musician to have achieved so easily without this personal introduction.

Poor in purse but all the richer in ambitious hopes, Wagner and Minna finally reached Paris, the goal of their desires, on 17th September 1839. The story of how fearfully these hopes were dashed, what desperate struggles the penniless young artist had to undergo with enemy forces that capitulated only before money, until the salvation that he had sought in vain abroad finally came to him two and a half years later from his own country, is long familiar. During these desperate years he had in Minna a faithful, devoted companion who shared every misery without a word of complaint, and met many a critical situation through her abilities as a housekeeper and clever economical manager. Her letters to Theodor Apel, to whom she sent a desperate appeal for help when Wagner was in the debtors' prison, furnish eloquent proof of her tender love, and, at the same time, of her unswerving faith in his art.

" Even if I myself had the means to get away from Paris (she wrote) I would never in the world leave Richard in such a predicament, for I know that this is not due to thoughtlessness but that the noblest and most natural strivings of an artist have brought him to this pass, which could happen to anyone without special backing. It was only after strenuous objections that I fell in with his plan of coming to Paris, but the more I know of his projects here, the more I see that it will only be for lack of adequate assistance if he goes under and doesn't reach his goal, which he otherwise might do. . . .

" Believe me, I don't usually share Richard's exalted hopes, but now know from what his own acquaintances say that he has only to take one more step forward to reach his goal. . . . In Richard there is a beautiful talent to be rescued that will otherwise be brought nigh to ruin, for he has already lost heart, and without courage his high destiny will be lost. A heavy responsibility rests, perhaps, on those who now cold-shoulder him. I can't give him up ; that is perhaps why I'm the only one to feel most keenly how shameful it is to let him perish."

Richard's diary in those days reveals his own feelings.

" What the next month will bring forth (he wrote on 29th June 1840) I do not know. If I have been worried in the past, I'm now on the verge of despair. . . . All resources are already exhausted. I still keep my poor wife in ignorance that things are already as bad as they are. I always hoped Laube would come to my rescue ere now. I would only then have told her that but for it we could have counted on nothing, and that I concealed it from her to save adding to her fears, worn out with anxiety as she is. But nothing will come of it apparently. On the first of the month I can't hide it from her any longer. God knows that will be a terrible day unless help is forthcoming.

" Told my wife today during our walk how it stands with our money affairs (he wrote next day). I pity the poor lass with all my heart. It's a bad business. I mean to work ! "

Ah, now the lovely song is done,
The fond song of my youth!
She whom I loved is now my wife,
A kindly wife in truth.

A virtuous and faithful wife
Is surely a great treasure,
She's more than a pastime to me,
She's all my fortune's measure.

I wish each one the same good luck
I am its greatest prizer.
But if I think just ten years back,
I'm sure I should be wiser.[1]

One bright spot in the monotonous round of those Paris days was Wagner's friendship with his stepsister and childhood playmate, Caecilie, who was married to Eduard Avenarius, manager of the Paris branch of the Leipzig publishing house Brockhaus. Minna was also devoted to her and really adored their little boy Marcel. She and Wagner were very fond of children, but unfortunately they were never to see their fondest dream fulfilled. After their return to Dresden their letters to Caecilie in Paris reflect the beneficent warmth and sincerity of the friendship formed there.

" Few events in my life are so vividly engraved on my soul (Wagner wrote his sister on his return to Dresden) as the hour and moment of our farewell. I shall never forget it. We have never found a leave-taking so hard as that from Paris. *Gott!* What are all the sufferings that we endured there in comparison with the consciousness of this intimate friendship that we carried away with us ! "

" And we two (he continued after the " Rienzi " performance), how often and with what feelings do we think of you all ! I admit that, intoxicated by all the success I have met with here, I was ready to call

[1] Translation of Olga Erbsloh Muller.

this the happiest period of my life, when bitter tears gave me the lie
and showed me the incompleteness of my happiness, since *you*, you,
were not with us ! What wouldn't I give to have had you both here !
For you must know we are still forlorn. In the evening we sit all alone,
alone, and nobody drops in as they used to do. Ach ! how the saddest
situations in life can leave such sweet recollections ! "

If we compare this with the contemptuous, almost spiteful,
way in which he refers to this friendship in his autobiography,
one can only marvel at the light-heartedness with which he does
violence to the truth under the influence of some subsequent ill
humour.

Finally, on 7th April 1842, the hour struck to return home.
" Rienzi " was to be given in Dresden. The goddess of fortune
who had been so lacking in graciousness to Wagner up till then
now seems to have declared him one of her favourites. A wave
of good luck carried him from triumph to triumph. The tremendous success of " Rienzi " was followed immediately by the
acceptance of " The Flying Dutchman," and finally by a life
appointment as conductor of the Royal Opera. At one fell swoop
the young man, who had only recently been at the point of
starvation, had become a fêted celebrity and, what was even more
important, a man in a brilliant position which apparently made
him independent for the rest of his life. Minna was beside herself
with joy and happiness. She saw her wildest dreams fulfilled, her
faithful perseverance and privations royally rewarded. Above all,
she rejoiced at the thought of not having to depend any longer on
the charity of others, which she (in contrast to Wagner) always
felt to be degrading and humiliating. " My dear ! I'm too happy
for words ! (she wrote jubilantly to Caecilie). I have attained my
heart's desire ! "

But the comet-like appearance of Wagner's name on the artistic
horizon had one unpleasant aftermath. His old creditors (and
they were by no means few) considered it an appropriate moment
to present their claims. This placed him in a very embarrassing
position. But a saviour appeared in the person of Schroeder-
Devrient, the " Adriano " in his " Rienzi," who voluntarily sent
him 1,000 *thalers*.

He now became an intimate friend, professionally and personally, of this gifted artist. Her interpretation of " Adriano "
and particularly that of " Senta " had made an indelible

impression on him. "The slightest contact with this extraordinary woman gave me an electric shock, and for a long time I heard and sensed her presence when the creative urge came over me."

In fact, he long played with the idea of writing an opera especially for her, and went back to an earlier draft, "The Saracen Maid," with this in mind ; but the libretto, which he had written hastily, did not please the singer, and so nothing further came of it. Devrient was also very fond of Wagner and soon made him her confidant in a very exciting love affair in which she was momentarily involved. There was only one thing about him that she could not tolerate, and that was the fact that he was married. She therefore often called him " the marriage cripple " in fun ; but their friendship was marred later on by a serious misunderstanding.

When Wagner got the idea of publishing his works at his own expense, thinking he could scarcely fail to make money by selling them to the theatres after the Dresden success, she placed the necessary funds (a by no means insignificant sum) at his disposal, and he then went ahead at once with the project. But when it came time to pay the bill it transpired that this generous patron was no longer in a position to live up to her promise as her new cavalier had appropriated all her property in the meantime. This placed Wagner in a very embarrassing position and he was forced to engage in financial operations that were fatal for him and undermined his Dresden position later on when the income from the theatre did not materialize to the extent anticipated. It finally came to an open breach between the two artists after the great success of Wagner's niece Johanna in the rôle of Elizabeth in " Tannhäuser."[1] Jealous of her charming young rival, whose Dresden engagement she claimed had been pushed through by Wagner only to give the management the excuse to discharge her, Schroeder-Devrient was blinded by her feelings to such an extent that one day she turned over to her lawyer Wagner's

---

[1] Johanna was the adopted daughter of Richard's brother Albert. On 12th August 1828 Albert Wagner married the actress Elise Gollmann, mother of Johanna, who was born 13th October 1826 of a previous liaison. Albert adopted the child at the time of his marriage, and later on had two daughters of his own : Franziska, born 28th March 1829, and Marie, born 25th January 1831. See *Richard Wagner und seine erste Elizabeth*, by Kapp-Jachmann. Hans Jachmann, co-author of this work, was Johanna's son. Albert did not meet his future wife until 1827 in Mannheim. See Glasenapp, *Wagner*, Vol. 1, page 169.

receipt for the thousand *thalers* she had previously loaned him and instituted suit against him. The poor young man, who was already in all kinds of difficulties, had no other recourse but to confess his situation to the Intendant, Herr von Lüttichau, and ask for an advance, which was granted, though under very humiliating conditions.

He ran across another of his old acquaintances among the singers at the Dresden Opera, namely, Henriette Wüst, to whom he had once paid court during his student days in Leipzig where she was studying with Heinrich Dorn. It was she who on 22nd April 1832 sang a scena and aria by Weinlig's unknown young pupil at a recital given in the Court Theatre, which was the first performance of one of his works in public. Now in 1842 she gave her mature art to the rôle of " Irene " in " Rienzi." The Wagners were soon great friends with her and her husband (the actor Hans Kriete), a friendship that outlived the Dresden days.[1] Several very amusing notes of Wagner's have been preserved which show on what an intimate and friendly footing the two families stood at that time. " Richard Wagner begs you to put a capon in the oven betimes (he once wrote on a visiting card) as he has no desire to be roasted himself."

If he was gay and informal with his artists he could, however, never warm up sufficiently in his intercourse with the leading figures of Dresden society. True enthusiasm for his works brought many ladies to his feet, as, for instance, the wife of the Chamberlain, Herr von Könneritz. Lüttichau later claimed she was to blame for Wagner's conceit and had turned his head by her flatteries. But there were no real mutual friendships in Dresden that might have had influence on his development and position. The only one of his lady acquaintances there who perhaps played a greater rôle in the life of the Herr Hofkapellmeister was Frau von Lüttichau, wife of Wolf Adolf August Freiherr von Lüttichau, Intendant of the theatre.

" This highly cultivated, sensitive and noble woman (he tells us in his autobiography) might have played an important rôle for me if it had been possible for me to see her more frequently and have stood on

---

[1] Wagner had been a witness at their wedding, but according to the unpublished correspondence of Wagner's friend, Anton Pusinelli, she became very unfriendly to Wagner later because of the latter's tardiness in repaying some money he had borrowed from her husband.

a more intimate footing with her. It was less the attitude of the wife of the General Director towards me as her continued invalidism and my strange disinclination under such circumstances to give the impression of officiousness that were responsible for my coming into closer contact with her so rarely. In my memory my thought of her is mingled to some extent with that of my sister Rosalie ; for I recall being faintly stirred to evoke in this sensitive, suffering lady, who was slowly dying (and in the coarsest surroundings) a gratifying interest in myself. My first hope for the satisfaction of this ambition was the interest she took in my ' Flying Dutchman ' in spite of the fact that it seemed so strange to the Dresden public after ' Rienzi.' She was therefore the first who, swimming against the current, met me on my new course. I was so pleased by this success that when I published the opera later on, I dedicated it to her."

" The Flying Dutchman " also made another friend for Wagner, namely Alwine Fromann, who as friend of Princess Wilhelm of Prussia was able in later years to do the Master (whom she so sincerely admired) many a valuable service. The Berlin performance of " The Flying Dutchman " in January 1844, under the composer's direction, had won her over to his art, and she at once wrote him an enthusiastic letter in which she thanked him for the great pleasure it had given her, and embraced his artistic concepts. Alwine came to Dresden for the first performance of " Tannhäuser," and the hitherto unknown admirer now became a loyal friend to the Wagners, who were both devoted to her.

" She was no longer in her first youth (he wrote) and with no pretensions whatever to good looks. She had to rely on her very keen, expressive eyes to communicate her great spiritual qualities. She was a sister of the Jena bookseller Fromann, and could tell many intimate personal stories about Goethe who stopped with her brother when he was in Jena. Holding the position of reader to the Princess Augusta of Prussia, she came into close contact with the latter, and those who knew of her relations with Her Royal Highness regarded her almost as the latter's friend and confidant. Nevertheless she lived in very poor circumstances and prided herself on maintaining a certain degree of independence by her modest talent for painting arabesques. She was always loyally devoted to me as she was now one of the few who, unperturbed by the unfortunate impression of the first performance of ' Tannhäuser,' quickly made up their minds and championed the work with great enthusiasm."

The bonds of friendship with Alwine grew even closer when Wagner was in Berlin for the " Rienzi " performance in the autumn of 1847. In the confusion and intrigues against him and

his work he found in this influential friend an energetic and tireless champion. The invitation that Wagner and Minna (who had
gone to Berlin for the performance) addressed to their " dearest
friend " after their return to Dresden shows how fond they had
grown of her.

" As we left Berlin on Saturday (he wrote) a thought came to both
of us ; dear Fromann, couldn't you make up your mind to come and
live with us ? We'll fix up a room for you, much nicer than that in
Berlin, and then you'll live with us and share our joys and sorrows as
long as we all live. Do you absolutely insist on living all by yourself ?
Or are you so fond of the Princess that you can't leave her ? We need
someone. Are you sufficient unto yourself ? Don't answer in a hurry.
Keep the thought in mind for a long time, and then when you can't
any more, make up your mind ! If you answer me immediately, I
know in advance that you'll turn it down. So take time, please ! "

But their friend did not accept the invitation. Wagner's wish
sprang from his hunger—so often apparent in later life—for the
companionship of those he loved and who understood him. As
he and his wife were denied children,[1] and a family circle represented his greatest happiness, his friends and sympathizers had to
fill the breach. The great world with its noisy turmoil and superficial acquaintances had nothing to offer him.

" You and our little home are my real country (he wrote Minna from
Berlin). I know nothing in the world that could take their place ! But
also think how we live and if I actually have anything else besides my
home ! You can never know how I long to hold you in my arms again,
to shake off that frigidity that finally grips one all over when one is
among strangers, remote from all affection. No ! I'm not too ambitious
—a lovely home means more to me than anything else in the world."

[1] See Exhibit 95b, Burrell Collection. According to Nathalie, Minna allegedly
suffered such severe internal injuries in an accident during their flight from Riga
that it was impossible for her to have children in the future.

CHAPTER III

MATRIMONIAL SHIPWRECK

THE " Kapellmeister years " in Dresden represented the zenith of Wagner's married life. In this safe harbourage the shipwrecked pair soon forgot their past sufferings and calamities. The storm had abated and they knew once more the calm peace and the ineffable comfort of being in an assured position.

" What is a youthful passion in comparison with such an old love ? (Wagner wrote Minna from Berlin in 1847). Passion is only beautiful when it finally ends in love of this type ; in and for itself it is suffering ! But a love like ours is a pure joy—and·a brief separation makes this plainer than anything. But heaven preserve us from a long one. Isn't that so, old dear ? "

But an envious demon already lurked in the womb of time. Genius began to follow paths that were beyond the grasp of an ordinary mortal. As time went on the working conditions in Dresden had become intolerable for Wagner. More and more frequently his intrepid efforts met with open opposition, even to the point of flat rejection. His ambition and creative urge were blunted by the continuous failure of his works outside Dresden. In short the only solution in his opinion was a radical change in existing conditions, and he felt this could only go hand in hand with a political revolution. On this he staked all his hopes ; but of course this was quite beyond Minna. She saw no ground for complaint in the musical situation in Dresden. With her far more practical mind she viewed her husband's political ambitions as impossible fantasies ; which they eventually proved to be. And she was filled with grim forebodings that his activities might cost him his permanent post, which in view of his huge burden of debts was their only safeguard against more years of misery and want.

" You know what he was when I married him (she wrote in a letter which is still unpublished). A forlorn, poor, unknown conductor out of a job ! As regards his intellectual development, I have the satisfaction of knowing that everything that he has produced was written while I was with him ; and that I understood him is attested by the fact that he always read me the draft of all his poems, his compositions, scene by scene, or played them over for me and discussed them with me. It was only his political activities that I failed to understand. With my simple mind I saw that no good would come of it, and as he now moved farther and farther from the paths of art, I always had the painful feeling that he was also breaking away from me."

A gulf now yawned between the two companions which was forever unbridgeable because it derived from fundamental differences in the two characters. Since it was a source of perpetual misunderstandings and nerve-racking worries, it might therefore easily lead to catastrophe. After the sacrifices of their early married life Minna felt that she had a right to expect that her husband would not thoughtlessly throw up a permanent post and again face them with an uncertain future without a penny in their pockets, merely to chase artistic butterflies that would always elude him. That this was not due to a love of ease or personal considerations, and that she was glad, in fact, to make any sacrifice, any renunciation, if she could see an end in view, is shown by her courage and patience during the trying years in Paris. But now she was not ready to exchange reality for illusions in which she had no faith. It is very unjust and stupid to blame poor Minna for this, and call her insignificant and small-minded just because she was unable to follow the audacious flights of a genius that was far in advance of its time. How should she be able to understand something that baffled even brilliant intellectuals and professional musicians many decades later ? And the question is moot whether the other women who later on (when it was much easier) seconded his ideas, backed him courageously, and turned up their noses at doubting Minna, would have acted any differently in Minna's situation in 1849, that is, *vis à vis du rien*.

On the other hand, Wagner had to obey his inner voice and disregard the demands of everyday life. His firm faith in his artistic mission raised him above all these secondary considerations ; but he suffered from the disharmony in his home and the lack of understanding in his immediate surroundings.

" When I came home (he wrote) badly out of sorts and excited over some fresh annoyance, some new mortification, some new failure, what did this wife of mine offer me in place of comfort and inspiring sympathy ? Reproaches, ever new reproaches, nothing but reproaches ! Domestically inclined as I was, I stayed at home none the less ; but in the end I did so not to relieve my feelings, talk things over, and receive encouragement ; but to keep my peace, to let my grief corrode my soul—just to be *alone* ! "

At last Minna's worst fears were realized. Wagner had to flee from Dresden. The revolution from which he had hoped so much had been quashed and the Herr Hofkapellmeister, who had greatly compromised himself, was now under a warrant of arrest. For the artist, this was equivalent to regaining freedom at last after bursting professional fetters that he felt were degrading and would only have proved intolerable in the long run. For the man, however, and especially for his wife, it meant that they must leave their safe haven again and once more become the playthings of chance, exposed to new struggles and privations. In the beginning, therefore, Minna was not at all inclined to accept meekly this new turn in her chequered fortunes. It required all Wagner's powers of persuasion to induce her to come to Weimar, where Liszt had provided a safe refuge for him, in order to bid him good-bye before his dangerous flight.

" But my wife finally decided to accede to my wish (he wrote Minna later from Italy) not in order to console me or seek comfort once again in my embrace ; but only to satisfy an obstinate man so that he might eventually get away—to save himself, it is true. I shall never forget the night I was waked in my refuge to receive my wife ; she stood before me cold and reproachful and said : ' Well, here I am, as you insisted ! I hope you're satisfied ! Now be off ! I'm also going back to-night.' I finally succeeded in getting you to Jena for a really affectionate farewell. This farewell was my consolation when I was far away from home."

Wagner had gone to Paris where on Liszt's advice and with the latter's promised assistance he was to try and put through an opera written especially for Paris. Minna had returned to Dresden. The things that were whispered to her about her husband in this " stronghold of bourgeois virtues and mag-nanimity where gossip and all kinds of nonsense were rife " did not conduce to reconcile her to him. She was firmly determined not to accede to his clamorous demand to join him in Paris until " he was in a position to support her there by his own efforts." For (as she wrote him) " after he had so recklessly trifled away and wrecked a position and a situation in general such as would never come his way again, it was hardly to be expected that any woman would take any part in his possible ventures as a means of future livelihood."

" My wife suffers and is embittered (he complained to his friend in Weimar). I hope that time will heal it. I must have a new domestic hearth or it is all up with me. My heart is bigger than my reason."

Since there was nothing to be accomplished in Paris for the time being he left for Zürich to write the Paris work in tranquillity after Liszt had provided him with the necessary funds. But he could make no progress without a home of his own. He was also tortured by anxiety and yearning for Minna. In his letters he endeavoured in every way to paint the future to her in rosy colours, to hold out hopes for successes in Paris and to try to bring her round.

" It is disgraceful the way Minna treats me and that she refuses to join me again (he wrote Nathalie on 10th July 1849). I am planning to sell all my future operas to a rich patron of music for a fixed income."

When Minna, who shortly before had complained " that he had played thoughtlessly and irresponsibly with their material welfare " at last wrote " as touchingly as could be " that she was willing to join him again and share all life's miseries with him, his joy knew no bounds. It now remained for Liszt to remove the last obstacles.

" O dearest friend ! (he wrote him). You are concerned for the best in me, for my soul, and for my art. Help me for my art's sake ! Believe me, I cling to no country, but I do cling to this poor, good, faithful woman, to whom I have brought little but trouble ; who is truly conscientious and lacks inspiration, and yet feels herself shackled forever to a rough devil like me. Give her to me ! Then you'll be giving me everything that you could wish for me. And see ! I shall be so grateful to you ! Yes, really grateful ! You will then see how everything flows from my fingers, the preparatory work for Paris, the article for the pamphlet and—even two drafts for articles will be ready next month and on the way to you. Where I can't fall in with your ideas, I'll win you over to mine instead ! I promise you that, so that we can go hand in hand and need never part. I will do whatever you bid me— only give me my poor wife. See that she comes to me soon ; that she's cheerful in mind and shows a degree of confidence. *Ach!* and that—in the language of the sweet nineteenth century—means ' unfortunately,' send her as much money as you can possibly raise. You see, that's how I am ! I can beg—I could steal to make my wife happy, even for a short time only. You dear, good Liszt ! see what you can do about it ! Help me ! Help me ! dear Liszt ! "

Minna, whom Liszt had generously supplied with money on 27th July, finally arrived in Switzerland the beginning of September 1849 with all the family pets and a part of their Dresden belongings which she had been able to salvage, thanks to Liszt's generosity. Wagner hastened as far as Rorschach to meet her. The two were now happily reunited, but the inner breach was only superficially healed, and when the hopes for a Paris success (which he had aroused in Minna) proved a delusion and a snare and he gave all his time to writing instead of energetically following up his Paris plans, the still latent discord between the two now became more acute than ever.

" I had hoped to win you over entirely to my side (he confessed to her later in a letter), to convince you of my ideas, to acquaint you at last with my real nature. You came, and how happy I was ! And yet— unfortunate creature that I am ! You hadn't come to *me* to share joy and sorrow with me, just as I was. But you had come to the Wagner who you assumed was going to write an opera for Paris ! In Dresden you were ashamed to say that you were coming to me in Switzerland ; but you let everybody think that you were going to Paris and that your husband (as you probably thought yourself) had a signed contract in his pocket. O, the great rift between us had to become more evident as the days went by. All my ideas and sentiments were an abomination to you ! You loathed my writings, though I tried hard to make you see that they were now more necessary to me than all this useless opera writing. You only bemoaned the loss of former conditions ; you only thought of the future in the light of a return to those conditions—in the light of a Paris success.

" My whole nature was hostile and objectionable to you. Every minute, *Ach !* in practically every movement I made, you found something to object to ! In short, I now felt so infinitely alone when I was with you because I saw that it was impossible to win you over to my way of thinking. To keep peace in the family, I turned again seriously to my Paris plans. The fact of being forced to do so, the disgusting struggle against my convictions, the impossibility of making myself clear to my immediate entourage and finding consolation, help, and advice there—this all resulted in a spiritual tension that was bound to aggravate my ill health very seriously, owing to the added mental stress."

As Liszt, Sulzer and other friends on whom he was then almost entirely dependent for support continued to bring up the Paris question and urge him to give his serious attention to the only thing that would guarantee his future, he finally gave in against his own convictions, and towards the end of January 1850 went back to France with its hated " *Schnettereteng* " language, as he called it.

" My sojourn in Paris belongs to the most loathsome experience that I have ever undergone ! (he wrote). Everything happened exactly as I knew and had foreseen. My sketch for an opera libretto (' Wieland der Schmidt ') seemed ridiculous (and quite rightly so) to everybody who thought in terms of the French language and the Paris Opera. The conditions at this opera house itself and all the impressions connected with it made me seem crazy even to myself. Finally, not being able even to get an overture performed—and with my fearful loathing of ' banquier ' music—all this brought me to a point (seeing that I was already suffering from the most depressing nervous tension) where I was really unfitted to excuse and explain myself to those of my friends who now probably only expected reports of Paris triumphs and success from me. I was at the end of my tether, for anything was preferable to going on living with those who considered the thing that was most repulsive to me as the very best for me."

He finally decided, no matter how dark the future might be, and even though everybody might desert him, to abandon the useless Paris scheme. And just then, in the moment of direst need, there came an unexpected ray of hope. He was suddenly offered an annual allowance which would enable him to give his full time and attention to his artistic work without having to worry about money.

He owed this piece of good luck to an unknown Dresden admirer, Frau Julie Ritter, the mother of one of his friends. This young musician, Karl Ritter, had come to see him after the " Tannhäuser " performance in Dresden, and was accompanied on this occasion by a young English friend, a Miss Jessie Taylor, who wished to congratulate him and have him autograph her score. Wagner did not see her again at that time, but became great friends with Ritter. Learning now of Wagner's financial plight through Ritter's Dresden friend, Theodor Uhlig, violinist of the Court Orchestra at Dresden, Karl's mother, who had only a very modest private income of her own, made arrangements with a wealthy friend and Wagner enthusiast with the object of placing an annual stipend at Wagner's disposition. This wealthy friend was none other than the aforesaid Miss Taylor who had since married and settled in Bordeaux, where her husband,

Eugene Laussot, was engaged in the wine business. Wagner accepted his good fortune in great delight, for now he could confidently abandon the Paris project.

"I hope this is the last time I shall have to mention the word money between us (he wrote sanguinely to Liszt on 6th February 1850). I'm now going to see Mme. Laussot."[1]

It appears that Wagner had accidentally run into Jessie Laussot again in Paris, and it was here they really began to get interested in each other. At all events, after Jessie returned to Bordeaux, he sent her a large picture of himself which he had had his painter friend, Ernst Benedikt Kietz, make[2] especially for her. Soon after this the Laussots invited him to Bordeaux for several weeks as their guest. He arrived there the middle of March and was warmly welcomed by his hosts.

"The family consists of the young married couple (he wrote) and Mme Laussot's mother, an Englishwoman who, however, also speaks German, as does the husband. This very charming and natural young man was really extraordinarily pleased to see me. They are intimately acquainted with my works and know what it's all about; and are proud of being able to do so much for me."

The only thing now was to win Minna over to the change of plan and surmount her opposition to any departure from the Paris plan, as well as to overcome her dislike of "accepting charity." In several cleverly couched letters Wagner tried to make the new situation clear to her.

"No one could possibly have been kinder, nobler or more delicate than our friend Mme. Laussot! I should have thought, dear wife, that it would have really been a moral inspiration to you to see what a deep impression your husband's works can make on wholesome, unaffected, and noble hearts; and that he can move them to such self-sacrificing and deeply sympathetic resolutions. Can you really bring yourself to despise such a success through my art?—for it was due to this alone—or rate it lower than these so-called 'brilliant' successes that are achieved to-day with the stupid, slovenly, heartless masses that make up our big theatre-going public? Should we despise these people and think only in terms of money? Good! then here's money for you—as much as we need for a quiet, even comfortable existence, and not swindled from the stupid masses, but offered me (and in the most delicate manner) by a noble heart through the sheer joy afforded by my creative works, even as they spring from my own real inner nature. What more do you want?"

[1] Exhibit 197, Burrell Collection.
[2] Exhibits 199, 200 and 201, Burrell Collection.

Mme. Laussot also wrote Minna on 7th April 1850,[1] and tried to dispel her scruples about accepting the allowance. She offered Wagner a sum of 2,500 francs a year for two years, beginning with 1st April 1850. Minna finally came round, though with a heavy heart. But she still nursed the secret hope that Wagner would return to Paris from Bordeaux and would push the performance of the " Tannhäuser " Overture which had been promised him. However, when she learned that he had already given up this idea and was about to return to Zürich without having accomplished anything ; and when reports furthermore came to her ears that other attractions were holding him in Bordeaux, she demanded that he should return to Paris immediately. The excited, implacable tone of her letter woke Wagner from his sweet dreams and showed him with bitter clarity that here any further understanding was impossible and that any attempt to resume their life together must only end in mutual martyrdom.

" The fundamental diversities of our two natures (he wrote Minna on 17th April 1850) have been proved time and again to my sorrow— and above all to yours also—since we have known each other, sometimes mildly, sometimes more fiercely. I finally thought I had won your heart. I fancied that you had yielded to the power of true love, and then to my fearful grief I felt more than ever the absolute certainty that we no longer belonged to each other. You stand before me— implacable. You look for honours in quarters that to me seem nothing short of a disgrace. And you are ashamed of that which is most welcome to me. . . . What can *my* love be now ? Only the wish to repay you for your wasted youth with me, for your share in our common tribulations ; to make you *happy* ! Can I still hope to achieve this by continuing to live with you ? Impossible ! "[2]

Therefore—their ways must separate ! Wagner wanted to forget by setting forth on an extended tour to Greece and the Orient.[3] Generous provision was to be made for Minna at all times. Perhaps in the course of time a reunion might be possible.

Naturally other and more impelling motives lay behind this sudden decision on his part than his pathetic eulogy on their lost marital happiness would suggest. For the rumours that reached

[1] Exhibit 202, Burrell Collection.
[2] Exhibit 204, Burrell Collection, dated 16th April 1850, represents an extended variation on the same theme.
[3] Exhibit 207, Burrell Collection. Letter to E. B. Kietz dated 4th May 1850.

Minna to the effect that her husband was languishing in Love's chains in Bordeaux were by no means compounded of thin air. The hot-blooded artist was strongly attracted to the pretty, clever woman whose hospitality he was enjoying, and his love was not unrequited. The young woman of twenty-two viewed the admired Master as her saviour, for she knew that he, like herself, was unhappy in his marriage. For the first time she had found someone who understood and loved her, and she probably nursed the belief that she could be a real comrade for her lover.

"I wish you could have seen the joy of love (he wrote his friend Frau Ritter) that quivered in every fibre of this richly blessed woman when she—not so much confessed, as let me see, through herself, through the involuntary, clear, and naked revolution of love, that she was mine! O, that you might have witnessed this joy, this happy ecstasy that gave life to every fibre of this creature, from the movement of her finger tips to the most subtle workings of her mind, when this young woman gazed at me—the sorely tried, unhappy man who in truth is fairly lacking in all the qualities that could effect such a miracle as that which now began to flower for me here and which I was able to savour to the point of the most blissful intoxication!

"You must sense the beauty and fullness of the love that drove this highly talented, wonderful woman to such intrepid, triumphantly rash decisions! ... But was it not Jessie's complete unconcern *vis à vis* these revolting bourgeois points of honour that delighted me so in her? Who understood better than she that I love my unhappy wife, that I am bound to her with a thousand chains of common ordeals and sufferings, and that I could only tear myself from the poor soul with a bleeding heart in order to wrest her from a destiny, the workings of which were incomprehensible to her and could only cause her pain and misery without her being able to interpret and understand them? Who better than Jessie could appreciate how miserable I was after this separation? For the very sincere proof that I gave her of this misery inspired her with the marvellous resolve to break with the whole world so as to come to me and compensate me for everything, to heal all the wounds of my life, even this latest wound? Who realized more clearly than Jessie that I must indeed separate from this poor woman, but never wrong her, never grieve her or treat her brutally in any way? She even offered to go to the other end of the world with me so as to spare the unhappy one the sight or even the knowledge of our love!

"How happy I was never to find in her letters a trace of that cruel and unworthy bourgeois hypocrisy! She was all love. We dedicated ourselves to the god of love and despised all the idols of this miserable world so completely as to consider them unworthy of mention."

Minna's letter had rudely awakened Wagner from this love-dream and decided him not to return to Zürich again, but to " break with everything and everybody connected with the past " by going with Jessie on an extended trip to Greece and the Far East. But since the situation in Bordeaux had also become untenable in the meantime, he left his hosts in the middle of April after a visit of four weeks, and first returned to Paris to await events. He informed Minna of his intentions in the afore-mentioned letter. The sorely tried woman, who had no idea then of the real reasons for this " desperate decision "—though she undoubtedly had her own suspicions—set out at once for Paris to find her husband. Anonymous letters had already informed her of what was going on. She had even received offers of marriage from Dresden on the grounds that Wagner had deserted her ![1] " Oh, this Richard ! (she wrote Kietz on 12th June 1850). If I were sure that there was a just God in Heaven, it would be a consolation ! "[2] Wagner, who had been informed by Kietz of her presence in Paris, left word that he was not there, and set out the same night for Geneva, where he was to await news from Frau Ritter, in whom he and Jessie had probably confided while he was in Bordeaux.[3] There he found a letter from Jessie in which she informed him " in the greatest excitement " that she

" couldn't avoid telling her mother of her intentions and that in so doing had at once given rise to the assumption that he (Wagner) was also involved, as a result of which her disclosure had been passed on to her husband and the latter now swore to find Wagner and put a bullet through his head."

Wagner therefore decided to leave for Bordeaux at once.

" I sat down and wrote a long letter to M. Eugene (he wrote in his autobiography) in order to explain matters in their correct light, whereby I made no bones of my opinion that I could not understand how a man could bring himself to hold a woman by force when she did not want to have anything more to do with him. I finally informed him that I should arrive in Bordeaux at the same time as my letter and immediately upon my arrival there would let him know at what hotel to find me ; furthermore, that his wife knew absolutely nothing of my step and he could therefore act without the slightest constraint."

[1] Exhibit 212b, Burrell Collection.
[2] Exhibit 211, Burrell Collection.
[3] Exhibits 203d and 203e, Burrell Collection.

Before leaving, Wagner sent an imploring letter to his motherly friend, Frau Ritter, begging her to hasten to his side in this decisive moment of his life.

"I am summoning up the last strength of my suffering body to hasten off to Bordeaux (he wrote) to see—not Jessie—but Eugene. Look upon me as a dying man, for there lies before me either a speedy death—or a new life. My forces are spent ; only a prodigy of love can bring me back to life again. *Do* come ! It is the last—or the first— day of my life ! "

But a bitter disappointment awaited him in Bordeaux. Eugene preferred to avoid any further dealings with him. He left for the country with his mother-in-law and his wife, from whom he concealed all Wagner's communications. He did this to gain time in order to enable his wife to recover from her infatuation ; but knowing that Wagner had come to Bordeaux without a valid passport he had him expelled by the police. Wagner, highly incensed by this treatment, wrote a detailed explanatory letter to Jessie, and in some mysterious way managed to have it hidden in the work-basket in her boudoir. At all events he returned to the Lake of Geneva without having accomplished anything. In the meantime, Jessie (who knew nothing, of course, of Wagner's letters) had to taste all the torments of an unhappy, betrayed love. Her mother, who had favoured the affair at first in order to console her daughter for her far from happy marriage[1] completely changed her attitude, and disclosed everything to her son-in-law as soon as she saw that things were taking a serious turn and would inevitably lead to a separation, which was not at all in keeping with her intentions.

The two then took energetic counter-measures, and first of all exacted from the desperate Jessie a promise to wait a certain time before leaving her husband, at the expiration of which period— if she still persisted in her determination—she would be given the longed-for liberty. As she knew nothing either of his correspond- ence or of his trip to Bordeaux she agreed to this.

In the meantime her husband and her mother (who held the purse-strings) tried in every way to open her eyes about Wagner, who was regarded as the " instigator of a sort of abduction

---

[1] Mrs. Taylor, who was very well off, had had a liaison with Eugene Laussot and had then given him to her sixteen-year-old daughter in marriage.

project," and in so doing they were not at all squeamish in their choice of methods. Mrs. Taylor had written to Minna and accused Wagner of " premeditated adultery," and had informed her that Wagner had told Jessie that he and his wife had not been legally married,[1] and Minna, of course, was by no means slow in furnishing the necessary and undoubtedly temperamental explanations to the contrary.[2] The Burrell Collection also contains a letter from Jessie to Minna dated 7th April 1850, across the face of which Minna had scrawled in pencil : " *O falsches, verrätherisches Geschöpf!* " (O false, treacherous creature !)[3] Jessie, who had received no direct word from Wagner himself, had to believe willy-nilly what her family told her, and particularly such documentary evidence as Minna's letter ; and she therefore considered herself basely betrayed and was on the point of committing suicide.

Wagner, who had received no sign of life from Jessie, was most rudely awakened from his dream of the past weeks, and had returned to Geneva in the depths of despair. Fortunately he found Frau Ritter there. Strengthened in her decision by Karl's disquieting reports of events, and greatly agitated, she and her daughter Emilie had hastened to Wagner in response to his appeal for help so as to prevent any rash action on his part.

" The women stayed with us about a week (he wrote in *Mein Leben*) ; we tried to divert ourselves by excursions in the beautiful Rhone Valley without dispelling Frau Ritter's great anxiety over recent events which she had just learned in detail, as well as over the shaping of my own future. As I heard later, it cost this delicate and nervous woman a supreme effort to undertake this journey, and when I urged her to move to Switzerland with her family so that we could all be together, she gave me to understand at last that I must not assume from this present—for her—almost eccentric undertaking that she was possessed of a physical vigour that in point of fact she could no longer claim. For the time being she commended her son (whom she wished to leave with me) to my charge, and then left me sufficient funds to look after the two of us for some time. She informed me that her own means were limited, and since it was now impossible to continue the arrangement with the Laussots, she was worried how she was going

---

[1] Wagner said this was a misunderstanding or a wilful and calumnious distortion of a remark that he had once made in jest.
[2] Exhibit 205b, Burrell Collection.
[3] Exhibit 202, Burrell Collection.

to provide a sufficient amount to guarantee my independence. At the end of a week we took a tender, touching farewell of this fine woman, and she and her daughter then went back to Dresden."

His association with this rare, noble woman (who always placed herself unselfishly at the service of the highest ethical aims) had a very calming and soothing effect on him. He called it the " brightest, most shining encounter " of his life. He next retired with his young friend Karl to the romantic solitudes of the Alpine valleys of the Valais, hoping there to find oblivion.

Then one day Karl received a letter from Bordeaux in which Jessie informed him that she had learned of Wagner's baseness, was breaking with the immediate past, and would burn unread any letters in his handwriting. The harsh manner of this rupture, which damned him unheard, wounded Wagner very deeply and restored his pride and self-control. He pictured this " childish turn of the catastrophe " very resignedly to Frau Ritter, and deposited with her the testament of his love

" of which I shall never be ashamed and which, physically dead though I may be, will fill me perhaps with happy memories and blissful feelings as long as I live. From the turn of events it already seemed to me that Jessie had undertaken something beyond her powers, and was not up to carrying out her plans. It did not escape me for a moment that it would take the most courageous revolutionary power to carry out her resolve, that this resolution and her feeling must be their own justification, and then only when these proved so invincible that all other conceivable considerations would seem feeble and impotent in comparison.

" Whoever rebels through the power of love—even though rebellion spells his ruin—he is *mine* ! And if this love is for me personally, it could only bring me happiness if it also spells my own ruin. In this and in no other way (after being informed of her resolution) did I view my affair with Jessie. And from no other point of view than this was I able to cast aside all personal considerations, no matter how painful they might be. But it was only as a rebel that Jessie could carry out her resolution and not by any accord and agreement with those who never in the world could treat—or come to terms—with her. (Can a prince declare a republic ?) The news, therefore, that Jessie was not strong enough to face the music, that it suddenly seemed preferable to her to come to terms and let others dictate to her and define her actions, made me more than doubt her force of character and the infallibility of love's intuitions.

" Our relations had suddenly changed altogether. If before, I thought I had the strength to defend the accomplished fact of Jessie's resolution before all the world, and also the ability to propitiate those who had been most grievously injured by it, I still knew that I was absolutely lacking in the skill required to negotiate for a loved one, whom I had no need to woo from others, but merely had to defend my having won her. I now had to realize that I only had to defend my own honour against brutal attacks (here of course with unbounded sincerity and by fully admitting my love and the immeasurably high value that I set on its realization and fulfilment); leaving Jessie, however, to rely for all time on herself alone. For she was now in chains from which she, and she alone, would be able to liberate herself.

" That she had the strength for this, I had every practical reason to doubt, after these recent experiences. However, what I could do, I did. And I confess to you that I did it, completely indifferent to the risk of having my brains blown out by an irate husband. Only Jessie could help herself and that only by thwarting (through unswerving perseverance and strength of character) all the plots which those in her immediate entourage would naturally set in motion to alienate her from me.

" But now the only power that could help her—the power of her love—she has rejected and betrayed. She herself is lost because—she is *weak*! The woman who was to have brought me salvation has proved herself a *child*! Forgive me—but I can't help but regard her as pitiable ! If she had been forced by present circumstances—and under pressure of her mother—to agree that explanations be demanded from me about my marriage—all very well ! One should have exacted this of me and painful as it would have been to me to have to engage in such heartless and disgusting pedantry, I would still have understood that it was necessary for me to reassure and appease a mother. . . .

" If the strength of Jessie's love had stood the test, I was fully decided to have a friend at some distance, and if possible after a certain time had elapsed, acquaint my wife with all that had occurred. In the meantime she would have become accustomed to our separation and I was then certain that she, who now had a real excuse and a thoroughly valid ground for a formal divorce from me, would also insist on this divorce. For my part, I would not only have considered it contemptible but also impossible to have sued for a divorce from my wife *before* this as I had no legal cause to do so. But that I was prepared even to be cruel to my wife, will show you the overwhelming strength of my love for Jessie. For if I set what Jessie's husband might mean to her over against what my wife must mean to me after our (for her, unspeakably painful) life together, then Jessie's sacrifice dwindled to absolutely nothing in comparison with mine. She also never showed the slightest trace of any love for her husband. But my Jessie never thought of this perfectly natural solution. Yet she was pleased all at once to see in those communications from my wife an ostensible ground for breaking with me !

" At the toss of a hat she felt I had insulted her ; she suddenly

recognized the happiness of love in a conventional middle-class setting
and was so enthusiastic about it that she never deemed it necessary for
a moment to request an explanation from me. But she was suddenly so
indignant over my presumable sentiments in this regard that she
elected to deny me the slightest consideration and sent me word
through my young friend that from then on she would burn my
letters unread. How was that possible ? What power could so suddenly
dethrone the most wonderful love and turn it out of doors like an old
dog ? O everything even the utmost baseness—is possible to the
heart that has surrendered the key to its innermost sanctuary—to
cowardice ! Woe, woe to the cowards and the weak ! Share with me
my deep, deep distress over the happy success of the cure employed
by a prudent mother and a solicitous husband to heal that heart of an
' unseemly ' passion. O, believe me ! love is really there ! I didn't
only imagine it ; it lives, it lives, and loving Nature sends forth its
bliss-giving shoots everywhere in full abundance into this most
miserable of worlds !

" But her mortal enemy has still a fearful power. Its weapons are
education, marriage, propriety, business ; and its mask is the hypo-
critical image of that love itself, against whose most frank-hearted
undissembling conduct it goes forth to battle, mercilessly and
murderously ; but always with a smile of affectionate concern ! And
here it has also been successful !

" They may well be proud of themselves, these clever healers. They
have captured here a lovely corpse ! They are preparing for the burial
with all the pomp of circumstance ; let those of us who loved her
strew sweet blossoms on her grave ! No, we will not revile her, the
dead, the murdered one—for she was—Love ! Never shall I be
ashamed of this love ! If it has died—and I am firmly convinced that
nothing can ever revive it—her kiss was still the richest delight of my
life ! Neither honour nor glory nor fame could ever outweigh this
pleasure for me. Farewell, Thou fair one, Thou blessed one ! Thou
wert dear to me above all else ; and I will never forget Thee ! Farewell ! "

As Wagner grew quieter, his feeling for Minna grew
stronger again.

" Poor woman ! (he wrote). She was so rich, had so much to give ;
whom wouldn't she have made happy ! Alas, that you lacked just the
one thing—the only thing without which all love is deception, all
loving care a martyrdom, all union a torture ; the understanding of
him whom you think you love, this understanding which is the sole
source of joy in the beloved, which alone enables us to bear all sufferings
joyfully. I had to leave you in order to love you again—even if it
meant the ruin of us both."

But when he learned that the Laussots had brought Minna
round by the report that he had " seduced " Jessie, and through

distortion of his statements regarding their marriage had tortured and wounded her most deeply, and that Minna had calmly accepted the insult, her love for him proving stronger than error and doubt, he was filled with sincere sympathy for this poor, unfortunate woman. He at once accepted Karl Ritter's offer to go and see Minna at Zürich in order to explain the situation to her and reassure her. When Ritter, on his return, described her attitude in glowing terms, it broke down all his defences, particularly when he heard that after her unsuccessful visit to Paris she had overcome her personal feelings and had rented and furnished a new house on the lake (as Wagner originally wished) in the hope of hearing from him again. He resumed direct communication with her again in a lamentable letter in which he tried to depict the whole Laussot affair as altogether innocent, and soon after returned to Zürich. Minna made a running marginal commentary on this letter,[1] summing up her feelings in the statement : " I owe our reunion not to this letter with its many untrue accusations and insults but to my great love alone." Be that as it may, she confessed to her Dresden friend, Mathilde Schiffner, on 2nd August 1850, that

" he came and excused himself as best he could. I, a weak woman who however loves him still, have forgiven him, but between us, dear friend, I certainly will not, and can *never*, forget it ! He can never make up to me for the unspeakable anguish he has caused me. May God forgive him as I have done. . . . People can know that I also had to undergo *this* hard trial, that men are the weak ones, not the women. What wouldn't I give if this slur did not rest on Richard ! I don't care what he did. But I've lost confidence in him ; though he almost carries me around in his hands ! We've been married too long, otherwise. . . ."

And thus ended on a note of reconciliation this stormy epoch in his life that had begun with the fatal Dresden political entanglements, had been intensified by misunderstandings of all kinds, and at last had been brought to the verge of catastrophe by outside agencies. Once more the two partners in battle ventured to pick up the old strands of life together again, and as the trials in Koenigsberg had once before matured them and bound them more closely to one another, so now this bitter experience appeared at first to have a salutary effect.

[1] Exhibit 213, Burrell Collection.

" I've got a new wife (he wrote Theodor Uhlig shortly after his return home on 27th July), even though she is just the same as ever yet I now know that, come what may, she will stand by me till death. As for me, I really had no idea of putting her, so to say, to the test. But as things have turned out, she has been through a fiery ordeal such as all must go through who nowadays consciously cast in their lot with those who recognize their future and steer straight for it."

CHAPTER IV

MATHILDE

" Mir erkoren—mir verloren! "
Isolde.[1]

THE new house that Minna had selected and rented during
Wagner's absence met with his full approval, and under her
efficient management (a talent that earned her unanimous praise
at all times) the Villa Rienzi was soon the gay centre of a little
group of congenial friends.

" I now feel very well again (Wagner wrote his friend Uhlig) and
if I had the choice I should want to live nowhere in the whole wide
world but here. We have a really delightful house on the lake with the
most wonderful views, garden, etc. I run down to the lake in my
dressing-gown to bathe—there's a boat there that we row ourselves.
In addition the people are of a fine type, sympathetic, obliging ; in fact,
touchingly eager to be of service whichever way one turns—more, and
far more reliable, friends than I could ever find in the whole of lovely
Dresden. They're all happy just to have me here."

Karl Ritter, who was then stopping with them, was ambitious
to win his spurs as conductor at a little theatre, so Wagner got in
touch with the director of the Zürich Theatre on his behalf ;
whereupon the latter immediately offered the post to Wagner
himself ! But when he declined it the director could only be
persuaded to engage Ritter on condition that Wagner assume the
oversight and guidance of the young novice. Wagner's refusal,
which was quite comprehensible on the grounds of prestige,
upset Minna very greatly, as owing to the continued drain on her
housekeeping funds she naturally looked at the matter mainly
from the practical standpoint.

" The director offered Wagner 200 francs a month (she wrote a
friend in a letter that was still vibrant with her recent sufferings) if he
would accept the post of conductor at his theatre. But Richard finds
it quite beneath his dignity to earn money and prefers to live from

[1] " Destined for me—lost to me."

67

charity or on borrowed money. Knowing my point of view on such matters, you can understand how this disgusts me, as it would any other woman—quite apart from what has gone before. What is going to become of me—of us—with such principles ? I nearly cry my eyes out sometimes and am really worn out with the worry that this man causes me."

Since Ritter soon proved himself incapable of conducting an opera Wagner had to come to the rescue (now without remuneration) and finally had to take over altogether, after young Hans von Buelow resigned as the result of a quarrel with the leading soprano. However, for several winters in succession Wagner consented to conduct a number of the subscription concerts of the Zürich Musical Society for a definite fee. This activity won for him many friends and admirers in the society, especially as he was able to raise these concerts far above the general level, thanks to the enthusiasm of the performers. In respect to his own work, he continued to develop his theoretical articles, as he was not interested in piling up opera scores that had no immediate prospect of performance. And, furthermore, he was not inclined to make any concessions to the temper of the age in spite of Minna's entreaties.[1] His financial situation was therefore pretty desperate. The efforts of Frau Ritter (who now frequently helped him out with small sums) to assure him a certain annual allowance, had not yet met with the desired success. The project had been recently broached to come to some such arrangement in co-operation with the family of Richard's brother Albert, whose daughters Johanna and Franziska were frequent guests of the Ritters.[2] When Wagner learned of the proposed arrangement he was horrified.[3]

" Let me dissect for you the collective concept ' Wagner Family ' into its component parts so that we will get a better idea of the business. Johanna is a good girl, but without character and highly dependent on others ! But I'm fond of her. Franziska strikes me as being very clever ; she's all for me, and she knows what she's about. I remember Maria as a talented, but spoilt, silly, and rather impertinent girl. The mother of

---

[1] Exhibit 232 of the Burrell Collection is a letter from Nathalie, in which she describes Minna's practical reaction to Wagner's literary activities " instead of creating immortal masterpieces " and her opinion regarding the choice of " Tannhäuser " (rather than " Rienzi ") for Paris.

[2] Shortly after this Franziska married Alexander Ritter.

[3] Exhibit 37(B), Burrell Collection. The quoted passage was deleted in the official Uhlig correspondence and was published for the first time in *Richard Wagner und seine erste Elizabeth*, by Julius Kapp and Hans Jachmann. The letters in the Burrell Collection are copies made by Uhlig's daughter.

the aforesaid three daughters I've come to detest. She is a stage
mamma who can absorb a lot of poison and then spews it out again
when occasion arises. For this she makes use of her husband, my
brother. He's a talented chap with a strong artistic instinct; but is soft,
weak and irresolute, and has come down pretty much in the world
through this eternal play-acting. In his letters to Switzerland, he
reproached me for not being more practical in my opera compositions
and for no longer considering the demands of small theatres and the
singers themselves, etc., but chiefly for allowing myself to be led astray
by that scoundrel Roeckel and losing my Dresden post. *In Summa*,
you won't be offended with me if I confess that the family, in the lump,
leaves me perfectly cold, with the exception, at most, of Franziska,
from whom I should like to hear more?

"However, this indifference was bound to change into something
else as soon as the following complications arose! After you met
Johanna in Soden, my wife received word from my sister in Chemnitz
that she was very happy that Johanna (that is, the Wagner family)
had now decided to do something for me—we surely had already
received a letter from her. Johanna had told the rest of the family
that she was now going to assist me financially (incidentally there has
been no sign of a letter or anything else). When I met Karl Ritter in
Altisbrunn, he told me his mother had written him and invited him to
a family parley in Berlin. I admit that I was weak enough to be suddenly surprised by this news and led to assume (particularly through
the choice of Berlin as place) that the Wagners had communicated
with the Ritters with a view to making common arrangements to
assist me, and that a conference on the matter was to be held in
Berlin.

"The thought of this was so painful to me that I couldn't sleep, and
urgently begged Karl to write to his family as soon as possible and
explain to them that I wouldn't accept the slightest thing from the
Wagners and that any co-operation between the Ritters and Wagners
on my behalf, as well as the mere thought that the Ritters would discuss
my situation and my future with them, would make me so unhappy
that I would even have to forgo the Ritters' allowance.

"Must I now go into minute details as to why I will have nothing
to do with the Wagners and why that suspected joint prospect should
have made me furious? Surely not? The Ritters are a new world for
me. Everything between us is a matter of course. We delight in each
other, and everything that the one does is designed to please the other.
There is no question of *gratitude* between us. And I'm therefore
expected to be indifferent if I have reason to fear that this wonderful
relationship is to be disturbed by the fault-finding of persons who
cannot understand me nor love me—who at most are ashamed of
what people may say because of certain disgraceful things—and ugh!
Just think over the last years of my life; look at the others, and look

at the Ritters—then you'll understand, I hope, why I was beside myself when that suspicion, that conjecture, struck me ! "

" Remember me to my niece Johanna (he wrote Uhlig in bitter irony on 12th January 1852). *Ach!* If she would only put in a good word for me ! Ask her nicely, she'll certainly do it, the good girl. Just tell her what a fix her poor devil of an uncle is in ! She's now in a position to help me achieve recognition, for I hear to my great delight that her lover is a Prussian prince who has done a lot for her—he even put through her Berlin contract. Perhaps if she's very nice to him, and Mamma has no objections, she can also do something for me ! "

Wagner once considered the eighteen-year-old Johanna worthy of singing Elizabeth in the première of his " Tannhäuser," and had taken the most affectionate interest in her further artistic development. He looked to her to be his chief exponent of the art of dramatic singing as he conceived it, and was dreadfully upset over the fact that under her father's influence she too soon adopted the usual prima donna practice and preferred to reap triumphs in the old virtuoso rôles, while she avoided *his* works. After the flight from Dresden, his brother Albert had broken off all intercourse with the " revolutionary." Only Franziska, who at the time was engaged as an actress in Schwerin, and therefore outside the range of parental influence, still stood by her out-lawed uncle. He used to pour out his heart to her, and sent her numerous invitations to visit him in Switzerland.

" I thought I already had to put you in the same category with Johanna (he wrote 21st March 1852), who in her childish subservience to her parents has come to ignore me completely. Her mother and father seem to find it distressing and dangerous for her to have any-thing to do with me. This anxiety on their part shows how conscience-stricken they are for their attitude towards me, and the promptings of a bad conscience are disturbing. I only wish they knew how they wrong me when they fear I might ever bother them. To my own kind I'm as open and frank as a child. But with those who don't understand me and don't want to understand me, I'm horribly proud."

Franziska finally succeeded in bringing her uncle and Johanna together again, and the latter then sent him a photograph of herself with a dedication that so moved him that, forgetting all his anger, he at once sent her the following acknowledgment on 2nd October 1852 :

" You see, Hans, that was really a *great pleasure* such as I've been yearning for ! You will have guessed that I've just received your autographed photograph ? O, you people ! If you only knew how much happiness we could give ourselves simply by showing others that we love them, you wouldn't be so miserly about it ! I've never cherished resentment against you ; at most a bitter astonishment—distressing doubts.

"But even if I had, your picture would have dispelled all my resentment. My one need is—love ! Fame, honour—nothing of this kind can refresh me. Only one thing can delight me and reconcile me to life, a sign that I am loved, even if it only comes from a child ! Of course, you are no longer a child. You are a *woman* ; your picture tells me that. Be completely a woman, all heart and love ! I know nothing more heavenly than such a woman ! and I'm happy when I find such a one, and *wherever* I find her !

"Just see how happy you've made me ! I'm to send you Minna's heartiest thanks also. She is delighted over the dress—because it comes from *you*—not because of the dress ! I'm charmed with the picture and the greeting from my foolish, good, dear Hans.

"Good-bye, dear child. Good-bye for to-day ! I can't write you anything better, and still it's the best I've written for a long time. All my books are not so dear to me ! Regards to your husband and the children. Farewell ! A thousand affectionate remembrances from Minna."

Minna expressed her own thanks in the following gushing letter of 1st November.

"Forgive me for not writing sooner to thank you for the lovely rich dress with which you greatly surprised and delighted me. Many prosaic household duties (since I have no maid) alone kept me from rousing myself to write to my now famous niece. I see with genuine pleasure that in spite of all the homage that rightly falls to you in your position you've retained your childlike nature and affection for us. Believe me, my dear Johanna, nobody knows how to appreciate that better than I, who understand your situation so well. I always follow your artistic career with the greatest interest and am delighted every time we hear or read something about you in our tiresome shut-in Zürich.

"When I saw you so universally acclaimed, I laid the paper aside with no little pride and said to myself : one never hears anything more about that ' wry face ' your little niece used to make in her tragic rôles. However, don't be cross with me for mentioning this little trait. But I love to recall it and wish that I could see you again like that. Unfortunately it will be a long time yet before I have my dearest wish of admiring you as an artist, though my husband is trying to persuade me to accept the Fromann's invitation to share her nutshell. But I must admit that my presence would revive so many unpleasant memories that they would spoil all the pleasure of seeing you.

" Moreover, there's my boundless anxiety as to how that
' Tannhäuser ' is going to take. In fact, if I could creep into a mouse-
hole just to hear and see you, this would fulfil my dearest wish, even
though I couldn't promise not to jump out of my hiding-place suddenly
to rush to you, press you to my throbbing heart (as I should be inclined
to do), smother you with kisses, and then return to my hiding-place
again. I believe I don't need to assure you now that I've never ceased
to think of you with affection ! In fact, I'll always think of you with
gratitude—how once when I was in an extremely desperate situation,
you wanted to help me through your friend, like a good angel !

" This is a very exciting time for us, since Richard's operas are
becoming more and more known. He has never felt his exile so keenly
as now, especially because of Berlin, as this to a certain extent is the
heart of Germany. A success *there* can help him as much as the reverse
can harm him. For this reason, your uncle is very upset that he
can't personally conduct the rehearsals and performances. I therefore
have a good deal to put up with on this account ! You must be patient
and make excuses for him. I must also ask your dear good father (to
whom I send my warmest greetings) to be patient and indulgent with
his restless brother.

" One can put up with these moods in the case of ' Tannhäuser,'
but if ' Lohengrin ' should ever have the good luck to be given at an
important German theatre then I don't know ! He hasn't heard this
music yet. I know what it means when a composer hasn't yet heard
his own work, especially when it's going to be given. Richard's
longing is so keen that he often speaks of going to Paris so that he
may at least have a good orchestra play it for him (*privatim*) scene by
scene, so as to get to know the music to some extent. Here the
orchestra isn't up to it. Although there's a theatre here, the conditions
are really miserable !

" How I wish that your uncle might soon be amnestied so as to
avoid this fatal Paris, where I should have to go with him. I had a
premonition that things would turn out like this and that some day he
would feel his banishment keenly when his operas were being
rehearsed for performance. But nobody feels it more than I do !
Would that I could undo it all !

" He has not been especially well. He is more irritable than usual.
His nerves bother him a lot, for which that horrid water cure that he
tried a year ago and now carries on at home is mainly to blame. But
when Richard goes in for anything, then he must see it through to the
finish—even if he is heading for a fall, no advice can stop him.

" We have just received letters from Dresden saying that
' Tannhäuser ' was given again before a packed and very enthusiastic
house, without further demonstrations. If this were also the case in
Berlin, it would lift a great weight from my heart. I can't help thinking
that the performance won't come off after all ! You will have heard

that the 'Flying Dutchman' was given here the end of last winter. Richard had to sweat a good bit in order to get passably good results with the wretched material at his disposal. But this opera was given four times in one week at special prices and with really crowded houses. Flowers were showered on us in profusion.

"However, all this trouble has spoilt Richard for ever wanting to put on any of his works here; though the director is pestering him for 'Tannhäuser,' he has still refused to give him the score. The performance probably reminded Louise (who is at present in Dresden)— or jogged her memory—that the composer is really her brother, for she has at last written to us after three years! She seems depressed, for which we are really sorry. We have no news of the rest of the family, even Klära—the only one who used to write me occasionally— has been silent for six months.

"We were very delighted to hear that Mariachen is soon to become a mother. We congratulate her heartily! It can't help being a pretty child if it takes after her at all, and I shall put on no end of airs on becoming a great aunt.

"Our life here is really very humdrum, but I won't die from boredom because I always have my hands full. Your uncle sees to that. We only have a little circle of good friends, but if we accepted all the invitations with which people seek to honour us, we would end up by having no time for ourselves at all. It's probably different with you. You live in the turmoil of the great world, which in your position you can't well avoid.

"You gave us real pleasure, my darling Hans, with your dear picture. You couldn't have given us greater pleasure, and it now decorates my little room, resplendent in a gold frame. This was the only place available in our little home, otherwise your uncle would have hung it in his room. But I'm very happy to have it and it looks so much like you that I'm often tempted to talk to you, at least I always wish you good morning and ask 'how are you, my dear Hans? are you in good voice?' etc. *Ach!* what beautiful days those were when I could really ask you those questions! But forgive me, my darling Johanna, for this long rambling letter. I'm robbing you of time that you could certainly put to far better use. Very best regards to your family! Write me when you have time, and rest assured that by so doing you will gladden the heart of your faithful, grateful and sincerely affectionate old Aunt Minna. I was interrupted at least thirty times while I was writing you this letter; therefore please think of my disconnected ramblings as really connected."

The Berlin "Tannhäuser" to which Minna alluded led to an active correspondence between Richard and Johanna and the latter's father. Hülsen of the Royal Opera had appointed Albert Wagner stage director there, and the latter now conducted the negotiations with his brother on behalf of his chief, who did not desire to come into personal contact with the " revolutionary " Wagner. But these came to nothing on account of Wagner's insistence that Liszt supervise the Berlin performance in his stead.[1] This led to renewed ill feeling between the brothers, as Richard reproached Albert for being too lukewarm in furthering his work.

This time Franziska also disappointed her uncle by failing to visit him as she had long promised.

" Why don't you let us hear something from you again ? (he wrote her on 4th February 1853). I have to send a bit of music to Herr Stock and am doing it through you so as to have the opportunity of telling you that *we are counting definitely on your promised visit* in the spring—or summer. At Easter we're going to take a larger flat in the same building—and there will be a guest room especially for you. You can be wonderfully comfortable with us. There will be no lack of excursions such as you will find nowhere else in the world ! Be a good girl now and come along, letting us know definitely very soon ! Your visit will do me, in particular, a world of good. I'm looking forward to it keenly. Don't go and squander your savings on anything else ! I withdrew ' Tannhäuser ' from Berlin—purely to save my honour ; because they would never have given it anyway. Perhaps you know more about it than I do. In a fortnight I'll send you a private copy of my Ring poem, which is now finished. You can feel yourself greatly honoured as I have only had a very few copies made. Kind regards to the Stocks ! Let us hear from you soon, and above all that you're coming to your

Uncle Richard."

All other sources failing for the time being, Wagner was again thrown solely on Liszt's mercy. He turned with confidence to his friend.

" With all the admirable qualities that my wife possesses (he wrote) she unfortunately doesn't understand my real character in the least. With regard to what I am and what I accomplish, the poor soul can't rise above those things that have to be put up with for the sake of those higher aims ; she only senses the depressing side of our situation, and nothing that I do can console her for that. My inner nature is a stranger to her. At the same time, I'm sorry for her—just for this reason—yes ! really sorry ! If I'm now to have any peace so that I can go on with my work without being disturbed, I must have provision for my immediate needs."

[1] Exhibits 230, 230B, 254A and 266, Burrell Collection.

The ever-ready Liszt did not disappoint him this time either, but sent him an official commission from the Weimar Court Theatre for the composition of *Seigfried's Tod*. Yet Wagner continued to procrastinate. The "Siegfried" drama which he had conceived some years before had gradually expanded to the gigantic project of the "Tetralogy." But he felt that the little Court Theatre in Weimar would never be able to handle it. While he was still seeking a way out of this dilemma he had an unexpected stroke of luck that made it possible for him to turn down the Weimar commission and, free of economic worries, dedicate himself to the execution of the "Nibelungen" drama. A substantial legacy suddenly relieved his patroness, Frau Ritter, of her tireless efforts to find the necessary help elsewhere, and made it possible for her to produce the proposed annual allowance of 800 *thalers* for Wagner out of her own pocket.

In the meantime Wagner had exchanged the Villa Rienzi in the Commune of Enge for a ground-floor flat in one of the Escher Houses, which were situated nearer town. Here he made some new friends who were destined to pay a great part in his life. Through Marschall von Bieberstein, an old friend from the days of the Dresden Revolution, he made the acquaintance of a very rich businessman, Otto Wesendonck, agent of a New York silk firm, who had recently settled in Zürich with his pretty young wife, Mathilde. The winter before they had heard Wagner conduct a Beethoven symphony, which had made an indelible impression on them, so that the desire to know the admired artist was therefore quite comprehensible, especially on the part of Frau Wesendonck, an idealist and very sensitive in an artistic way. Her taste was thoroughly unspoilt ; in fact, as she expressed it, she "was quite untaught, a blank white page as it were." The two families were soon on the most intimate of terms. Mathilde and Minna were also good friends at first, as testified by two letters from Frau Wesendonck to Minna that have been preserved in the Burrell Collection.[1] As for Wagner, with his congenital proclivity to teach and convert others, he was highly delighted to initiate the clever pupil into the world of his art and ideas, convey to this receptive soul the breath of genius.

[1] Exhibit 245, dated from Ems, 4th July 1853. Exhibit 292, dated from Paris, 11th January 1856.

" The Master (wrote Frau Wesendonck in her Memoirs) began to initiate me more closely into his intentions. First he read the texts of his three operas, which delighted me ; then the introduction to them, and then all of his prose writings one after the other. Since I loved Beethoven, he played the sonatas for me. If a concert were scheduled in which he was to conduct a Beethoven symphony, he was indefatigable in playing over the different movements (before and after the rehearsal) until I knew them thoroughly. He was delighted when I was able to follow him, and my enthusiasm took fire from his own."

Shortly after this, in the spring of 1852, Wagner made a second valuable acquaintance in the family of Dr. François Wille, who lived at Mariafeld, near Zürich, and to whom he had been introduced by his friend, George Herwegh. If it was chiefly the artist, the idolized genius, who was fêted at the Wesendoncks, the pure human friendship and simple hospitality of the Wille circle was on a more modest foundation, even though here too lively discussions of artistic and philosophical questions (Schopenhauer in particular) with the head of the house were the order of the day. Frau Eliza Wille had already met Wagner fleetingly in Dresden in 1843, but it was only later on that he came to appreciate the real value of her friendship. The Willes were also the first to hear the complete poem of the " Tetralogy," which Wagner read on three successive evenings towards the end of December 1852. This informal reading was followed in February 1853 by another in the banquet hall of the Hotel Baur au Lac in Zürich in the presence of a large invited audience.

How Wagner would have liked to bring the Ritter family into this circle of his Zürich friends ! He was always distressed that this woman above all others—who meant so much to him— always lived so far away, which made it hard to arrive at a complete understanding and a feeling of unbounded confidence.

" A feeling often comes over me that I ought to write to Frau Ritter again ! (he wrote Theodor Uhlig).[1] I sometimes feel so terribly ungrateful towards her ! If it weren't for this great-hearted woman, I should now be the most wretched of mortals. Yes, all imagination, even thought, fails me when I try to picture and think *what* I should now be if it hadn't been for her ! I can only imagine it would be something perfectly horrible !

" Yet there is a spirit of discontent in me that goads me on—to the point of self-destruction—against the things dearest to me, even

[1] Letter 54, Appendix B, Burrell Collection.

against this woman. I believe this is only because of the fact that she is far away from me and—persists in staying there. If she were near me and I could live on intimate terms with this family, then I believe this torturing discontent would vanish ! I will therefore hope that this wish also will be fulfilled, as otherwise almost everything the Ritters do for me is beginning to frighten me. Sometimes it seems to me— don't laugh !—as though I were merely being paid for the 'Tannhäuser.' This is the damned mistrust of the proletarian *vis-à-vis* the capitalist."

A decisive turning-point in the life of the exile had now arrived. For five long years during which he did battle in one theoretical article after the other, like a militant apostle of a new art, the fount of musical inspiration had been sealed up within him. The wonder world of the Nibelungs was now to awaken him to new life. But before he could arrive at the necessary tranquillity, the inner desire and the serenity to create, he had to absorb new impressions from the outside world. He required (as he wrote to Otto Wesendonck)

" a certain saturation with outward life, then through a beautiful counter-pressure be forced to fling what is inward joyfully to the surface again."

Since the real world was cold and hostile towards him he wanted to create round him an imaginary world, the enchantment of which had a very stimulating effect on him. First of all he must have much pleasanter surroundings. The stuffy ground-floor flat in the Escher Houses was exchanged for a more commodious one on the second floor of the same building, and this was then furnished as luxuriously as possible. That all Wagner's personal wishes were taken into consideration when the flat was enlarged and altered was due to the unselfish kindness and civility of the owner, Frau Clementine Stocker-Escher, who was an enthusiastic admirer of his. She was also an excellent amateur painter in water colours, " full of artistic talent," as Wagner said, and to her we owe an excellent portrait of Wagner at that period which was lithographed on its completion and enjoyed wide circulation. Minna was far from pleased with the new layout of things (the refurbishing even extending to her own person). She clung to the old surroundings to which she had grown attached, and these had now been sacrificed to a large extent to the new order of things.

" Richard is very happy in the new flat (she wrote a friend on 15th November 1853). Once more he couldn't resist furnishing it very prettily and naturally ran into debt as a result. This is also a trait of genius ! He has showered me with presents, for instance, a silk dressing-gown that would not disgrace a queen, then two hats and a little coat of some curious woollen material. A still greater surprise was in store on our return. He had made away with all my dear old furniture and had replaced it with red silk and velvet upholstery. There were also red curtains with embroidered net among the innovations. I must confess, dear friend, that I was more pained than pleased. It was as though I were in a strange room—not my cosy one where I was truly perfectly contented. I first had to have a good cry. The dear foolish man ! My happiness doesn't lie in such outward glitter. . . . And why all these silly gauds ! My life has been so gaudy as it is that this no longer suits my mood."

If the man in Wagner felt uplifted and strengthened by this new milieu, the hunger of the artist, who had been reduced to very modest fare in these humdrum Zürich surroundings, was now to be appeased at last with a grand banquet. He organized a big three-day musical festival in Zürich, chiefly to derive new inspiration from his earlier works, and particularly from " Lohengrin," which he had not yet heard.

" Everybody revelled in it (he wrote). It was really a festival for the world around me. The women were all kind to me and I laid the whole festival at the feet of *one* beautiful woman ! "

This " one beautiful woman " was his friend Mathilde Wesendonck, whose husband had guaranteed the largest part of the expenses of the festival, amounting to 9,000 francs. The only soloist was Frau Emilie Heim, wife of Ignaz Heim, conductor of a local choral society. She was one of the most admired beauties of Zürich and

" had a really fine voice and a warm tone (as Wagner wrote in his autobiography). But she was thoroughly unmusical and I had a lot to do to get her to hit the right notes and particularly to keep the proper time."

Wagner was long one of her admirers. He always called her Sieglinde, since her curly, blonde hair and typical Germanic build seemed to him the prototype of his daughter of the Volsungs. The Heims also lived in the Escher Houses and the two families saw a great deal of each other. In one of the two letters from Frau Heim to Minna that have been preserved in the

Burrell Collection she recalls " with emotion and delight the many beautiful hours and wonderful evenings " they spent together in " music-making or inspiring conversation."[1]

A long-awaited visit of Liszt (who unfortunately only stayed a week) and extensive Alpine tours furnished the needed recreation after the exertions of the concerts. Georg Herwegh also joined in these excursions. His wife was in Zürich at the time, and soon became a great friend of Minna's. Later on she had harsh words to say of Wagner, " this pocket edition of a man," as she called him, " this folio of vanity, heartlessness and egoism." But she left us a very excellent description of Minna.

" She was a stately, pretty person (she wrote in her Memoirs). Without being on her husband's intellectual level, she was far superior to him in many important qualities such as disposition and real kindness of heart; and it was these qualities that made others love and respect her. Her conversation was not precisely sparkling with wit, but—which was far more important—during those most difficult days when they often lacked the necessities of life, she knew how to spare her adored husband and artist (as far as it was possible to do so) all worry over their daily bread and the bitter prose of those hours. Of course, one couldn't expect exquisite tact from her; for this she was far too passionate a nature, too little able to control herself, and had too little education. But whoever appealed to her admirable heart could be sure of finding understanding and a ready ear.

" When she married Wagner, she was the beautiful, idolized tragedienne; he still obscure, that is, an insignificant looking, comparatively unknown musician constantly burdened with debt. Vanity therefore played no part in her choice. But to have so much breath left later on in a life of struggle, renunciations and the bitterest humdrumness, to keep up with a man like Wagner in spite of everything, to maintain his *niveau*, this at all events would have required a much more versatile temperament and a buoyant energy that the good Minna verily never possessed, and in any event never had the time to cultivate. The kernel was admirable. The world will never know all that this good and faithful proletarian soul did for her husband."

Wagner never seems to have liked Emma Herwegh especially. At least he felt she was not a very good influence for Minna. While up in the mountains he once sent this conceited reply to a question of Minna's inspired by Frau Herwegh :

" You wicked woman ! you haven't the slightest confidence in me ; but behind every action, behind every word you suspect something,

---

[1] Exhibit 305, dated 30th March 1858; and 336, dated 20th September 1859.

see something that doesn't exist. You silly women ! Don't you realize that the greatest pride must lie in the fact that your husbands, after a period of the most complete liberty and freedom, always come back to you in the end after all ? "

Before he finally settled down to work on " Rheingold " after his return from the mountains, he first went to Basle to meet Liszt, as arranged. Here he also became more intimately acquainted with the Princess Carolyne Sayn-Wittgenstein and her daughter, Marie, who had accompanied Liszt. He had previously met them only casually at a " Tannhäuser " performance in Dresden, and he saw them again at the Altenburg in Weimar at the time of his flight. *Mein Leben* describes the impression made on him by this strange woman, who played such a vital, and at last such a pernicious, rôle in Liszt's life.

" It was impossible for anyone coming into contact with Princess Carolyne not to be fascinated by her bright manner and the charming way in which she entered into everything that interested us (he wrote). She was as much interested in the more important questions that stirred us, as in the most casual details of our personal intercourse with the world. She flattered everybody into a sort of ecstatic state that made them feel that they had to give the very best of which they were capable. The Princess's daughter, on the other hand, displayed a certain ardent, rapturous quality. Then barely fifteen years of age, in dress and in bearing she gave the impression of a girl just on the threshold of womanhood and earned from me the honorary title of ' The Child.' "

Liszt wanted to go to Paris from Basle to see his three children, and obeying a sudden caprice the whole party broke up and went along with him. One of the first evenings after their arrival was spent quite *en famille* with Liszt's children, the two sisters Cosima and Blandine, who were living very quietly in Paris in the care of a governess. Liszt's promising son, Daniel, was also present and made a " touching impression " on Wagner through his great vivacity and his striking likeness to his father. As for the two girls he noted nothing about them but their " persistent shyness."

Wagner had arranged with Minna to meet him in Paris so that they might spend a few happy hours there together in memory of the difficult days of old ; but she was not to arrive " till Liszt and the Princess (particularly the latter) had left." Then he un-expectedly ran into the Wesendoncks in the street, and sent for Minna to come as soon as possible so that " at a pinch she could be along if he had to take part in any larks." " Frau Wesendonck was delighted when she heard you were coming, too," he added. As this shows, Minna and Mathilde were on a very friendly footing at that time. Minna arrived shortly afterwards and spent a very happy week there with Richard and their good friends from earlier days. But then an irresistible force drew Wagner back to his work. " I'm now past all help (he wrote). The game's up ! It's perish or compose—that's all ! " They rushed home practically head over heels, and Wagner threw himself feverishly into the composition of " Rheingold," and then plunged at once into " Valkyrie." The only impediment to his work was the lack of money, which had now become critical as the orders for his earlier works, on which he had built his hopes, failed to materialize.

" This niggardly existence of ours (he complained to Liszt), with never enough to go on, is exhausting my poor wife more and more, and I can only keep her from worrying if we have a certain economic security."

The domestic atmosphere was therefore sometimes very tense and uncomfortable, especially as he himself was inclined to be very irritable during these periods of great creative intensity. He therefore sent for Minna's daughter, Nathalie (then employed in a hotel) to run the house for them in order to relieve Minna.[1]

" Through many years of hard work, worries, and anxieties of many kinds which I had to go through in our very chequered life (wrote Minna to Caroline Uhlig, widow of their old Dresden friend, Theodor Uhlig), my health is finally so shattered that I've been suffering for a long time from the most severe blood disorders and gouty pains."

She sent her friend very pressing invitations to visit her soon in Switzerland.

" It would do me so much good (she wrote on 28th January 1854) to have a dear friend with me for once who is frank and sincere. Last summer I had lots of visitors ; but unfortunately only those of whose sincerity I had the very best reasons in the world to doubt, and that is quite against my nature. I'm only a simple person, but I like to meet everyone on the most sincere footing. . . .

" Nothing would entice me to lovely Dresden but the fact of your being there and the desire to see the children of our faithful and

[1] Exhibit 252, Burrell Collection. Wagner's letter to Nathalie dated 19th November 1853 offering her a yearly salary of 200 francs and " appropriate presents as a member of the family."

F

unforgettable friend again, as well as my poor brave family. Besides, I don't want to come because it would remind me too often of my lost happiness ! I still am terribly homesick ! My husband, thank God, is well and happy, except when he hears about bad performances of his operas ; then he feels his exile doubly hard. Naturally things would be altogether different if he could be present ; but as the matter stands there's nothing to be done. I saw right from the start that it would be like this. O, these stupid politics !

" Since Wagner got back from his many trips last October, he has been working very industriously, which makes me very happy. Then he's always in a good humour and it's pleasant to be with him. He has already finished ' Rheingold.' This is part of a huge work that he has started and hopes to complete in a few years' time."

Since it became more and more apparent that Minna's illness was a chronic heart trouble, in August of that year Wagner, after procuring the necessary money from friends (this time Otto Wesendonck and Sulzer) decided to join her in a cure on the Selisberg, a health resort on the Lake of Lucerne. Here Minna took a milk cure, and on its completion left for Germany to visit her relatives. While there she did everything she could to help her husband. For instance, in Dresden she pressed the matter of his amnesty, and to this end even had a private audience with Minister von Beust, leaving with him a personal petition addressed to the King on behalf of her husband, " the misled, guilty, erring one who is paying heavily through the fettering of his art." For the time being her efforts were in vain. She also tried to persuade Intendant von Huelsen in Berlin to give " Tannhäuser " under Wagner's conditions, after several attempts to achieve this had failed.

On this trip Minna also had an opportunity at last to hear her husband's works again. Her letter to her Dresden friend shows that she was by no means lacking in appreciation or understanding of them.

" During the rest of my trip (she writes) I had many exciting pleasures ; for instance, the day I arrived in Leipzig I was at a large party where they sang many selections from ' Lohengrin ' very admirably. This was a foretaste of the Weimar performance that moved me very greatly in spite of the fact that the leading singer at this opera house was really dreadful. Many passages he couldn't sing at all and had to keep silent ; and as an actor he was a big booby without a voice. But the music moved me really enormously. However, it was a shame that everything sped by so fast. I would have liked to have held it up so that I could really have assimilated it all. In Frankfort I heard a really admirable ' Tannhäuser ' performance, with the exception of Tichatschek and Mitterwurzer. Otherwise the rest were all better —fresh, lovely young voices. The staging was as good as in Dresden ; the orchestra, conductor, both absolutely first rate ! In short I was carried away with joy and delight. I cried the whole time so that next day the papers spoke of my very evident emotion."

The " Tannhäuser " negotiations were reopened after Liszt had met the director of the Berlin opera at a court function in Gotha. But this gave rise immediately to a heated argument between Richard and his brother Albert. Under the pressure of the continual lack of funds, Richard used the resumption of the negotiations to borrow immediately a thousand *thalers* from his niece Johanna in a very tactless way. This was too much for her father, who wrote his brother in his daughter's name, without mincing any words.

" Your last letter in which you announced to Johanna the—overhasty —withdrawal of ' Tannhäuser,' as well as many others to Franziska, etc., in which you have spoken contemptuously of Johanna and us, her parents, were of a nature to set our children against their parents. Naturally, if we weren't to blame for the delay in producing your ' Tannhäuser,' we were still—in your opinion—in a position to prevent it.

" However, I will let that pass, as I am used to seeing you notice people only if, and *so long as*, they are useful to you. When this usefulness is over the person also no longer exists for you. Gratitude for past favours is unknown to you ! It's all a confounded obligation ! This has always been the case : take Brockhaus, Koenig, Lüttichau, Pusinelli, Tichatschek and all the rest who have been kind to you in one way or another. Much as I esteem and love your talent, it is anything but so as regards your character.

" Since your last letter, the first cheep out of you to Johanna is again—give me 1,000 *thalers*. A mere trifle ! In Johanna's name and my own I reply to this ; if your opera is once really put in rehearsal in Berlin and I then receive from you a valid assignment, confirmed by the management, of the Berlin royalties, then I'm willing—if you need and wish it—to advance you a flat sum against them after the second performance. But to do so now without any guarantee would be unconscientious on my part with regard to Johanna's future.

" Believe me, without going into details, it's not too much to say—if Johanna were to satisfy all the demands made on her by the various families, she would soon have little enough to live on herself, let alone provide for her future. Johanna supports her parents, she has outfitted Marie for us in Hamburg and is now going to do the same for

Franziska ; brother Julius who amounts to nothing, knows nothing, and does nothing, costs her a pretty penny, not to mention all the rest. She is therefore doing enough, and as for you, I know that you have enough to live on decently if you could once adjust yourself to circumstances."

This put a definite end to all personal intercourse between the two brothers. But Wagner showed a conciliatory spirit towards Johanna when artistic matters frequently brought them into contact. Spurred by Minna's description, Alwine Fromann now tried through her Court connections to remove the obstacles that were still blocking the way for " Tannhäuser " in Berlin. Meanwhile, moved by Minna's accounts of her audience with Huelsen and the existing conditions in Berlin, Wagner began to waver in his opposition. He finally withdrew all his conditions, and " Tannhäuser " was at last given at the Royal Opera on 7th January 1856. Here, as in Dresden, Johanna had an enormous success as Elizabeth.

During Minna's absence Wagner now turned to Mathilde Wesendonck more than ever for companionship. Their friendship had grown more and more cordial, but the relationship soon underwent a change. Now he was no longer the kind mentor and teacher of an eager, adoring listener but the genius dispensing gifts to his tutelary goddess, his Muse. If previous to this he had given some particular concert or other solely on her account, he now dedicated all his creative work to her.

" What he composed in the morning he used to play over on my piano in the afternoon to see how it sounded (she wrote in her Memoirs). This was between five and six o'clock. He called himself the " twilight man." Aridness was quite unknown to him. He provided the stimulus if there was none to be found. If he was ever visibly tired and exhausted when he entered the room it was beautiful to see how after a short rest and refreshment his face would clear and his features would lighten up when he sat down at the piano."[1]

The overture to " The Valkyrie " bears the dedication : " G(esegnet) S(ei) M(athilde)."[2] It was inevitable that this ideal relationship, moving at first in spheres far removed from the earthy, should in time draw imperceptibly nearer reality, ever more pregnant with danger, and that the flame of love secretly

[1] As told to A. Heintz and published in the *Allgemeine Musikzeitung* of 14th February 1896.
[2] Blessed be Mathilde !

glowing in the hearts of both should one day violently rend the veil of the beautiful illusion. Their environment and common obligations were still strong enough to restrain them to some extent.

" Through a precipitate marriage with an estimable woman (Wagner wrote Liszt, in his distress), but one having absolutely nothing in common with me, I have sent myself to Coventry for life ! God ! how gladly I would run out naked into the world—be nothing, absolutely nothing ever again—but a happy, loving and beloved person ! Now, *this* I can never be again. I shall never be able to love happily again— only unhappily—an outlaw—an impossible person ! "

He derived consolation and help in this trouble through his acquaintance with Schopenhauer, whose principal work, " The World as Will and Idea," had been brought to his attention by Herwegh. This gave him strength for resignation, an " anodyne for the storms of his heart."

" It now gives me pleasure to live for my wife. If one measures love by sacrifice, then certainly no one was ever loved so much, since for no one have such heavy, conscious sacrifices been made. . . . But as I have never in my life known real happiness in love, I am going to erect to this most beautiful of all dreams a memorial in which from beginning to end this love shall for once drink its fill. I have outlined a Tristan and Isolde in my mind."

His absence in London on a concert tour during the summer of 1855, by separating the two friends, temporarily postponed the threatening conflict, and Otto Wesendonck chose—not altogether without motive—to pass the winter of 1856-7 in Paris.

But Wagner's intimate association with the Wesendoncks was sufficient to rouse the " moral indignation " of the Zürich tea-parties, and on poor Minna's return good friends whispered all sorts of things in her ear and began (naturally out of squint-eyed envy) to cut Mathilde Wesendonck. Since Minna herself repeatedly broached this subject in her letters to Wagner when he was in London, he felt obliged to discuss his point of view in detail. His remarks throw a characteristic light on the situation. Inspired by memories of their first visit to London in 1839 he spoke really touchingly and sincerely of their personal relationship.

" Believe me, dear Minna (he wrote 4th May 1855) even if we don't always happen to see eye to eye in many things and now and again give vent to our feelings over this and that, neither of us can now look back over our lives without seeing what great proofs of love and endurance under the most difficult and often the most distressing circumstances bind us together. Just imagine what memories overcame me upon arriving in this London again where sixteen years ago we wandered about in such fear and poverty ! And truly if I could now make things tranquil and pleasant for you, it would certainly give me the deepest satisfaction. But that I still don't really understand how to do this and go on bringing misery and distress upon you, that is my peculiar destiny, which I often heartily deplore for your sake.[1] This time I was very deeply touched to see how difficult the parting was for you again. Whatever I can do from this distance to make the separation pleasanter for you, I will most certainly do.

" I hope Sulzer will not be as timid about visiting a grass widow (he continued, alluding to Minna's reports of local gossip) as the ' blameless ' Wesendonck, that good chap who I hope will not think that only the husband's presence keeps the wife from all sorts of stupid nonsense that she otherwise would inevitably carry on with the other man. For example, he certainly hasn't such a poor opinion of his own wife ; as I fortunately also do not have of you, which is why I gladly give you permission to receive any visitors you may care to.

" This brings me to your reports of the bad name which Frau Wesendonck has earned with Mesdames Mueller, Heim, and Baumgartner. If the lady has really become suddenly so unpleasant that nobody can stand her any longer, things must be very bad indeed, and I for one should be very sorry, as Frau Wesendonck up to a short time ago was generally regarded as a very kind, likeable person. If everyone is ' feeling sorry ' for Wesendonck on account of his wife's reputation, that certainly manifests a very charitable attitude towards him but not towards his wife, who is thus brought into disrepute. And I cannot think that pity of this kind is very sincere.

" I hope, however, that you will set Frau Heim and Frau Mueller a good example and show yourself more forgiving and indulgent in respect of particular circumstances that may arise but which are in fact quite excusable and not so dreadful. Naturally you can't be forced to do this, and if you really don't like Frau Wesendonck then I myself wouldn't consider the gratitude presumably due her sufficient ground for obliging you to consider an acquaintance that is repugnant to you. But if your dislike is due to any kind of suspicion that your honour is implicated, I think I may assure you that this suspicion is absolutely unjustified and unfounded, and that on the contrary you can rest absolutely assured that no one deserves your confidence and your friendship more than Frau Wesendonck, in the same way that I, granting all the differences in our characters and abilities, have a firm and hearty confidence in him—a confidence that I hope he reciprocates as he has every cause to do."

[1] In a letter of 26th June 1836 (Exhibit 72, Burrell Collection) Wagner admits he was " born to bring her (Minna) misfortune, grief, pain and anguish—a grey and black leaf in her book of life."

This fortunately cleared the air for the time being in the feminine world of Zürich. But the argus-eyed guardians of morality were still on the look-out. Minna's suspicions were soon allayed, especially as she felt that the trouble undoubtedly lay in an entirely different quarter. Her neighbour, Frau Heim (Heimchen, as they called her), whom Wagner was then coaching in selections from " Valkyrie " for a private performance, and who (as Minna wrote) " almost devoured him with her eyes," struck the latter as far more dangerous, as did also Frau Johanna Spyri, the wife of the editor of the *Eidgenoessischen Zeitung,* in whom Wagner, for a time, seemed to be very interested. Later on, Minna and Frau Heim had some unpleasant tilts, and jealousy finally made it impossible for them to live next door to each other. As for the " Valkyrie " performance, Frau Heim was eventually replaced by Frau Pollert, who had once sung the rôle of Isabella in the one memorable performance of " Liebesverbot " in Magdeburg and was now a member of the ensemble of the Zürich Theatre.

The middle of October 1856 Liszt arrived in Zürich for an extended visit, accompanied this time by the Princess and her daughter.

" When the Princess Carolyne took up her residence in the Hotel Baur, a very gay life overwhelmed my modest home as well as all Zürich (Wagner wrote in *Mein Leben*). The strange excitement with which the lady immediately infected everything that she drew into her personal orbit also fairly intoxicated my good sister Klära, who was visiting us at the time. It was as though Zürich all of a sudden had turned into a sort of metropolis ; carriages rushed back and forth, servants announced arriving and departing guests, dinners and banquets followed one on another, and we found ourselves surrounded by an increasing number of interesting people of whose existence in Zürich we previously had no idea.

" It was principally the professors of Zürich University whom the Princess succeeded in shaking out of their rut. First she would enjoy each one by himself, and then she served them up *en masse*. If I dropped in for a moment on my daily constitutional, I found her dining *en particular*, now with Semper, another time with Professor Köchly, a third time with Moleschott, etc. But the atmosphere was always free and easy. The more modest affairs at our house, when the Princess helped the hostess serve the guests with typical Polish patriarchial *Gemütlichkeit*, were particularly cosy. . . .

" The Princess seemed to be extraordinarily bent on getting to the bottom of the ' intrigue ' affecting the fate of the gods in my *Nibelungen*. One day she received me *en particular*, just like one of the Zürich professors, in order that I might elucidate this point fully to her ; whereby I must admit that I had the irrefutable feeling that she really wished to understand the most delicate and mysterious elements, but in somewhat too much of an arithmetical-mathematical way so that at the end I almost felt as though I had been unravelling some French comedy of intrigue to her. Her vivacity in all such matters was as great as her peculiarly good-natured disposition. For she really took it as a good joke when I said to her one day, touching the first-mentioned trait : ' If I were continually in your society, I would be done for in a month ! ' "

All this constant excitement, the hectic life and bustle, was not at all to Wagner's taste. He tried as best he could to keep out of it and made an effort to draw Liszt away (he was really concerned about the latter's health) without, however, being able to offset the far weightier influence of the Princess, either in this matter or in their disagreements on artistic matters such as the finale of the " Dante " and the " Faust " symphonies, for instance. In fact, she even felt called upon to remove her lover from Wagner's personal orbit, particularly as she viewed Liszt's unselfish championship of his friend as detrimental to his own artistic interests. A joint excursion to St. Gall, where the two Masters conducted a big festival concert, closed a visit that on the whole had been highly stimulating and pleasurable, though the activities of the Princess frequently disturbed their companionship. Wagner then returned to his work on " Siegfried " with fresh enthusiasm.

The question of where to live was now one of his major worries. Existing conditions were intolerable in the long run on account of the noisy neighbours (five pianos and a flute) and also because of the aforesaid tension in their relations with the Heims.[1] He longed with all his heart for a simple country house with a garden and hoped to get the requisite funds for this through the sale of his " Nibelungen " to Breitkopf & Härtel. He was constantly on the look-out for a suitable place ; but nothing worked out as he hoped.

When the negotiations with the Leipzig publisher came to

[1] " The beautiful and spacious flat in the Escher Houses (wrote Frau Wesendonck in her Memoirs) had become insufferable to him on account of the many pianos in the neighbouring flats. He made an agreement with a smith living across the street whereby the latter was to do no hammering in the morning—Wagner's working hours—because he (Wagner) was composing Siegfried's ' Forging Song.' "

naught he had to relinquish his dream with a heavy heart. Then, as on so many occasions in the past, Otto Wesendonck came to the rescue. The latter was building a handsome villa on a hill overlooking the city in the Commune of Enge, and directly alongside his property stood a modest little cottage that could be fitted up very comfortably for a small family. On his return from Paris, Wesendonck offered this to the harried artist for life tenure at a very low rent. Wagner's joy knew no bounds. He took the keenest interest in the alteration and renovating of the house, and could hardly wait till it was finished and they could take possession. Finally, at the end of April 1857, the great day arrived. Deeply happy, he breathed a sigh of relief. " Well, at last, that's accomplished ! "—a home of his own in God's free and lovely world, his own little patch of ground—this dream of his life for so long —he had now attained at last. How he revelled in it all ! " The last move in this world " was now over. He could not say enough in praise of his " Asyl," as he called it, and he wished he could show all his friends over the place right away. He at once invited them all to visit him and share in his pleasure.

" My study is furnished with the pedantry and elegant cosiness familiar to you (he wrote Liszt). My desk stands alongside the big window with a marvellous view of the lake and the Alps ; peace and quiet all around. A pretty little garden—already in very good shape with quiet nooks and big enough to stroll about in, while it affords my wife the pleasantest of occupations and keeps her from getting notions in her head about me. For instance, a good-sized kitchen garden demands her most solicitous care. As you see, I've won a very attractive site for my retirement, and when I think how long I have yearned for such a place and how hard it was to achieve even a prospect of ever attaining it, I feel obliged to recognize this good Wesendonck as one of my greatest benefactors."

His cup of bliss was full to the brim when the first greeting that he received in the new home was a very kind letter from Frau Ritter, which dispelled a shadow that had been weighing heavily on him for some time. During Liszt's visit to Zürich, he and Karl Ritter got into a heated argument that eventually led to Wagner's complete break with the latter. Karl's mother took sides with her son, and Wagner was obliged—with great reluctance—to forfeit his annual allowance. Now after a long sad period of silence a conciliatory letter arrived from this noble woman which proved the most welcome of gifts.

"I was afraid to open it (he wrote her in acknowledgment), and with my eyes filled with tears I read of the wonderful and noble love that you, beloved lady, extend to me! This letter warmed us through and through and made the first day in our Asyl a glorious sun-flooded festival."

In working on the "Nibelungen" Wagner looked round for someone to sing the Brynhilde, and this brought to mind his niece Johanna. Since he had had no direct contact with her for some years he asked Hans von Buelow to make discreet inquiries if he might count on her for the festival production of the "Ring" in 1859. Johanna's spontaneous and happy acceptance drew from him one of the most sympathetic documents that the man Wagner ever penned.

"I want to write you very calmly to-day (he wrote her on 3rd June 1857) and thus hope to avoid some of the erroneous impressions caused by my otherwise impetuous manner. It has always been a fault of mine to overdo the mood of the moment. My former letter, in which I turned the 'Tannhäuser' matter in Berlin over to you, must have convinced you of my unreserved confidence in you. It represented a great change in my already sceptical attitude towards you.

"Let me explain that a little. As I never do anything by halves, I set very great hopes on you, when your youthful talent was developing semi-unconsciously in Dresden. To me it meant that you were to follow along the same path as *I*—and this path was the one in which I fled the spurious with ever greater repugnance, so as to be able to refresh myself only with the genuine. You were to be my singer, my exponent, and one evening at a 'Don Giovanni' performance when you seemed to me to be especially good as Donna Anna, I conceived a really passionate liking for this . . . hope of mine. Your heart was good, and willing—yet you couldn't understand me. While I was sketching out 'Brynhilde' I had to conduct 'Favorita' for you and see you and Tichatschek wasting yourselves on 'Zampa.' Believe me, it was not poisonous gossip but only the sad feeling—*she's going to be just like all the rest!*—that irresistibly estranged me from you. I saw you going the usual way of a coming prima donna and—that might have all been quite immaterial to me if—I had not made the mistake (as mentioned above) of thinking too highly and too—how shall I say it—ardently, loftily, of those I'm fond of. Exactly the same feeling estranged me from your father. I remembered him from our youthful days as an especially gifted dramatic singer; though the theatre had also lowered him far below the level of his intellectual qualities, I was nevertheless delighted when, while working along with me in Dresden, he pulled himself up and went forward *with* me.

"In that fatal epoch when all his thoughts were centred on you and your brilliant career, he again dropped away from me. He followed the useful, practical—in short, the external side of theatrical success for your sake—and—in this he may have acted for the best as a father; but I had had too high hopes for him not to watch him also from a distance with bitter grief. I felt that all of you no longer belonged to me; and this at a time when I was ruthlessly pursuing my ideal of the Genuine and Real, with an energy that was completely indifferent to my own best interests. You may say I was wrong. Well and good! And you may have been right to go your own way. Mine led me to the most extreme poverty, to the most harrying and forlorn of situations. Yours led you to fame and wealth! Nevertheless, I stuck to my guns, and your father's advice that he sent me in my exile to 'be more practical in my compositions—to make things easier for the singers— the "Tannhäuser" was so difficult that nobody could produce it,' etc., made me realize with a smile how little my brother understood me, he who now only seemed to be worried lest your growing success might lead me to impose on you in any way.

" Tell me, dear child, can you understand all this and realize that my coolness was not dictated by outside agencies but that it derived only from the conflict between our own innermost natures? Now you see what sort of a chap I am! At the start of the 'Tannhäuser' negotiations, my attitude towards Huelsen and Albert was one of the coolest, most sceptical prudence. But when *you* finally wrote me, all my old hope and love revived. In a flash all was forgotten. Full of enthusiasm I left everything to you. That was dangerous. Because I got too excited, and you couldn't understand my enthusiasm.

" The news that 'Tannhäuser' had been postponed in favour of Feensee brought back to me again all the old Dresden pictures of 'La Favorita' and 'Zampa,' etc. I was angry with *myself* for overdoing things again and—I made *you* suffer for it; which after all was wrong because as a matter of fact it was all due to my expecting too much. I was unspeakably bitter. You see I'm as hypersensitive as a lovesick girl. I now only followed up your repertoire, a repertoire of the same strange variety; and I had to see her for whom I had designed my 'Brynhilde' treating us to a parody of it beforehand in Dorn's amateurish work and thereby breathing life into something that without you could never have dared to show its face in public. So—forgive me—dear child! but I must first surmount my bitterness and realize clearly that I'm a fool and that after all you're not here just for my benefit. But I'll drop the subject. I don't want to grow bitter again, but only to make it clear to you how matters stand between us and that my bitterness is not due to indifference but to quite the opposite. There is practically nothing more that I can say to you.

" The reason why I once asked you for money, with all that followed, I must explain to you in person sometime. At all events it was a bad business. You'll hear all about it some day. I couldn't help Minna's not calling on you in Berlin, but I quite approved of her action. As matters then stood between us, no good could have come of her visit. She can't forget the way your mother treated her in Dresden after my flight, when Countess Kaminska wanted to give her money to pay a debt. If it really happened as my wife says, then I can't really blame her for holding herself aloof. It's only strange that you should think a thing like that could affect my relations with you ! O my dear child, in such things I'm so very broad-minded that I can throw off anything, anything ! and nothing—not even the greatest ignominy, prevents me from following the dictates of my heart where I think I shall find the sympathy which is so vitally necessary to natures like yours and mine.

" You must believe this if you really want to understand me ! But now enough of these explanations. Time has made me view things more calmly as far as you are concerned. I heard how deeply pained your father was over the ' Tannhäuser ' scandal in Berlin—and all my anger vanished ! Even at the risk of his paying no attention to it, I told him how touched and grateful I was. I am really sorry for him. If he is absolutely incapable of distinguishing me from any other ordinary individual, then I must strike him as very hard and insulting. But when I look at him calmly and forget the feelings I once also cherished against him, I can only regret having shown myself so bitter towards him.

" As regards my ' Brynhilde,' you have again been often in my thoughts. I finally couldn't resist asking Buelow if he thought I could win you for this undertaking. The manner in which you responded to his inquiry could easily have led me to commit my old error and have given way too unreservedly to a new confidence which—as I learned— would be too heavy for you. I will therefore restrain myself and only say that it is consoling to think that I shall still see you sometime in one of my works. At all events, rest assured that you will have no further trouble from me from now on. My own life is teaching me gradually to temper my demands on people and I have the pleasure of thereby being more just to them. Nevertheless I know that you also are not indifferent towards me, and you are certainly worthy of being loved, just as you are.

" Therefore be a dear, and if possible don't put off your visit to us till next year. We're only a day's journey from Soden. We now have a lovely little house and garden with a wonderful view, which I owe to the rarest friendship and sympathy. You would be very pleased with it. Or do you insist on being the last ? Louise Meyer is coming from Vienna very shortly, then Tichatschek, Niemann, Buelow. Don't let us have to urge you. Come and convince yourself that things aren't so bad as they seem, even with my poor much-tried and tormented wife. She is now planting her garden, and it agrees with her. Give my kindest regards to your fiancé, and in this connection I send you my warmest good wishes for your happiness. May he make you happy.

And also remember me to your father and mother. Tell them that things are never so black as they look by night ; and it is now daytime for me."

Johanna's visit to Zürich did not, however, materialize. But Wagner had the pleasure of a visit from the Buelows, who spent three weeks at the Asyl while on their honeymoon.

" Buelow contrived most wonderfully with my manuscript (he reported to Frau Ritter in Dresden) so that we could perform the two ' Siegfried ' acts with tolerable precision. In addition, ' Rheingold ' and ' Valkyrie ' went really wonderfully—quite worthy of public performance. I have seldom felt so good and so happily inspired as through this intimate visit. In the morning everybody had to be very quiet as I was writing ' Tristan,' and every week I read a new act to them. Then the rest of the day we nearly always made music, and Frau Wesendonck came over very conscientiously every time, so we always had a most grateful little public.

" Buelow's mastery of the piano is tremendous ; with his innate musicianship, his incredible memory and all the amazing facility that is peculiar to him, his imperturbability and unfailing readiness were of admirable service to me. When you know Cosima you will agree with me in thinking the young couple most admirably suited to one another. With all their great intelligence and real talent there is so much that is light and buoyant about the two of them that one cannot help but enjoy being with them. I only let them go at last with great reluctance, and then only with the solemn promise to come back again next year."

At this first more intimate contact with Wagner—she had previously only met him once in Paris—his very powerful personality and the deeply moving tragedy of the " Tristan " poem had a depressing effect on Cosima. To add to her confusion she felt that her inner life had been upset by an external power. She had only been married a few weeks, and a certain indefinable feeling of fear made her shy and reticent towards Wagner, who treated her as a familiar old friend. When she was questioned about her behaviour she excused herself by saying that she was not proficient enough in German to be able to parry Wagner's sparkling flow of conversation. She listened to the reading of " Tristan " " in silence with her eyes lowered," and when she was questioned she " began to cry." Wagner alluded to this later in a letter to Buelow.

" But first of all I must tell you that Cosima's reserve towards me really distresses me since I think I can now be sure that the reason she gives[1] is only a pretext and that on the contrary she really feels very embarrassed in my presence. If my manner seemed strange to her, if a blunt comment here and there, some little joke, has hurt her feelings, then I should have every reason to regret having gone a bit too far in my familiarity—which I'm always only too ready to admit and regret every time I alienate some sincerely worthwhile person by such behaviour. This time I am perfectly sure it is only a question of a misunderstanding. My altogether ruthless familiarity with persons who are sympathetic to me has already alienated many. May your dear young wife's present feeling towards me be of no long duration."[2]

In the midsummer of 1857 the Wesendoncks took possession of their new home on the Green Hill and destiny was fulfilled. The question involuntarily rises : how could Otto Wesendonck —in view of his recent experiences—make Wagner his next-door neighbour and a constant guest in his house ? An answer is found in a passage of a letter written by Wagner to his sister Klära Wolfram on 20th August 1858.[3]

" Wesendonck in the face of his wife's unconcealed candour *couldn't* help but become increasingly jealous. Her greatness lay in the fact that she kept her husband always informed of her feelings and brought him gradually to the point of giving her up altogether. The sacrifices and struggles this entailed can be easily imagined. That she succeeded was due solely to the depth and nobility of her affection— entirely divorced from any self-interest—which gave her the strength to reveal herself to her husband in such greatness that the latter— when she finally threatened to take her life—had to step aside and thereby prove his steadfast love for her by supporting her even in her anxiety for me. After all he wanted to keep the mother of his children, and for their sakes (it was they who proved the most invincible barrier between us) he accepted the renunciation. So though he was con- sumed by jealousy she was still able to interest him in me to such an extent that he often assisted me financially. When at last it was a question of finding me a little house and garden after my own heart, it was she who persuaded him, after the most incredible battles, to buy for me the fine piece of property adjoining his own.

" The wonderful part of it all is that I hadn't the slightest idea of

---

[1] That her knowledge of German was still inadequate.
[2] There is a letter in the Burrell Collection (Exhibit 340) in which Cosima tells Minna that she would like to write Wagner but always loses her courage. " I am silly enough to be still shy towards him," she wrote.
[3] This letter was not included in the original Wagner-Wesendonck correspondence and was published for the first time in the Berlin *Taeglicher Rundschau* of 23rd September 1902. The Burrell Collection contains a letter from Klära Wolfram to Minna dated 3rd June 1858 (Exhibit 309) offering her a home and telling her she " would take it much amiss " if she forgave Wagner. " He has much to thank you for (she continued) and he has repaid you very poorly for it."

these battles she went through for my sake. Her husband always had
to maintain a friendly, natural manner towards me on her account. No
frowning looks should reveal the real situation to me ; not a hair of my
head should be ruffled. The sky above me must be serene and cloudless, the earth soft and smooth to my tread. Such was the incredible
triumph of the glorious love of this purest and noblest of women, and
this love that always remained unexpressed between us finally had to
reveal itself when I wrote ' Tristan ' a year ago and gave it to her.

" Think, dearest sister, what this love must mean to me after a life
of struggle and suffering, of excitement and sacrifice, such as mine !
Yet we both saw at once that union between us was unthinkable ; so
we resigned ourselves, renouncing all self-interest—we suffered—bore
up patiently, but—we loved each other ! "

After this personal confession on Wagner's part, the odious,
even contemptuous, way in which he speaks of Otto Wesendonck
in *Mein Leben*, without ever mentioning his innumerable kind-
nesses, is doubly distressing and disgraceful. This love which (as
he said) " remained unexpressed " was finally revealed when he
unlocked his emotion to his friend in " Tristan." The apparently
abrupt transition from the " Ring " (the composition of which
was finished up to the end of the second act of " Siegfried ") to
" Tristan " shows very clearly how greatly Wagner's creation was
rooted in spiritual experiences. After his acquaintance with
Schopenhauer's philosophy had set the innermost chambers of
his soul at odds with the original revolutionary-optimistic note
of his " Nibelungen " drama and he then began to write the
music for the buoyant, rapturous love scene of the third act of
" Siegfried," his genius deserted him. The emotions aroused
within him by his blissful yet painful emotional experience with
Mathilde Wesendonck categorically demanded expression. So
the joyous hero had to retire into the background, and the storm
within him dissolved in the febrile ardours of " Tristan," bringing
him healing and relief.

" I completed the poem and brought you the last act (he wrote
Mathilde from Venice on 18th September). You led me to the chair in
front of the sofa, put your arms round me and said : ' Now I have
nothing more to wish for ! ' On that day, at that hour, I was reborn.
All life till then had been preamble. Then the epilogue began. In
that wonderful moment alone I really lived ! And do you know how I
partook of it ? Not boisterously, tempestuously, deliriously ; but
solemnly, deeply affected, gently elated, free, as though in a trance. I
had detached myself from the world—painfully, yet ever more and

more definitely. Everything in me had become negation and defence. Even my creative work was torture to me. For it was longing, unsatisfied longing to find in exchange for that negation, that defence, my own assenting wedded mate. That moment gave this to me and with such unequivocal certainty that I was overcome with a sacred peace. A lovely woman, shy and hesitant, threw herself courageously into a sea of trouble and suffering in order to create this marvellous moment for me, to say to me : ' I love you.' Thus you dedicated yourself to death in order to give me life. Thus I received your life in order to take leave of the world with you, in order to suffer with you, to die with you. Now the spell of yearning was broken."

The two then surrendered themselves unreservedly to their newly won happiness. The days in the Asyl were among the most beautiful of Wagner's whole life. Close to the woman he loved so passionately, who watched over him like a guardian angel, in whom in their daily intercourse he found understanding and sympathy for everything that touched him personally. In addition to all this came the creation of a work like " Tristan " that was veritably saturated with his heart's blood. Mathilde Wesendonck's " Five Poems " written during this period, and for which Wagner's genius found such exquisite settings, gave a penetrating glimpse into the consecration and tenderness of this unique liaison.

The attacks of hostile forces rebounded from the sheer spiritual force of the lovers. As early as September of that year a little tension was noticeable between Minna and Mathilde, but it soon blew over.

" I really had to relieve my feelings to young Frau Wesendonck (Minna wrote). She behaved in such an overbearing and idiotic way to me all at once that I refused her invitations. But then she apologized to me and now I'm friendly with her again for Richard's sake."

And there were also little friendly altercations with Otto Wesendonck who felt that his rights as head of the house had been infringed upon by Wagner's invasion of his home and the great consideration paid to him. And these altercations were soon followed, as we have seen, by a violent spiritual reaction. But far more menacing for the lovers was a danger that slowly but surely developed within themselves. Some day the fatal hour must strike for them when the idealistic-romantic basis of their

liaison would go to pieces and naked reality, stripped of all their
fantastic dreams, would call for a decision : union or renunciation.
This moment arrived at the beginning of 1858. In his first
despair and helplessness Wagner turned to Liszt for help.

" I am at the end of a conflict which involves everything that a man
holds sacred (he wrote his friend). I must come to a decision, and
every choice that presents itself to me is so cruel that in deciding, I
must have the support of the incomparable Friend whom Heaven
has sent me. . . .
" Since I hope to find the way that will cause the least distress, I'm
planning first to go to Paris where—in the eyes of the world and
particularly of my good wife—my professional interests might well
call me."

That Liszt, in spite of these cryptic allusions, understood at
once what his friend meant is shown by his inquiry : " Is your
wife remaining in Zürich ? Where is Mme. W. ? " But Wagner
had overestimated the acuteness of the conflict, that came to a
head in a sudden argument with Otto Wesendonck.

" For a moment it seemed as though I must be prepared quickly and
definitely to take defensive measures (wrote Wagner). But it soon
became apparent how very mild everything here is in reality. *For* me,
nothing but tenderness, loyal devotion, a total submerging of self,
unique anxiety on my behalf. *Against* me, *sincere suffering* combined
with infinite kindness and unshakable consideration for the delicate
suffering figure in the conflict. Therefore it was only a question of
finding a vent for the oppressive suffering, and of gaining a little time.
An extended or a permanent separation would be absolutely unthinkable. This would mean death in a quarter where even my temporary
absence is the principal cause of all the suffering. The essential thing
for me is to allay somewhat the sufferings of the good-natured Otto
Wesendonck. This is possible, and I hope to return in a few weeks."

After Wagner's heart had found peace he returned to Zürich
from Paris.

" When a month ago I communicated my decision to your husband
to break off all personal intercourse with you (he wrote Mathilde), I
had . . . given you up. But I was not yet altogether clear with myself
about this. I only felt that nothing but a complete separation or—a
complete union could safeguard our love from the horrible contacts
to which we saw it exposed in the recent past. Consequently the feeling
of the necessity of our separation was offset by the potentiality of a
union—envisaged even though unsought.

G

" This implied in addition a convulsive nervous tension that was intolerable for both of us. I went to you, and it was clear and definite to us that any other contingency represented an outrage that could never even be taken into consideration. This in itself lent a different character to the necessity of our renunciation. The spasm passed off in a gentle reconciliation. The last trace of egoism vanished from my heart and my resolve to visit you both again now represented the triumph of the purest humanity over the last stirrings of selfish longing. My only wish was to reconcile, to soothe, to comfort, to cheer—and thereby to guarantee myself the only happiness that can still be in store for me."

And now when they thought that they had won through to clarity and spiritual contentment through their own will and effort, brutal reality (from which they were prepared to demand the impossible) broke the lovers' bond. Minna, with growing jealousy, had watched for a long time her husband's daily visits to the Wesendoncks, and Mathilde's frequent visits to Wagner, which were carried on behind her back and had already set the servants' tongues wagging. The day therefore came when she finally lost her self-control and learned the truth which her husband very wrongly had concealed from her, that is, if he wished to avoid any misunderstanding. And who can blame Minna, who when once she discovered the truth—and with her practical matter-of-fact mind—looked on it as a perfectly prosaic love affair, and then proceeded to act accordingly, and was unable to believe Wagner's protestations regarding the purity and other-worldliness of the relationship ? How many women would be likely to act differently in these circumstances ?

For a long time little was known regarding the details of those fateful days on the Green Hill, especially as there was nothing to go on but Wagner's one-sided account in his much-quoted letter to his sister Klära and his even more naïve account of the affair in *Mein Leben*. But numerous letters of Minna (who has often been one-sidedly blamed for her share in the catastrophe, and who in common justice should also be given a hearing in the matter) made it possible (in combination with other authoritative material) to reconstruct more exactly the occurrences of those eventful days. Wagner research then learned for the first time the contents of the fatal letter that Minna intercepted and read, which (as well as Wagner's numerous love letters that preceded it) was missing from the published correspondence with Mathilde Wesendonck.[1]

" Mme. Wesendonck (wrote Minna) visited my husband secretly, as he did her, and she forbade my servant, when he let her in, to tell me that she was upstairs. I paid no attention to all this. It so often happens that men have love affairs. Why shouldn't I also have to put up with it from my husband ? I wasn't a bit jealous. Only I might have been spared these vulgarities, these insults ; and my ridiculously conceited husband should have concealed it from me."

" On the 7th of the month (she continued in a letter dated 30th April 1858) I simply had to find out for certain about Richard's affair with Frau Wesendonck. After all sorts of things had been whispered to me from various sides, things I didn't believe, I couldn't help but notice that Richard went over only too often when the good man was

[1] When the *Diary and Letters of Richard Wagner to Mathilde Wesendonck* was published in 1904 the book created a sensation. In his effort to depict Cosima as *the* woman in his life, Wagner had carefully destroyed all traces of this earlier love tragedy so that only a very few of his closest friends knew the secret, and it would have remained hidden for ever from the world if Frau Wesendonck had destroyed all Wagner's letters, as he begged her to do. She considered it her duty, however, to preserve intact this spiritual confession of an artist, which is one of the most valuable and informative that has ever been published. She therefore sacrificed consideration for private individuals to her duty towards posterity and left instructions that upon her death (which took place in 1902) everything should be published just as it was, " complete and unaltered." Wahnfried was shocked when it learned of the existence of these documents and of their impending publication.

After some time had gone by permission was finally granted for the publication of the book, but only after the deletion of certain passages, which was contrary to the express wish of the deceased. This was very short-sighted on the part of the authors of this step as it reacted to the detriment of Cosima and Otto Wesendonck, whose character was thereby completely falsified before the world.

For twenty years, in my various Wagner publications, I fought indefatigably against this sin of " official " Wagner literature, and in the course of time finally succeeded in restoring a whole series of earlier Wagner publications to their original form, for instance the Wagner correspondence with his friend Theodor Uhlig (now a part of the Burrell Collection) in which at least a third had been deleted or toned down; the correspondence between Wagner and Liszt, in which all references to the serious dissensions between the two men (so important in connection with the entire relationship between them) had been deleted as well as all references to the Buelow catastrophe, etc. It is therefore not surprising that owners of Wagner documents were tireless in bringing me material that was at variance with the published versions.

In 1931 I received a copy of Wagner's letters to Mathilde Wesendonck that contained all the passages that had originally been deleted at the behest of Wahnfried. In consideration of Cosima Wagner the owner had refrained during her lifetime from making this material available to the public, but after the latter's death felt it his duty to place this material at the disposition of Wagner research. This included the intercepted letter to Mathilde Wesendonck, the pertinent portions of which (together with the Uhlig deletions) I published for the first time on 12th September 1931 in the German musical journal *Die Musik*. The intercepted letter is now in the Burrell Collection (Exhibit 306).—J. K.

not at home, and then this daily correspondence and the running back and forth of this woman's messengers who wanted to know ' if Herr Wagner had slept well ' ; asking him to come over—' the conservatory was heated ' ; in fact she even came over in person, but forbade my maid to disturb me. I also stupidly stayed downstairs in my own rooms and left them to themselves.

" On the 6th of the month they were both here. On the 7th I noticed that Richard was extraordinarily restless. Every time the bell rang he came out holding a big roll in his hand that he wanted to send over to Frau Wesendonck.[1] But he wouldn't let it out of his hand, and hid it in great embarrassment when I offered to attend to it for him. That all made me a little suspicious. When he finally couldn't wait any longer he called our servant. I accidentally happened to be there when the latter went by and asked him for the roll of music. I undid it and took out the thick letter that was rolled up inside, opened it, and read the most jealous love letter ! "

This eight-page letter, which formed part of Minna's estate, read in part as follows :

" Morning Confession
Just out of bed

" O no, no, it isn't de Sanctis[2] whom I hate, but myself for catching my poor heart again and again in such attacks of weakness. Shall I offer as excuse my indisposition, my consequent sensitiveness and irritability ? Let's try and see how it goes ! At noon the day before yesterday an angel came to me who blessed and refreshed me. This made me feel so happy and gay that in the evening I felt a sincere desire for friends so as to share with them my inward happiness. I knew I would have been very charming and friendly. Then I heard that no one in your house ventured to give my letter to you, because de Sanctis was with you. Your husband was of the same opinion. I waited in vain and finally had the pleasure of receiving Herr von Marschall who spent the evening with us. Every word he said filled me with dreadful hatred against all the de Sanctises in the world ! The lucky man ! he kept her from me. And through what gift of pleasing ? Simply through her patience ! I couldn't blame him for taking his being with you so seriously ; for anyone who has anything to do with you takes it so seriously. See how seriously I'm taking it ! To the point of tormenting you. But why does she cultivate this pedantic fetter ? What does Italian mean to her ? Well that I could easily answer. But the easier it was for me to answer, the more the bore annoyed me. He merged with Marschall in my dream and from this a figure emerged which I recognized as representing for me all the misery of the world. And so it went on the whole night.

[1] Sketches for Act I of " Tristan."
[2] A professor at the Zürich University.

" In the morning I was reasonable again and could pray really fervently to my angel—and this prayer is Love. Love ! This love represents the deepest spiritual joy—the source of my redemption ! Then came day with its awful weather. I was denied the joy of your garden—my work still wouldn't go. So my whole day was a battle between ill humour and longing for you ! And every time I felt a real yearning for you, our tiresome pedant—who stole you from me— came between us and I had to admit to myself that I hated him ! Ach, poor me ! I had to tell you ! I simply couldn't help it ! But it was really silly of me and I merited a good punishment for it. What is it to be ? Next Monday after the lesson, I'll stay for tea and I'll be terribly nice to de Sanctis all evening, and to the joy of you all, I'll speak French !¹

" What twaddle I'm talking ! Is it only the pleasure of talking or the pleasure of talking to *you* ? Yes, to you ! Yet when I look into your eyes I can't say another word ! Then everything that I could say is quite useless. You see, everything then becomes so indisputably true to me ; I feel so sure of myself when these beautiful saintly eyes rest upon me and I submerge myself in them ! Then object and subject no longer exist—everything is blended into one—a deep infinite harmony ! O there is peace—and in the peace, sublime, perfect life. O fool, who would seek to win the world and peace from without ! A blind man who could not have known your eyes, and found his soul in them ! Salvation dwells only within, in the intrinsically spiritual, only in the innermost being ! I can only speak and explain myself to you when I don't see you—or may not see you.

" Love me, and forgive my childishness of yesterday. You were right to call it that !

" The weather seems to be mild. To-day I'll come to the garden ; as soon as I see you, I hope to find you undisturbed for a moment !

" Take my whole soul as a morning greeting !
" 7th April 1858."

" Now, what do you say to that ! (continued Minna). At noon I told my husband that I had opened and read this fine letter. He was a little startled. But I said I couldn't stand this deception against the poor man, I'd go away ; but he must call this woman his own forever.

---

¹ Here follow approximately fifty lines referring to a Goethe dispute the day before. In his work on the Burrell Collection, Mr. John Burk has the following to say regarding this : " The writers of *The Truth About Wagner* obtained access to this letter in this collection and published what they considered its more purple revelations. What they quite ignored was the main purpose and content of the letter— an elucidation of Wagner's attitude towards Goethe's *Faust*, engendered by a discussion of the subject the night before. Characteristically, Wagner visualizes Mathilde in Gretchen and inevitably transforms her into the vividly present Isolde. That Minna should take these Tristanesque rhapsodizings in a gross sense would have been acutely embarrassing to Mathilde or Otto, or anyone who understood Wagner."

Richard tried to talk himself out of it with his wonderful blarney, but it didn't go down with me. He wanted forcibly to make a fool of me and convince me of the purity of his relations with good and evil. How ridiculous! I stuck to my convictions!"

"Yet next day I was sorry for her (Wagner wrote his sister Klära). I went to her and said : 'Minna, you are very ill.' We drew up plans for a cure for her. She seemed to calm down. The day of departure for the health resort drew near. She insisted on speaking to Frau Wesendonck before leaving. I categorically forbade it. The important thing for me was to enlighten Minna gradually as to the nature of my relations with the former so as to convince her that our marriage was not in jeopardy and therefore she should only be sensible, level-headed and noble, give up all idea of silly revenge and avoid making a scene of any kind. In the end she gave me her solemn promise.

"But it gave her no peace. She went over after all, behind my back, and probably without realizing it herself, wounded that sensitive woman in the grossest way. As she said to her : 'If I were a common woman, I would go to your husband with this letter!' Frau Wesendonck, who was conscious of never having had a secret from her husband, couldn't do otherwise than tell him at once of the incident and the cause of it. This represented a brutal and vulgar intrusion into the tenderness and purity of our relations, and many things had to change. Returning from a walk, I met Herr and Frau Wesendonck in their carriage just as they were starting out for a drive. I noticed her embarrassed manner, and on the other hand the queer, smiling, smug expression on her husband's face. It was clear to me at once what had happened. For I also found my wife in extraordinarily good spirits. She offered me her hand very straightforwardly and announced her readiness to be friends again. In reply to my question whether by chance she had broken her promise, she answered with an air of assurance that she, of course, as a clever woman, had to straighten out the affair. Thereupon I pointed out to her that she would probably find that her breach of faith would have very bad consequences. But first of all it seemed to me imperative to think of building up her strength, and to that end she was to betake herself, within the next day or two, to the health resort recommended to her—Brestenberg on Lake Wallwyl. Minna was also willing to get started with the treatment of her ailment, and so after a few days—during which I avoided any inquiries as to what had happened next door—I accompanied her and her parrot to the health resort which is pleasantly situated about three hours from here, and adequately equipped. When I left her, in bidding me good-bye she was overcome by the distressing seriousness of our situation. I could say very little to comfort her, other than that I would try to neutralize the dreaded effects of her breach of faith on our future."

Minna had undertaken the conversation with Mathilde Wesendonck on the advice of Frau Herwegh with the good intention of candidly warning the young woman betimes and thereby averting a calamity. She thought she had achieved her aim.

" Frau Wesendonck was also most grateful and friendly towards me (she wrote) and accompanied me as far as the stairs still holding my hand ; we had come to an understanding and all was well. Afterwards, however, she changed her mind and told her husband that I had insulted her dreadfully, without telling him the plain truth of the matter. To Richard she made an awful hullabaloo about how deeply and dreadfully I had insulted her, in spite of the fact that I had the delicacy not even to show this woman the fatal letter which I actually had in my pocket. But that's the way with these common, petty natures ; they're incapable of anything but gossip and mischief-making. I didn't want to forbid the person concerned mentioning my conversation with her—any sensible woman would have understood that by herself—and, circumstances permitting, all might have remained as before, at least outwardly."

The Wesendoncks were very angry with Wagner for leaving his wife in the dark regarding his relations with them and thus subjecting Mathilde to such a distressing and humiliating experience. .

" But I felt a very great sympathy for you in those days when you thrust me from you (Wagner wrote Mathilde in his Venetian diary), when—no longer at the mercy of suffering, but of passion—you fancied yourself betrayed and felt that your noblest impulses were misunderstood ; then for me you were an angel forsaken by God. And as your state of mind quickly banished my own confusion, it made me resourceful in bringing you refreshment and healing. I found the friend who could bring you comfort and moral inspiration, relief and reconciliation."

The discreet intervention of Frau Wille finally succeeded in obtaining Mathilde's forgiveness for Wagner, a loving service that he never forgot. But they made it very plain to him that " from then on it would be impossible for the mortified victim to cross his threshold or have any further intercourse with Minna." That this was equivalent to his leaving the Asyl, he at first refused to recognize. In order to give the wounds time to heal, Otto Wesendonck took his wife to the Italian Lakes for a month to divert her thoughts to other things.

In the meantime Minna's efforts to find a cure in Brestenberg for the heart ailment that had taken a catastrophic turn as a result of recent events proved in vain. There were days, in fact, when her death seemed imminent from hour to hour.

"My health is not improving at all (she wrote her friend Frau Herwegh on 14th June 1858). Next Thursday I will have been here nine weeks and my poor heart still thumps and pounds as though it would jump out of me. In addition I have such bad nights that I usually have to pace up and down my room for two or three hours. The doctor still shakes his head over the unusual symptoms of my illness. For instance, in the morning I can usually only stay ten minutes in the wet compresses while others usually require an hour to get warm. Another strange thing is that my pulse and heart-beat are quite different, the latter beating twice as fast as the pulse. This is unfortunately a very bad state of affairs, and I wouldn't wish it on my enemy. Sometimes I get perfectly furious, but I always keep myself and my heart in check so that hardly anyone knows what I suffer.

"My dear husband might be really kind and ease my pain if he didn't allow himself to be influenced by certain people. His heart is kind, but very weak! That is why he often writes me very dear, kind, comforting letters; but even oftener still flings the basest and most insulting things at me in his letters, praising others to the skies, and trampling me thoroughly underfoot. That, my dearest Emma, is what is still eating my heart out! It is only very seldom that I can cry over these outrages, and that's very bad for me. But my heart suffocates me as though it were being wrenched. It's really dreadful how shabbily Richard treats his wife, whom after all he has made so ill. May God help me! Sunday a week ago I was at home, but only for twenty-three hours, so that I had no time to see you. I wish I hadn't gone. Dear Richard vented his spleen on me until two in the morning."

This meeting of the two produced a definite revulsion of feeling in Wagner.

"I noticed from her manner that she no longer thought it necessary to attach any further importance to the recent domestic happenings (he wrote), particularly as she more or less imagined it was here a case of a 'little love affair' which she had put to rights. As she expressed herself on the subject with a certain unpleasant levity I had to explain our situation to her clearly and definitely one evening, as much as I should have liked to have concealed it from her now out of regard for her health."

"After the terrible confessions I had to make her (he wrote in a letter to Alwine Fromann) the poor woman has become for me quite a different person from what she was formerly. I only see how dreadfully she must suffer and I now can only—suffer with her. Even in her low spirits she was in a gentle mood for the first time and only bewailed her lot—which tore my heart. From that moment, my mind was made up. I never seriously contemplated leaving her or—even perhaps seeking another ' happiness.' Yet suffering, on the defensive, I had always kept my wife at a distance. Now after I have had to inflict this dreadful wound, I entered—fully aware of what I was doing—into an active relationship with her. I was now anxious to console her, reconcile her to her fate, be wholly and sincerely all that I now could be, *must be*, to her ; and this not from any sense of duty, but in response to a still small voice of the heart. . . .

" I could only hope to reconcile and calm Minna deeply and sincerely if I brought her to a sense of justice. In fact I could only expect to bring her real comfort, true elevation of spirit and self-respect if she was able to estimate more correctly the nature of those relations that she so odiously misinterpreted, and if she realized that here there was *only suffering*—and that suffering was a noble tender one ; but nothing whatever to get angry about. But how was *I* to make this clear to her ? Any attempt to do so on *my* part would practically represent only a new insult, a new complaint against her. For on this point she was extraordinarily touchy, emotionally. And reason and insight couldn't combat the effect of my voice when I raised it in the cause of justice and to bring her to a sense of understanding. How I longed for you at that time ! Alwine ! Only a woman, a friend, could now achieve that which was beyond *me*. But you didn't come and I was left alone with the unhappy soul in the fearful desolation, seeing any hope of reconciliation recede farther and farther every day."

We may well believe that Wagner did not fail to make the most touching efforts to bring Minna to her senses, and—as his letters show—tried with amazing forbearance and kindness to clear up the misunderstandings and find a *modus vivendi* with his old comrade. But what had always succeeded in the past now failed utterly. In the old surroundings, so pregnant with disaster, where (in view of the ever-glowing fires of inner distrust) wounds that had scarcely healed were continually rent open and the demon of passionate misunderstandings pursued his quarry so unremittingly that any tolerable life together was out of the question in the long run. Even Minna's return from Brestenberg produced a new crisis on the Green Hill. Their manservant had rigged up a sort of triumphal arch to celebrate the return of his mistress, and Minna noted at once

" with great satisfaction that this floral arch must hit our neighbours in the eye, and thought this was sufficient to make it plain to them that her return could not be regarded, perchance, as a humiliating experience. She insisted, with triumphant gratification, that these festive signs should not be removed for several days."

However, Mathilde, who had not yet recovered from her deep mortification and disapproved of Minna's return to the Asyl, viewed this ostentatious reception of her rival as a new affront. Which necessitated further explanations that were disagreeable and very distressing to all concerned. The oppressive atmosphere which lay over everything was to some extent mitigated by the numerous guests that arrived at the Asyl during July and August. The most welcome to Wagner were naturally Hans and Cosima von Buelow, who announced their arrival in accordance with their promise of the year before.

" I'm now expecting the Buelows shortly (he wrote Liszt) and am looking forward keenly to seeing them. I've taken Hans especially to my heart. Cosima is more drawn to the Herweghs. I seem a little repellent to her. All the same we're excellent friends."

It is indeed a curious turn of fate that in such a momentous hour shortly before the drastic upheaval in Wagner's life, the three women—Minna, Mathilde and Cosima—who played such a decisive rôle in his career, should have come together. The visit of the Buelows naturally suffered greatly through the tension in the atmosphere, and as the days went by the situation became more and more impossible.

They arrived in Zürich in company with Cosima's mother, Countess d'Agoult, and stopped at first at the Hotel Baur au Lac. When Hans went to call on Wagner he found him in the midst of a " terrific row with Minna," in which he informed her that he was only waiting till their Berlin friends had left to give up the Asyl definitely, and leave her. Under these circumstances Buelow was reluctant to accept Wagner's hospitality, but the latter wrote him next day that

" my wife begs you to come to us at once. She also has great hopes that your visit will help us resume our connections with the Wesendoncks, which is so necessary, and sends you a very hearty welcome. If it were silly to ask you to forget what has happened, I nevertheless beg you not to mention it again. Let us assume you only arrived to-day. Under the present circumstances you can now be of greater assistance than ever to us, and to me especially, through your presence in our house."

Since the Buelows considered it their duty as Wagner's friends to stand by him now in his desperate straits, they moved over to the Asyl. This time also there was a great deal of music, from the " Nibelungen " and from " Tristan." But the atmosphere was nevertheless very tense. As in the previous year, Wagner's proximity again had a disturbing effect on Cosima, and completely upset her inner equilibrium. Without being in love with him as yet, his tragedy and the great love song that he glorified in all his creations, revealed to her the deep tragedy of her own life—her own marriage—which though founded on great mutual esteem, sympathy and warm friendship, still lacked the passion that strikes down to the core of things and the fervour of which in " Tristan " she now sensed so keenly.

She still remained shy and bashful in Wagner's presence ; but inwardly, inflammable material had collected that some external incident might easily bring to explosion. This occurred when she left for Geneva to meet her step-sister, leaving Hans behind with Wagner. Karl Ritter, who was also passing through an emotional crisis as a result of his recent separation from his young wife, accompanied Cosima on this trip.

" When Cosima left for Geneva to meet her sister (Wagner wrote Mathilde from Venice) it so happened that Karl could offer himself as travelling companion as far as Lausanne. We only learned through an inquiry on the part of Karl's wife that he had gone on with Cosima and had stayed with the two sisters until their return. When she got back Cosima was in an extraordinarily excited state and this manifested itself especially in a convulsively fervent tenderness towards me. Moreover, on departure next day, she fell at my feet and covered my hands with tears and kisses so that I gazed at this puzzle, amazed and startled, without being able to find the key to it.

" Now Karl has recently disclosed to me the passionate incidents that took place between him and Cosima, and the fact that they both were on the point of taking their lives in Geneva. Cosima, in a wild burst of passion, suddenly demanded that he kill her. He thereupon offered to die with her ; but this she definitely refused. After the two had taken a trip on the lake, Cosima with the intention of drowning herself, Karl with the idea of following suit, the former only abandoned her project because she was unable to dissuade Karl from his determination to die with her. Thus everything was left in a passionate, vague suspense. The two parted with the promise to let each other know in three weeks' time how things stood with them—their mood—and what they had decided to do further. We must now wait and see what will be the upshot of this conflict. Greatly shocked as I was by this news I nevertheless sensed a slight feeling of deep satisfaction that sprang immediately from an involuntary comparison with our experiences, our situation.

" How differently we came together ! How differently we learned to know each other. And how differently arose for us therefrom the sweet compulsion to unite ourselves in death—to die united ! In our case, years brought it to flowering. If I loved you at once, yet how deep and wide were the ramifications of this love through the finest fibres of my being before I ventured to confess to you definitely and more distinctly that I wanted to die with you ! And thus our love developed into a vessel which enclosed within it the noblest elements of the whole world. When, overcome at last by this tremendous burden, we confessed our love to one another, we knew that we must die just because of this superabundant burden. To give it to the world, then blissful and serene, redeemed of all sin, to lose ourselves—united—in the universe, that is our love, that our death !

" So I gazed sadly upon this couple, who have still such endless disillusionments in store for them. I also calmly advised my friend to temper his pride. For such a violent storm can never last. Just how the heaven of love may manifest itself to them now depends altogether on how the reality of their attraction for one another develops. However, he declared himself ready under all circumstances to follow Cosima's example. In this I could only uphold his stand, for in matters of love you women show us the way, and to free himself from the vulgarity of existence the man cannot do better than imitate you, follow you, when you love. Happy is he to whom an angel points the way ! Sorrow is the meed of him whom the devil takes in tow. Happy me ! An angel beckons me ! "

" As sequel to the Cosima-Karl affair ! (he continued in a later letter). It happened with them just as my feelings prophesied. My friend thought he could count on something incredibly intrepid. I wasn't worrying very greatly on that score. Such a sudden, violent outburst in the case of such a young person cannot spring from any deep self-confident impulse. She wrote him at the end of three weeks, regretted her impulsiveness, admitted feeling ashamed, thanked him for his tender indulgence, begged him to forget ! He felt bitterly hurt and won't answer her letter. How deep this goes, I'm not at all certain. But from what meets the eye I assume that it doesn't go any too deep.

" It all had a painful effect on me. I found no real pathos there. But Cosima surprised me most of all. At that time there was something very fanatically melancholy about her. At all events I consider her the finer nature of the two. I can understand what was actually taking place in her soul. If she sticks it out (for Hans, this good, talented but not exactly remarkable, decisive and sensitive individual cannot satisfy

her) then I shall be exceedingly curious about her further development.
She deserves your consideration. But this has again given me a real
abhorrence of youthful marriages ; except in the case of quite insignificant persons, I never have met anyone who in time didn't have the
feeling of having made a great mistake. And then what misery !
Soul, character, disposition, all must be stunted unless extraordinary
new relationships (and then only very sorrowful ones) come along."[1]

On 16th August the Buelows left the Asyl. " Hans dissolved
in tears, Cosima sombre and silent," in the words of Wagner.

" My wife is very lovable again (wrote Buelow on his return to
Berlin). I wish you could come to know her otherwise than as she has
so far been in your home. Her loquaciousness is always throttled in
your presence, her frank expansive nature retires into itself. This
implies a compliment for you, even though out of place. ' *Ehrfurcht
hielt sie in Bann*' (awe held her spellbound). Now she is always afraid
that you might consider her childish and altogether too insignificant
to be able to love and understand you. And yet she is one of the very
few who is capable of doing just that. . . .

" I haven't yet thanked you for your hospitality this year. As painful
as it was to me to see you suffer and the most sacred elements of your
existence jeopardized, I wouldn't for anything in the world have
missed being with you at this time. Once again your presence charmed
and refreshed me so much that I can go on living on it for a long time
to come. If I could only have meant something to you, could have
protected you from evil, even though I could have brought you no
good. But that's the way it goes in life, unfortunately. One person
has the good will, *the other* the power. Don't despise my helplessness."

This romantic episode on the Lake of Geneva that unquestionably meant nothing to Cosima in a deeper sense and in which
Karl Ritter played an altogether secondary rôle (quite casual,
in fact) was the first tragic note in the married life of the
Buelows. That it did not lead to catastrophe at this time was only
because the proper protagonist was lacking. Cosima had sufficient ability and talent to have made her own mark in the world
like her mother—a personality in her own right. But she voluntarily renounced this and placed her life in the service of a mission.
Genius and Wagner's sweeping passion which transcended all
bounds showed her in a flash (when she witnessed the tragedy on
the Green Hill) that her own marriage with Buelow was a mistake
and that she would never succeed in making of her husband the
great creative artist she had hoped. Wagner's genius left this

[1] Deleted from the published Wagner-Wesendonck correspondence.

talent (which placed itself so whole-heartedly at his service) no possibilities for individual development. It was this painful realization in the midst of the boundless excitement of the experience that suggested to Cosima the idea of suicide, and she saw in Karl Ritter only a welcome tool for her purpose. The latter's all too exuberant acceptance of her romantic plan, due to a passing depression, undoubtedly sobered her very quickly and brought her to her senses. She came back to Hans, determined to try once more, and with redoubled effort, to fulfil her mission at his side. She even wrote an opera libretto (" Merlin ") for him, and hoped to inspire him to undertake creative work of his own. If Buelow should now fail and renounce his independent career in order to limit himself to acting as the faithful disciple of another (certainly an honourable rôle but inadequate for the vaulting ambition of one who had sacrificed her own career) then the tragedy of this marriage must become apparent. That her plan was hopeless from the start is shown by the following effusion that Buelow addressed to Wagner on 24th August 1859, indicating how small and insignificant he felt alongside this Titan with whom his wife wanted to " force him into artistic competition."

" A man like you (he wrote) who has not his counterpart, who is something apart and belongs to another world than this vulgar and trivial one, how then could friendship ever fall to his share ? One looks *at* friends—one looks *up to* you. For example, I, who am not exactly one of the sorriest members of the guild, would even be willing —*in the deepest seriousness*—to become your bootblack and commissionaire ; but I haven't the cheek to lay claim to being called your friend."

And then signed himself " your true vassal and servant."

A letter from Minna to her Dresden friend, dated 2nd August 1858, tells the story of the days immediately following her return to the Asyl.

" It's no trifling matter to be faced with a separation after being married for nearly twenty-two years (she wrote). At least, I can't take it so lightly. If it lay with me, I assure you it wouldn't happen. As far as indulgence towards men is concerned, I'm just as open-minded as any other woman and I've already overlooked many things, preferring not to notice them. For six whole years I followed along blindly. Now Richard's honour simply won't allow him to stay here, as the husband has learned of the affair, I don't know how.

" When I returned, my husband attacked and threatened me in such a violent manner, demanding that I associate with that woman again, that I also gave in and wanted to make this tremendous effort ; that is really the utmost that a woman in my position could do. But the husband—and, in the end, this woman herself—won't have it that way. She—as my husband shouted at me—is furious, quite beside herself, that I'm here and will no longer permit me to remain, out of jealousy. Only Richard alone should stay here, which of course he can't do.

" Richard has two hearts. He is ensnared by the other person while he still clings to me through force of habit—that's all. As this woman won't tolerate my staying with my husband, and he is weak enough to do what she wants, I've decided to live alternately in Dresden, Berlin and Weimar until it shall please either Richard or God to call me. My health naturally doesn't improve under such circumstances ; not all the waters in the world can help when such an emotional turmoil is going on inside one. I regret every *groschen* that I gave out here.

" The palpitation of my heart very often keeps me from sleeping. I'm also short of breath. As soon as I go up the stairs I have to stop to get my breath—to say nothing of my nerves. Both are dreadful in every respect. In a fortnight, as soon as our visitors have gone (I would like to keep them as long as possible) I shall have to get busy with selling and packing the furniture, which also grieves me greatly. Richard will be going off beforehand—I don't know where—perhaps to Italy. That is my immediate unhappy future, which I would never have dreamt of. May God forgive those who have brought this new trouble upon me. I never speak to Richard about this affair. We're outwardly on good terms ; he suffers sometimes, but not on my account ; while I suffer only on his. I hate the world where weak creatures make such torments for each other."

Wagner's departure was postponed from day to day, to his great distress, even after his friends had already all left. For he had great difficulty in raising the necessary funds for himself and Minna. At last, on 17th August 1858, he left his cosy Asyl. This was indeed one of the most tragic moments in Wagner's turbulent life, when after little over a year he almost had to flee from the place which he had thought was to be his permanent abode and go abroad once more, solitary and homeless, after having taken possession of it amid such rejoicing and with such jubilation. The " Tristan " fate in all its tragic force now broke over him and Mathilde.

" The last night in the Asyl I went to bed after eleven (he wrote in the diary for Mathilde). I was to start next morning at five. Before I closed my eyes it came vividly to mind how I always used to put myself to sleep by imagining that one day I would die here. I should be lying thus when you came to me for the last time ; when you openly before everybody clasped my head in your arms and received my soul in one last kiss ! This death was the most lovely of mental images for me and was entirely associated with the locality of my bedroom. The door opening on the stairs was closed ; you entered through the portières of the study ; thus you put your arms round me ; thus, gazing at you, I passed away.

"And now what ? Was I also bereft of the possibility of dying thus ? Chilled and with a hunted feeling I left the house where I had been shut up with a demon that I could only escape by flight. Now where—where—am I going to die ? And so I fell asleep.

"A wonderful rustling sound awoke me from my troubled dreams ; on awakening I distinctly felt a kiss on my brow ; a deep sigh followed. It was so vivid that I sprang up and looked about me. Everything was quiet. I put on the light ; it was just on one o'clock, the end of the hour when spirits walk the earth. Had a spirit been keeping watch over me in this troubled hour ? Were you awake or asleep at that time ? What were your feelings ? Now I couldn't close my eyes again. I tossed about in bed for a long time in vain till I finally got up, dressed myself completely, closed the last trunk, and—sometimes pacing back and forth, sometimes flinging myself on the sofa—anxiously awaited dawn.

"This time it came up later than I was accustomed to from my sleepless nights of last summer. The sun crept up blushing from behind the mountains. Then I took one more lingering glance across the way. Heavens ! No tears came to my eyes, but it seemed to me that all the hair on my temples had turned white. Now I had said farewell. Now everything within me was cool and determined. I went downstairs. There my wife was waiting for me. She offered me some tea. It was a terrible, wretched hour. She went along with me. We walked down through the garden. It was a marvellous morning. I did not turn round. At the final parting my wife broke out in lamentations and tears. For the first time my eyes were dry. Once more I counselled her to be gentle and magnanimous and reap Christian comfort for herself. But the old revengeful violence flamed up again. I had to admit to myself that she is past all help. Yet I can't revenge myself on the unfortunate creature. She must work out her own sentence. And so I was dreadfully serious, bitter, and sad. Yet I couldn't cry. And so I left. And see ! I don't deny it ! I had a feeling of well-being. I breathed freely. I went forth into solitude. There I am at home—in that solitude where I can love you with every breath I draw ! "

"The parting from Richard almost broke my heart (wrote Minna). My grief could not have been any greater if it had been his funeral. The parting was so hard for me because I had the feeling that it was a

From a painting by C. Dorner

MATHILDE WESENDONCK IN 1860

At left
FREDERIKE MEYER

At right
MATHILDE MAIER

parting for life. Richard could do nothing but cry when he sat in the train. Before this he had neither thought nor glance nor sympathy for me. When I walked down the path with him into the garden from where you can see the Wesendoncks' house he walked at my side like a blind man, keeping his eyes fixed across the way without the slightest thought of my grief, as I walked by his side until I took him by the hands and turned him gently towards me saying : ' Richard ! do look at *me* ! ' I couldn't shake off the feeling that I would never see him again in this life. And yet if Richard were to send for me, I assure you I couldn't see him again—not yet. A year or more must go by before I could make up my mind to join him. May he long keep well, and stay away from me ! I don't believe I need to tell you how fond I was of my husband and how loth I was to be away from him, even for a week. When I couldn't be with him I wrote him nearly every day. Now here I am ! I have to write him and can't think of anything to say ! "

After superintending the break-up of their Zürich home Minna left for Dresden in search of quiet and health under the care of Wagner's old friend, Dr. Anton Pusinelli. It was not to be a permanent separation. They were only to go their own ways for a time in order to forget and regain peace of mind. When the news of the catastrophe at the Asyl became known most of their friends rallied sympathetically round Minna, among them Princess Wittgenstein and Wagner's two sisters, Klära and Caecilie. Cosima von Buelow also sent Minna an invitation to come to Berlin which, however, she declined. Wagner did not wish to settle down with Minna again till time had healed their wounds and he was in a position to make a permanent home for them without the constant worry over money. But it must be in a larger place this time, where both of them would have outside interests, for (as he said) " we were far too buried in Zürich and were thrown too much on our own resources, which over a long period was bound to have a demoralizing effect and make us grumble at being condemned to sit moping in such a hole."

Wagner had fled to Venice by way of Geneva. Here he lived in complete seclusion and aloofness from the world, giving himself up wholly to his love-dreams and the completion of " Tristan."

" Yes, I hope to recover for your sake (he wrote Mathilde). To keep you means to keep myself for my art. This—to live to be a comfort to you—this is my task ; this is in accord with my nature, my destiny, my will—my love. Thus I am yours and thus must you too recover

H

through me! I shall finish ' Tristan ' here—let the world rage as it will. And with it, I may then, I *shall*, return to see you, to comfort you, to make you happy. This is now my loveliest, holiest wish."

Although Wagner had left the Asyl in outward tranquillity he inwardly cherished a jealous anger against the person on whose account he had been forced to make this renunciation.

" Parents, duties towards children! (he wrote Mathilde). How remote all this sounded in my hallowed, mock-serious-hearted mood! When I thought of you, parents, children and duties never once entered my mind! I only knew that you loved me and that everything that was lofty and sublime in the world must be unhappy. From this height it horrifies me to see outlined so clearly just *what* made us unhappy!

" Then all at once I see you in your magnificent home, see all that and hear all those to whom we must forever remain incomprehensible, those who—strangers to us—are near us so as to anxiously keep from us all that is close to us. And I'm furious at having to say : you are supposed to sacrifice everything for these people who know nothing about you, comprehend nothing about you, but demand everything from you! I cannot, and do not want to see and hear it, if I'm to complete my earthly mission in a fitting manner. Only from the depths of my soul can I draw strength, but—all outside agencies that insist on regulating my decisions rouse me to bitterness.

" You hope to see me for a few hours in Rome this winter? I'm afraid—I shan't be able to see you! To see you—and then to part from you to another's complacent satisfaction—am I already equal to that? Most certainly not!"

If Wagner's relations with Mathilde Wesendonck were destined to end in tragedy, to fade out in painful, yearning resignation, this was inherent in Mathilde's character itself. Unlike Cosima, her gentle nature had not been endowed with the ruthless energy that could carry her love triumphantly over all the obligations and barriers imposed by ethics and society and could only find perfect peace in permanent union with the beloved. Mathilde remained the bride of his soul, who for her lover's sake forced her husband to renounce all physical claims on her, but then sacrificed her personal happiness to the obligations she had previously assumed.

" She belonged to those absolutely happy women for whom nothing counts but home, husband and child (Wagner wrote later in an outburst of bitterness to Frau Wille) and who every time they are forced to decide, prove that there can be no higher happiness for them than that which they possess."

Wagner was forced to bow to her will, and give her up. But it took time for him to adapt himself to a compulsion of this kind —so essentially foreign to his nature—and the flame of his passionate temperament often flared up suddenly in wild desire.

" I awoke from a short but deep sleep, after long fearful suffering, such as I have never known (he wrote Mathilde from Italy). I stood on the balcony and looked down on the flowing black waters of the canal ; a tempest was raging. No one would have noticed my plunge —my fall. I would have been rid of all torment as soon as I jumped, and I clenched my fist to raise myself to the balustrade. Could I—with my gaze fixed upon you—upon your children ?

" Now All Souls' Day has dawned ! All souls are at rest. Now I know ! I will soon see you again—certainly in the spring ; perhaps already in the middle of the winter. Look, my child, now my soul is free of the last thorn. You undoubtedly sought it in the wrong place. It wasn't my wife—it was your husband who drove me from your side. Forgive me if I again touch the wound. My own has healed— since last night. Now I am capable of everything."[1]

After his flight from the Asyl he was at first entirely cut off from any direct communication with Mathilde, who returned his letters unopened. The lovers only gleaned scanty news of each other through their mutual friend Eliza Wille. Both, wrestling with their passion, confided their hopes and longings to their diaries. That autumn, after they had exchanged these intimate confessions and Wagner had read Mathilde's notes, which revealed to him that she, too, only mastered her passion after a hard battle, he was on the point of forgetting all their vows and resolutions and hurrying to her to take that which he felt was his.

" Did I desist out of consideration for myself ? Most certainly not. But out of consideration—for your children ! For that reason—once more—and for ever—stand firm ! That holds for some time yet. I feel as if—as if—I might—soon behave towards you in a finer way, one more pleasing to, and worthier of you ; and this I want so much to do ! "

While he poured forth his desires and longings to his diary for Mathilde, with all the ardour and passion of his temperament, he was also endeavouring to comfort Minna, cheer her up, calm her with promises of better days to come in the near future. And this he did with really touching patience and indissoluble affection for

___
[1] Deleted from the Wagner-Wesendonck correspondence.

his old comrade who had gone through so much trouble and misery with him. Letters and telegrams followed one after the other,[1] and in letters to old Dresden friends (chiefly to Tichatschek and Pusinelli (Minna's physician) he implored them to help his wife. Minna's health also soon began to improve a little. Unfortunately her constant intercourse with gossipy old friends was not exactly conducive to her forgetting past events or viewing them in a more sensible manner. She therefore returned again and again to the "Wesendonck affair" with complaints and reproaches. And Wagner, with the veritable patience of an angel, tried repeatedly to make her see these things in the proper light.

"To ensure us a peaceful evening at the end of this troublous life (he wrote her on 7th February 1859), to look after you and sweeten your toil to the best of my abilities, is my one and only earthly aspiration and endeavour, while otherwise I scarcely belong to the world any more. I daily turn over in my mind how best I may set about the attainment of this final goal, do this and that to this end—then another letter arrives from you—and the same old story begins all over again! I'm supposed to have said this or that at some time or other, somebody or other knows this or that; and again everything has been in vain! I try to straighten things out. But I only make bad matters worse!

"I have no other aim on this earth than to take care of you, and have your welfare sincerely and loyally at heart. God is my witness! Child, child! keep your promise and—not another word about the past!"

Minna was also moved with the best intentions, but trifles, gossip or misunderstandings were enough to cause all the old nonsense to flare up again within her. Her nerves broke down, and in the most passionate outbursts she heaped reproaches and insulting accusations on her husband. If he defended himself it irritated her and led to endless arguments. If he kept still and said nothing she took it as an admission of guilt, and taunted him with it triumphantly. He therefore soon realized how hopeless it all was, and that Minna could only recover if she were with him and under his personal care. He was therefore firmly determined to consider taking up life with her again just as soon as he had regained sufficient control over himself.

It was a sorrowful event that brought him into touch with the Wesendoncks again. Otto Wesendonck had written him of the death of their little four years' old son Guido.

---

[1] Six telegrams in the short period from 18th to 26th August 1858 are in the Burrell Collection, Exhibit 314.

" I was deeply touched (Wagner wrote in *Mein Leben*), and as I was badly in need of rest in every respect I at once planned a short trip across the Alps with the idea of perhaps spending Christmas Eve with my old friends—in a really charitable sense. I wrote Frau Wille of my project and strange to say, her husband replied in her stead, giving me a highly unexpected account of the tremendous and exceedingly unpleasant stir caused by my sudden departure from Zürich, and particularly by the way in which my wife had carried out her share of the undertaking—all the brunt of which had fallen on the Wesendoncks. Since I further learned as a result of this how skilfully and cleverly Wesendonck had acted in the matter, this automatically led to a renewal of our friendly intercourse and provided a basis for better relations."

Wagner's flight from the Asyl naturally had stirred up a lot of gossip in Zürich, and the most idiotic and piquant stories were going the rounds and were also given full credence, thanks to those good ladies who had long watched with envious eyes the artist's intimacy with this distinguished, cultivated woman.

Minna, too, had done much to foster the local gossip by advertising her furniture for sale at a low price " owing to sudden departure." The Zürich Philistines were amusing themselves in lively fashion at the expense of Otto Wesendonck, for whom all this local notoriety and gossip were naturally painful in the extreme. As the gossip refused to die down he invited Wagner to come to Zürich as their guest for a few days in order to deprive the rumours of any foundation in fact. Wagner, who had moved to Lucerne the end of March after completing the second act of " Tristan," accepted the invitation the beginning of April. In the course of the summer he visited the Wesendoncks again on several occasions,and they came to Lucerne twice to see him. Thus the meeting with the beloved, of which he had dreamed so often, now became a reality, and yet it seemed to him only a dream after all, and one far inferior to those of his fancy. Reality, with the constraint that went with it, had a sobering effect on the radiant picture born of his solitude and loneliness. Only when the memory of their meeting had faded again did Mathilde once more become for him all she had been—the immortal mistress of his heart, the transfigured gleaming lodestar of his life and creative work. " We do not see each other where we are (he wrote). It is only where we aren't that our eyes behold one another."

The resumption of personal relations with the Wesendoncks aroused fresh resentment in Minna.

" My conceited husband's visit to Zürich was no way to counter the gossip that that woman brought down upon herself by her common behaviour (she wrote Frau Herwegh). Yet that, as he wrote me, was his sole object. I can't help laughing now at the innocence of our good Wesendonck. They've reckoned without their host. The only way to have enticed the people back again into those magnificent and now deserted rooms would have been for *me* to have associated personally with this woman again—which Heaven forbid for all time ! But I'm now afraid of new gossip that won't do any of those concerned any good. My shrewd spouse is soon to repeat his visit to the Wesendoncks in Zürich from nearby Lucerne, and this time they're to give a big party so that the appearance of being on apparent good terms with his weak host will contradict all rumours with éclat. . . .

" The stupid new agitations that I've had to suffer again through my good husband have given me a serious and prolonged setback, as so easily happens in the case of heart trouble (she continued on 29th August 1859). Isn't it enough to make me lose all confidence in him when he keeps on breaking the promises he has only just made me ? That is, that only blessings are now before me, that I won't have to put up with any more insults ? No, my dear Emma, it takes a very special type of character to forget under such circumstances, and get well.

" I wouldn't trade my husband for any other in the world. On the contrary—I only want to end the short span of life still left to me in peace and quiet in some corner of the world, believe me.

" ' Lohengrin ' was finally given for the first time at the Court Theatre in Dresden on the 6th of the month. I'm very fond of this opera and the principal rôles were in better hands than in Berlin. I often have to turn to Richard's works to give me moral encouragement —give me strength—otherwise I couldn't write him a friendly letter (this quite between ourselves). In me he certainly has a glowing admirer of his earlier works. I feel as if I had helped compose them, as during this time I had to look after him, and shoulder all the domestic responsibilities alone. How very different things were in the last years of our life together."

Wagner had long realized that Minna could never recover in her Dresden surroundings. Since he felt that after the hard lessons of the past year they should now be able to take up life together again, especially as in the meantime he had recovered the necessary repose and self-control in order to be able to curb his temperament even at crucial moments, to comfort her and to allay her anxieties, he began to make serious plans for their reunion in the autumn of 1859. The principal reason was his great anxiety about her health. " I can't help seeing that she won't be able to get on so well under anyone else's cure and protection as under mine."

" I am extremely sorry (he complained in a letter to Alwine Fromann) that she chose Dresden of all places to settle in. The unfortunate part of it is that she associates almost exclusively with uneducated women, who though no doubt very well-meaning, are not even remotely capable of exerting a beneficent effect on such a highly excitable person as she. Almost every letter brings me some new tale —so-called tittle-tattle, some heedless alarm that has come her way. And these—I can only say—unhappy associations of hers can only be broken up by removing her from this environment. As she herself longs so desperately for a quiet retired life, I consider mine absolutely cut out for her to share. I therefore feel sure of the success of my plan in every way, because I know exactly what lays before me. I know that *I* alone can have a really salutary effect on Minna, and this fact cuts out my work for me. So I have no choice. This I could only have if I were convinced that leaving her in her present surroundings and mode of life would have the same favourable effect on her."

That this resumption of their life together would be nothing but a purely platonic companionship is shown by Wagner's request to Minna's Dresden physician, his friend Pusinelli.

" I implore you to advise Minna against resuming any sexual relationships with me (he wrote on 3rd October 1859). From a medical standpoint, I also consider it very important to prescribe the strictest rule for her in this respect, as she is to a certain extent irresponsible and too run down mentally."

As Germany was still closed to him and he could not settle in Karlsruhe (as suggested by his friends, the Grand Duke and Duchess of Baden) he decided to take up his residence in Paris again as soon as he had completed " Tristan," if only for the sake of hearing a good orchestra or string quartet from time to time— sources of inspiration which he had missed so keenly during his years in Switzerland. After negotiations with publishers had proved futile the funds for the new venture were willingly put up by Otto Wesendonck in the very tactful form of a business transaction in which the latter bought from Wagner the rights to the " Nibelungen " scores for the sum of 24,000 francs.

" I spent four days in Zürich as the guest of the Wesendoncks (he wrote Hans von Buelow on 7th October 1859). The man is very devoted to me and is to be admired in the fullest sense of the word. A beautiful and certainly very unique relationship has been established

—a proof of the power deep earnestness can have even over the least gifted natures. Thus the man stands between me and his wife (whom he has had to renounce completely) as (I can really say) the most genuine of friends to both of us. I am exceedingly proud of this development. I was guided solely by a most earnest desire not to deprive the poor woman of my presence. Now the almost incredible has been achieved. We exchanged visits repeatedly between Lucerne and Zürich. I always stopped with them and I do everything I can to help this loyal woman through her difficult life ; and her husband is genuinely delighted when I come and stay. I'm now taking my unfortunate wife back again. She's a little better ; but to get on, she now requires the most tender care and attention. Only I can vouchsafe her this. She clings to me with all her being, and this definitely dictates my attitude towards her."

The middle of September he then set out for Paris. This marks the close of his sojourn in Switzerland, so rich in hopes and disappointments. The free little land of Switzerland had sheltered him for almost a decade, but his own ambition—to find a home for himself and his art—was also denied him by an adverse fate. And yet this epoch denotes a culminating point in his life and creative work, since all his most sublime creations were produced during this period, as he himself readily recognized and admitted. It was during this period also that fate brought into his life the woman of whom he could still say many years afterward :

" She is, and remains, my one and only love ! It was the zenith of my life. The anxious, exquisitely restless years which I spent in the increasing charm of her presence, her affection, hold all the sweetness of my life."

How this tragic love revibrated in Mathilde's heart is shown by a little cycle of poems entitled " Mignon " which she dedicated to Wagner. These afford a deep glimpse into her wounded heart, which had to pass through all the phases of a yearning but unhappy love.

I

So tenderly, so heart in heart
You kissed me in my dream!
I feel it still, that love-true kiss,
Awakened though I seem.

And yet in life my waiting mouth
Your lips have scarce brushed o'er.
No look, no cry, revealed to you
How sad my heart, and sore.

But in my dreaming you called me
Your own beloved love.
When I awoke, I heard it still,
That word so full of love.

Oh, do not scorn the dream that gives
High courage to my mood.
Life looks on me with hateful eyes,
The dream alone is good.

Then what is falsehood, what is truth,
What life, and what dream stuff?
Let me go dreaming on and on
For I have lived enough.

2

Oh, the kiss is without gladness
Kiss of dreams that is not real
For a bitter lack and sadness
In my deepest heart I feel.

Oh, the loving is but sorrow,
Loving that is but in dream!
Joy and happiness the morrow
Scatters with its dawning gleam.

One embrace in its hot fire,
Arm in arm and breast to breast,
Burning would assuage desire,
Leave me joyful, leave me blest.

3

Oft I wanted to beseech you
For that moment so supreme,
But a dread inexplicable
Forced to silence all my theme.

Fearful tortures then came o'er me,
Tore my suffering soul apart,
And my very blood ceased flowing,
At its source was struck the heart.

Leaden was I, as with dying,
Knew no solace from that wound,
Quivering in all my being,
Cast me down upon the ground.

Then the harpist's song resounded
From the tiny attic room,
Sobbing, I fell down before him,
Waked all night in utter gloom.

4

I bore it gladly, just to see you,
And your mere presence stilled distress,
Though I could only stand and watch you,
Yet you were there, my happiness!

Every one loves you—you love many,
Your being as the sun is shown
Whose smile brings ever joy and blessing ;
My heart loves you and you alone.

When deepest agonies assailed me,
Tortures that I could not endure,
The doctor knew what sorely ailed me
And she herself prescribed the cure.

You came, and lo! I seemed recovered,
A miracle had made me o'er.
You gazed in wonder on that being
You ne'er saw beautiful before.

But when you to the friend had spoken
Those rapid words : " faith to the last,"
Ah, then indeed my heart was broken—
A pang, a cry, and all was past.

(Translation by Olga Erbsloh Muller.)

Chapter V

YEARNING AND SEEKING

AFTER an arduous search Wagner finally found the accommodation he desired in Paris in a small detached house quietly situated at No. 16, Rue Newton. However, he was obliged to pay three years' rent in advance amounting to 12,000 francs, and since the landlord was not at all disposed to shoulder the expense of the repairs and renovations that Wagner considered necessary the latter was obliged to pay for them out of his own pocket. As the sumptuous furnishings also swallowed up a good deal of money, Wesendonck's payment for the " Ring," which was intended to defray the cost of Wagner's stay in Paris, barely covered the initial outlay. But as his first thought was to provide himself with an attractive comfortable home and he felt that he had now found one which promised to be permanent for several years, he spent the money with a light heart, confident that he would soon be successful in Paris. As so often in the past, here again he was to find that he had reckoned without his host.

Minna, to whom he sent almost daily reports of his progress, finally yielded to his entreaties to join him in Paris, though she rebelled inwardly at the thought, especially as all her Dresden friends counselled her strongly against it.

" I should and ought to be indifferent by this time as to where I'm to be dragged to next (she wrote), but in point of fact I long for solitude and tranquillity—not for the bustle of society where there are so many silly people, especially women, who even here envy me the possession of this great artist. I would rather they envied me my good husband—the man himself."

Wagner displayed a touching anxiety to have everything ready before Minna's arrival and thus spare her any kind of work. He engaged the servants and a companion and drew up a fixed schedule for her.

" You must entrust yourself absolutely to my care and treatment (he wrote her) for it is my duty to see that you, my poor wife, have this spiritual and physical care, with true devotion. That means, however, that you must effect a great change in the domestic activities which formerly engaged so much of your attention and are now such a strain on you. Once and for all you must have nothing to do with all the fuss of housekeeping. You're to be the lady of the house ; you'll keep the accounts, and everything shall and must be done exactly as you wish ; but you're not to raise a finger yourself. Now you're only to give the orders."

Well-meant as this undoubtedly was, Wagner's recipe for the rôle of a great lady with a retinue of servants was ill-suited to Minna's lively bustling temperament, and their discussions on the subject in their letters held out little promise that any good would come of the venture. Nevertheless Minna finally undertook to try it out, and arrived in Paris on 17th November 1859, though Nathalie, who had hitherto always lived with them in Paris, Dresden and Zürich, now stayed behind in Dresden. Since Minna, as long as she lived, was curiously ashamed to tell the girl (who was always passed off as her sister) that she was her mother, their relations during the latter years were far from pleasant. For Nathalie felt, as Minna's " sister " (as she was also designated in Minna's will) that she had a right to be treated on an equal footing, and only gave in very stubbornly and with bad grace to Minna's parental authority. Wagner therefore did not want her to come to Paris, but wished her to remain in Dresden and continue her studies, the expenses of which he gladly assumed.

Since all his efforts to have his works produced in Paris were ineffective he conceived the bold plan of founding a German opera house in the French capital, and even succeeded in finding a few wealthy persons who looked favourably on the scheme. However, before such a project could take definite shape it was essential to generate public interest in his works and win the backing of influential people in the social and artistic world. He felt the easiest way to achieve this end was to give concerts of his own works, and hold large weekly receptions, as was then customary in Parisian society. While the concerts were successful from an artistic point of view they left him with an alarming deficit of 10,000 francs ; but his Wednesday receptions in the " salon " of the Rue Newton were a great success. The élite of the intellectual and artistic worlds of Paris soon became regular visitors at the home of the German master. " But Wagner dominated the company so completely (wrote Malwida von Meysenbug) that one really saw and heard nobody but him, and quite overlooked the others."

Years before, Malwida had become an enthusiastic admirer of his through reading his book, *The Art Work of the Future*, and had made his acquaintance personally during his visit to London in 1855. This, however, had ended on a very discordant note as the result of a heated dispute over Feuersbach and Schopenhauer.

" We parted in a very bad humour (he tells us in *Mein Leben*). Now it was almost a shock to meet her again in Paris. But all painful recollections of those London arguments were soon wiped out when she at once explained to me that our dispute at that time had the decisive effect of making her turn her attention immediately to Schopenhauer's philosophy. She informed me that she was now a zealous follower of mine, and interpreted this avowal at once in the sense of a friend, anxiously concerned for my welfare in every way. When, in keeping with the laws of propriety, I next introduced her to my wife as a friend, she could not help seeing at a glance the extreme unpleasantness of our merely pseudo-marriage, so she took steps with affectionate solicitude to rectify the drawbacks resulting from the conditions she had observed. And now she could not fail to see to what a difficult pass the heavy expenses of the three concerts had brought me."

So she immediately set about raising a subscription for him among the members of the German Colony in Paris. But as an announcement of this project found its way prematurely into the papers and caused some malicious comment, Wagner was obliged to issue a statement that he must decline any such assistance. Malwida's attempt to interest a rich Jewess of her acquaintance[1] in Wagner was more successful.

" She did not conceal from herself or from me (he continued) what a disagreeable task the cultivation of this acquaintance would be. Nevertheless she relied on the good nature she attributed to this rather grotesque woman, as well as on her vanity which would certainly prompt her to try to repay me for the honour of attending my receptions. Mrs. Schwabe, who regularly attended my soirées and just as regularly fell asleep during the music, now found herself induced by the solicitous Meysenbug to offer me her personal assistance. This amounted to about 3,000 francs, of which at that moment I was most certainly urgently in need."

But welcome though this assistance was, it could only relieve matters temporarily, and his situation remained as desperate as

---

[1] Mrs. Schwabe was the widow of a wealthy Manchester business man.

ever, for none of his Paris schemes worked out. He therefore accepted an offer from Brussels to repeat the Paris concerts there. But the large receipts on which he had counted also failed to materialize.

The one pleasant memory of this time was provided by Liszt's friend Agnes Street-Klindworth[1] and her father, with his inexhaustible fund of anecdotes, and in whose house he felt really at home. The lovely Agnes, who was perpetually changing her lovers, seems to have harnessed Wagner also to her chariot, and it was to this family that he owed his introduction to Prince Metternich, the Austrian Ambassador in Paris, whose wife Pauline was very influential at Court owing to her intimate friendship with the Empress Eugénie.

At first the Tuileries looked with disfavour on Wagner's project of producing his works at the Paris Opéra. This attitude was due to the influence of Fould[2] who, as a friend of Meyerbeer, was hostile to Wagner. But an improvement gradually set in, thanks to Hans von Buelow's influence with Count Pourtales and Count Hatzfeld of the Prussian Embassy.

One evening at Court, Princess Metternich (who had heard " Tannhäuser " in Dresden) spoke of it in such enthusiastic terms that the Emperor, out of courtesy to his friend, immediately commanded a production of the work at the Opéra, in French. Which removed all Wagner's obstacles, for since those in high places realized the futility of opposing the Princess, all his wishes were readily granted in the beginning. But there was still a long way to go before actual performance, with the hoped-for receipts and Wagner's financial situation—already highly critical—was brought to the verge of catastrophe by a misfortune which in fact could not have been foreseen.

The house in the Rue Newton that he had renovated at such great expense was scheduled for demolition as it lay in the direct line of an avenue that was to be cut through at this point. It then dawned on Wagner why the landlord had so obstinately refused to make even the smallest improvements in the property. The wily Frenchman, who of course had long known of the

---

[1] The " friend " to whom the letters in the third volume of Liszt's collected correspondence are addressed.

[2] Secretary of State and Minister of the Household to Napoleon III.

municipal project, had taken in the unbusiness-like artist completely. All protests, even an appeal to the courts, were unavailing, so poor Wagner had to vacate the house, and all his money was lost. His removal to the Rue d'Aumale exhausted his last resources and there was nothing left to defray the expenses of Minna's very urgent treatment at a health resort.

But help came unexpectedly. Frau Marie Kalergis, a friend of Liszt's, who had been present at the original performance of " Tannhäuser " in Dresden and had frequently entertained the two great masters at her house in Paris in 1853, now returned from a long journey.

" Count Paul Hatzfeld turned up at my house one day to ask me to call on Mme. Kalergis—who had just arrived in Paris—to receive certain communications from her (he wrote in *Mein Leben*). She greeted me with the statement that she regretted all the more not having been present at my concerts during the winter as she thereby had missed the opportunity of giving me timely aid when I was in a tight place. She had heard that I had suffered heavy losses, which she had been told amounted to 10,000 francs, and she now begged me to accept this amount from her.

" Although I had thought it only proper to deny flatly my losses to Count Hatzfeld, seeing that the Prussian Embassy had also been approached in connection with that odious subscription, I now saw no reason whatever to practise any dissimulation towards this big-hearted woman. I felt as though something were now being fulfilled which I thought all along I had the right to expect, and in return I likewise felt immediately impelled to repay this unusual woman—at least be something to her. All the uneasiness that my later intercourse with her caused me, sprang from my failure to satisfy this one desire, a situation due to her strange character and restive life. For the moment I tried at once to prove to her in some way the sincerity of this desire. For her sake I improvised a performance of the second act of ' Tristan ' in which Mme. Viardot (whom I got to know much better on this occasion) and I shared the voice parts while I had Klindworth come over from London especially at my expense to provide the piano accompaniment. This very remarkable intimate performance took place at Viardot's house. Besides Mme. Kalergis, for whose sake it was arranged, Berlioz was the only person present."

Another very valuable service was rendered him by this patron. The efforts of her relative, the Saxon Ambassador Baron von Seebach, together with the personal intervention of Princess Wilhelm of Prussia with the King of Saxony (which was due to the efforts of Count Pourtales), finally succeeded in obtaining permission for the exile to set foot on German soil once more in safety. He had been urged to make use of his first trip to Germany to express his thanks to Her Royal Highness, so he took advantage of Minna's stay at Bad Soden in the Taunus for this purpose, fetched her there when her cure was finished, paid his respectful homage to the Princess in Baden-Baden, and returned to Paris with his wife after a week's tour of the Rhine.

Minna's health was still far from satisfactory and the perpetual excitement and financial worries in Paris did not conduce to her improvement. Wagner's optimistic expectations of their reunion therefore failed in every respect to materialize. His initial effort to spare Minna any share in his personal worries and to treat her only with calmness and gentleness merely resulted in renewed confusion, since she felt herself slighted, and viewed his mysterious taciturnity as an indication of something wrong. Yet on the other hand, if he entered into any discussion with her, this usually ended in a stormy scene, both being highly strung and irritable.

" When I thought I was strong enough to resume our life together (he later confessed to Minna) I had counted, of course, on a tranquil, less anxious and agitated existence on my side. It is with real horror that I now look back on this—our second terrible Paris experience, when worry, anxiety, anger, tension and suffering of every kind finally reduced me to such a wretched and irritable state that I can only wonder how I stood it all and did not at some time or other entirely lose control of myself.

" And could there have been anything worse to add to the innumerable worries I daily had to endure than to receive untimely reminders of past events that you persistently misunderstood ? The slightest insult, the merest sarcasm on your part, given the miserable state to which I was then reduced, was bound to goad me finally to frenzy. That you will fail to understand this and continue to regard such violent outbursts on my part as evidence of suppressed hatred towards you, or of glowing passion for another, can only make me wilder still."

It is sad to see these two human beings, who were really making a sincere effort to come together, clashing again and again in spite of everything and wearing each other out in a futile struggle as though under the power of a hostile demon. Minna's complaint had a bitter ring.

" I am becoming quite melancholy and am going to pieces—I'm well on the way to it (she wrote a friend). Richard is kind, but he's

COSIMA LISZT AT THE TIME OF HER MARRIAGE TO
HANS VON BUELOW

nothing to me, not even a friend, because he never confides in me and I don't like, or dare, to ask questions. . . . I'm the housekeeper here with nothing to do but order three servants about and put up with their annoyances. But I also have the entrée to the drawing-room to show the guests my silk dress. But not once have I had an affectionate or cosy chat with my husband, and that is sad for an old companion who has shared every misery with him, as I have. No confidence, no friendliness like there always used to be. He keeps everything to himself, never a cosy discussion, or talking things over, which often would help. I often don't see Richard the whole day long except at meal times—not even in the evening. But I never ask where he has been. I know, but now I'm not as stupid as I used to be. But this lady notices that I won't have anything more to do with her, and for some time has given up her frequent visits to my husband. It's better for him to go to her. I don't want to have anything more to do with such creatures or wait on them any more, and that's that.

" Here I'm not the wife—which does not disturb me—for this, love is lacking and I shouldn't be subjected to such brutality on the part of my husband. I'm also not a housekeeper because I don't draw any wages. Furthermore I'm not a friend, for that the confidence is lacking, unworthy persons having robbed me of it. Therefore what reason do I have for being pleased with things ? Because of the silk dress that I must wear as the wife of the celebrated Richard Wagner ? I haven't the vanity for this, and it will be hard to get it in my old age, seeing that I never had it when I was young.

" Why am I here after all ? Why didn't I listen to the warnings of kind, sensible Tichatschek, or my own intuition ? I haven't got over my homesickness by any means. Nothing has changed. Just think, dear Mathilde, the word *gemütlich* doesn't exist in French—and the actuality much less. They're only interested in outside entertainment such as trips, riding, mistresses, soirées, etc. Besides I can't stand the language any more and much prefer to avoid all French intercourse, which is superficial. For this reason I'm not learning it. I prefer to speak German."

Minna's indefinite but significant reference to the fact that " nothing was changed " is explained in a letter to Emma Herwegh, dated 24th March 1860.

" On Wednesday our little drawing-room is open to acquaintances and friends. A lot of people come to see us. Otherwise I never see anybody here that I like. Blandine is quite a common—I won't say vulgar—person, and even among all her acquaintances her reputation is not good, though that doesn't mean anything in Paris. She rather repels narrow-minded people, among whom I unfortunately must include myself. Frau Ollivier often comes to see my husband without having the decency to ask for my insignificant person. I'm used to

I

that sort of thing and let them do as they like, without paying the slightest attention. But I still can't forgive myself for coming here.

" If sooner or later anything startling of this kind happens again I shall go to Switzerland and stay there. I won't go home. I should be too ashamed, for everybody tried to dissuade me from coming here and prophesied all sorts of trouble. . . . Believe me, I don't deceive my Richard in any way ! On the contrary ! As I already told you, I live on the top floor and know nothing about what's going on down-stairs. My post is brought up to my room by our manservant. My husband is entirely indifferent to anything that has to do with me— who writes to me, or what they write to me, etc. When I received the letter just before your last one in which you asked me for two tickets for M. and Mme. Challemel, I turned down the page at this place and gave it to Richard as I've already asked several times in vain for a couple of concert tickets, while having to hear that Frau Blandine had whole boxes almost thrust on her to choose from.

" Hans von Buelow was here nearly two months and during that time gave four concerts which were well attended and aroused great enthusiasm. You will have met his wife in Berlin. She is another rather fast creature. It's her fault that Ritter left his wife ; the poor young thing is grieving herself to death. Buelow looks perfectly wretched. He often had dinner with us.

" I've found a dear old lady and friend in Liszt's mother who lives alone here. I go to see her very often and grow more and more fond of her—she has a rather forlorn life ; the granddaughter has no use for a chaperone ! Frau Ollivier has behaved abominably to Buelow, so that he left without bidding them good-bye. Mme. d'Agoult is not here. She's been in Italy for some time now."

Wagner's suspected liaison with Liszt's eldest daughter, Blandine, wife of the attorney Emile Ollivier (later Minister of Justice), to which Minna alluded in her letter, aroused consider-able gossip in Paris at that time. This was the real reason why Princess Wittgenstein broke off all connections with Wagner about this time, and did not look him up in Paris in 1860.[1] Wagner had met the Olliviers through Liszt when he was in Paris in January 1858.

" Blandine made an extremely pleasing impression on me (he noted in *Mein Leben*) through her gentle manner, her gaiety and a certain quiet wit added to a very rapid grasp of things. We understood each other almost immediately. The slightest remark sufficed to make it clear at once to the other what we each thought about the things and persons with whom we came into contact."

---

[1] Wagner literature scrupulously avoided all mention of this liaison, which was all the easier since the passages relating to it were deleted from the published Wagner correspondence.

Then when Wagner finally settled in Paris, he became very intimate with the Olliviers, and his friendship with Blandine, in particular, took such a form as to rouse Minna's justifiable jealousy.

" I hardly ever see Blandine now. Her husband is always ill and my wife is definitely suspicious of her" (wrote Wagner to Hans von Buelow on 21st May 1860).

However, apart from Blandine's passing annoyance at being given seats in the body of the house for the " Tannhäuser " performance, instead of a box, as she wished, Wagner's relations with her and her husband remained unimpaired, and when he finally left Paris for good he presented her with his writing-table as a precious keepsake, in accordance with her expressed wish.

When he returned from Germany in August 1860 he took " Tannhäuser " seriously in hand. The much-harassed Master, who had been tormented with the most absurd suggestions, such as the introduction of a ballet in the second act and other things of a similar nature, found a devoted helper in Princess Metternich, her powerful influence in the highest quarters usually managing to smooth away all difficulties.

" Your kindness to me (wrote Wagner) and your generous enthusiasm for my work are so infinitely valuable to me that I am very unhappy at finding no remotely adequate expression for my gratitude. ... Permit me, in gracious consideration of my situation, to let it all depend on the night preceding the performance whether a poor person like myself will be permitted to spend a few priceless hours on Tuesday with your Royal Highness. With profound respect, I venture to present to my most gracious patroness the text of my ' Tristan and Isolde.' May it find some favour in your eyes. In deep appreciation of the inexpressible kindness you are pleased to show me, I beg to offer you my sincerest thanks."

But nothing could save " Tannhäuser " from its fate, as the permanent subscribers to the opera had already signed its death warrant because of the composer's refusal to comply with their demands for a ballet. So after three tumultuous evenings Wagner finally withdrew it.[1] The vulgarity and rudeness of those bent on

---

[1] The Burrell Collection contains a number of interesting items treating of the Paris " Tannhäuser " performance, such as several letters from Minna to Nathalie and letters of condolence from her German friends. See Exhibits 332C, 357B, 361E and F, and 380.

defeating the work went so far that Princess Metternich, universally known as Wagner's patroness, was booed publicly in her box
and subjected to the most painful insults in *la presse vendue*. But
though she had compromised herself rather seriously in Paris
society by her championship of Wagner owing to the turn things
had taken, she was not to be frightened off, and remained loyal
to him and tried to obtain at least some financial compensation
for the composer, who by this undeserved blow had been
deprived of the sum he anticipated in return for a whole year's
work. That Wagner (contrary to his account in *Mein Leben*)
gratefully recognized at that time the great services the Princess
had rendered him is shown by his enthusiastic letter to her.

"Most gracious Princess! (he wrote on 21st March 1861). It has
not been possible to pay my respects to you in person since those—for
me—so stormy days. But to-day my heart gives me no rest until I
express to Your Highness—in some part at least—the feelings that
sway me almost entirely. Everything that I have recently gone through
(and it often struck to the innermost core of my artistic being) has been
made unreal and driven completely into the background through the
indescribable delight of being honoured by Your Highness's sympathy.
Perhaps you, my noble patroness, have yourself suffered on account of
me and my work. Nothing could pain me more deeply than to know
that you had been caused the slightest anxiety through your wonderful
interest in my work. I have never yet brought anyone luck! Only
worry, serious worry, has been the lot of everyone who showed even
the slightest interest in me. To you, also, most noble princess, I can
offer one reward. I shall pass away but my works may possibly live
after me. You who are in the bloom of health will long survive me.
When I am no more, perhaps my music will some day bring you the
thanks of a sincerely devoted person."

The Wesendoncks had also taken the most lively part in the
numerous hopes and disappointments of the Paris venture, and
the frequent letters exchanged between them at this time mirror
the futile trials and tribulations of the " Tannhäuser " scandal in
all its details. Otto Wesendonck repeatedly helped his friend out
of his financial difficulties, and also went to Paris for the performance, though Mathilde did not accompany him at this time.

"My child (Wagner wrote her sadly), what has become of our
happiness of the Calderon evenings? What malignant star robbed me
of my worthy Asyl? Believe me, whatever you may have heard to the
contrary, when I left the Asyl, my star was doomed to set; nothing is
left me but to die! Never—never—think of it in any other way!

Hold firmly to that thought! Otto's presence here during these
unhappy days was almost more of a worry to me than a pleasure,
though I must admit with all my heart that his solicitude and sympathy,
his whole personality, touched me very deeply. But I could show him
no real personal attention. It was one hectic rush."

In reply to Mathilde's question regarding his lady friends in
Paris he gave the following obviously somewhat tendentious
account which was deleted from the published Wagner-
Wesendonck correspondence.

"Mme. Ollivier is very talented and a really brilliant creature,
although much gentler than her sister. In wondering how it happens
that we see so little of each other I find that a certain lack of sincerity
on her part has somewhat repelled me and so I don't find her sufficiently attractive to accept Ollivier into the bargain. In spite of all his
graciousness he has one incredible characteristic, namely, the manner
of an agitated and agitating attorney. The same may be said of all my
acquaintances. The positive chances of a more frequent intercourse
are so unequal that I've adopted a generally reserved attitude and—all
according to mood—am perfectly content with what chance may
bring my way.

"Among others, for instance, is a democratic old maid, a Fräulein
von Meysenbug, who is here as a governess for Russian children. She
is incredibly homely, but when she was presented to me the odds were
in her favour because once in London, in a fit of ill humour, I treated
her pretty roughly after one of her gushing outbursts as a world
benefactress. Memory of the incident touched me, and as a result of
my repentant mood she now feels happier in my presence. My own
writings had so over-excited the poor soul—but now she has calmed
down and is enjoying the 'Tannhäuser' rehearsals.

"From the so-called upper circles of society is a lady whom I once
knew superficially and who has received greater attention from me this
time than ever before. This is the Countess Kalergis, niece of the
Russian Chancellor Nesselrode, of whom I have already told you. As
a well-known diplomatic *intrigante* she formerly filled me with frank
disgust. Last summer she was in Paris for a time, hunted me up, and
persuaded me to bring Klindworth over from London to accompany
her. I sang the second act of 'Tristan' with Viardot-Garcia—just
among ourselves. Berlioz was the only other person present. We also
did excerpts from the 'Nibelungen.' This was the very first time since
I left you. The thing that attracted me particularly to this lady was the
sense of a strange boredom, a contempt of the world and a disgust to
which I might have been indifferent had I not noticed at the same time
her ostensibly deep yearning for music and poetry which under such
circumstances struck me as significant. As her talent in this direction
was also considerable the lady was not altogether without interest for

me. She was also the first person I've met who surprised me by manifesting very spontaneously a really splendid comprehension of my situation. But yet I was really very glad when she too left again. For I don't need any of that.

" I have already told you my opinion of Princess Metternich. However, she's a queer sort. They tell me she dances charmingly and sings in quite an original way. Recently she asked me if I hadn't written any fugues ? she so loved to play them ! I looked at her in amazement, remembering her bad Vienna piano that was always out of tune, as well as her incredibly naïve questions. But—I said to myself—anything is possible here ! But I still had no opportunity to convince myself of her talents. Up to now I've had to decline her invitations and only put in an appearance when I had to approach the lady in connection with some pending order or other, and here I always preferred to address myself to her, because this always seemed to give her great pleasure. Her husband, the young Prince, is quiet and really good-natured but without any real warmth. He also composes, and asked permission to dedicate something to me.

" Frau von Pourtales, wife of the Prussian Ambassador, appears to be not without depth, and at all events has very excellent taste. I've discovered a really strong personality in the wife of the Saxon Ambassador, Frau von Seebach. She is very homely and coarse in outward appearance. I was surprised to find a certain delicate fire glowing here under the lava. She can't understand how anyone can fail to perceive the tremendous passion in my creations and considers it dangerous to take her young daughter along to ' Tannhäuser.' What strange creatures one runs across ! But they are only acquaintances—persons one must be reminded over and over again that one has met !

" The husbands of the aforementioned ladies are all notable for their good nature but very meagre talents. I've an idea that they lead on the whole a much coarser life than the ladies. On the contrary, here one comes up with the usual experience that intelligent men generally have very insignificant wives. But then I like them the best, I mean the men. The wives do not bother one and there are no obstacles to further acquaintance. But in the last analysis, this is also of very little moment.

" Ah, child ! let us drop all that ! And believe me, one just manages to drag along with great, great effort and is hardly disposed to say how it is managed. It's vain to wish for things ; toil and vexation are the only things that make one forget one's misery."

After the " Tannhäuser " fiasco Wagner naturally had nothing to gain by staying on in Paris. So he decided to give up his house there as soon as he could raise the necessary funds and go first to Vienna, where plans were being made for the première of " Tristan " as a result of negotiations that had been going on in the meantime. But he was firmly determined not to resume life with Minna again until he was sure of being able to avoid such vexatious struggles and agitations as he had had to go through in Paris and might have to face in Vienna. He must first be able to look forward to an assured future.

" These two years in Paris (he wrote Minna) weigh on my conscience like a terrific nightmare. I really meant well, but once more my good intentions led to hasty and ill-considered action ! I can only say that I admire you for the way in which you have survived this terribly and continually vexatious time. But I almost take comfort in this for your health's sake, for I tell myself that you may yet really get quite well if you lead a more tranquil, and less anxious existence."

As soon as Wagner's Paris patrons (Metternich, Pourtales and Hatzfeld) had settled his financial obligations and provided him with a considerable sum of money, he immediately settled his affairs in Paris.

" I got rid of my house by fortunately sub-letting it, thanks to a tip of 100 francs to the concierge. It was planned that Minna should continue her last year's cure at Bad Soden, after which she was to go to her old friends in Dresden. We decided to store all our furniture— well packed—with a shipping agent in Paris."

" I'm looking forward to my Germany where I have still always been happiest (Minna wrote resignedly before her departure for Soden on 19th July). We can only stay together if Richard is six months in one place—and I in another. If he comes back, I must be here, as I'm always in his way and annoy him. So this is what it has come to for an old and very sorely tried woman—and stupid people still envy me my lot ! "

Wagner stayed another three weeks with Count Pourtales at the beautiful Prussian Embassy with its famous black swans, as he was still busy with the translation of the " Flying Dutchman " for his French publisher. On leaving the Embassy he wrote an album leaf, *Ankunft bei den Schwarzen Schwaenen* as special homage to his kind hostess. At the beginning of August (1861) he finally left Paris, where he had undergone such bitter experiences for the second time in his life, and went to Soden to bid Minna good-bye. Here he also made the acquaintance of her friend Mathilde Schiffner, a Dresden dressmaker, who lived in the same house as Minna's parents. As she had often come to the assistance of the two old people, Minna out of gratitude had struck up a friendship with her, but Wagner thoroughly disliked her as he felt she was one of the worst gossips, whose pernicious influence over Minna he had been made to feel only too often. The Soden visit was therefore exceedingly unpleasant for all concerned, and after two days Wagner continued on his way. A letter from Minna to Caecilie Avenarius re-echoed vividly the discord and ill-feeling that still hovered in the atmosphere, and at the same time closed the balance sheet of the unfortunate Paris *étape*.

" First of all my sincerest thanks for your dear, kind letter, with its expressions of sympathy which brought me indescribable comfort (she wrote). Believe me, such evidences of friendship are the best medicine for my poor heart. Would to God Richard had only written me a little kindly during the past four years ; had treated me a little humanly during the time we were together. I would still be well, for heart ailments like mine are only caused by great emotional stress and through continued irritation. That has long been a well-known medical fact, and if it hadn't been for my iron constitution I should have been under the ground long ago. That much is certain.

" First of all I also have to thank you for your dear invitation to visit you in Berlin ! As welcome and tempting as this is, I still can't accept because I'm leaving for Dresden for a couple of months to put myself in the hands of my excellent physician Pusinelli. For several months now, a new complaint has been added to the painful palpitation of my heart ; that is, I suffer almost continually from severe pains in my neck. At least the doctors consider this even more serious than the palpitation alone. The difficulty in breathing is now much worse than formerly. I have to do everything very slowly and may only take short walks. . . .

" Yes, indeed ! If I only had one pleasant memory during all these last years ! God knows Richard doesn't seem to be able to wait to see me under the sod ; and yet I let him do as he likes and never ask, ' Where are you going ? ' ' Where have you been ? ' I scrupulously hand him over Frau Wesendonck's letters, without betraying the slightest emotion, much less saying a word. And in return he shouts at me in the most brutal way and grabs me so roughly by the arm that I still had black and blue marks from all his fingers when I was in Soden.

" I must confess that in spite of never having committed a fault, and I a sick old woman at that, I've behaved so nobly in the matter of his love affairs that I haven't ever said a word, no matter what he did. That horrible word jealousy was only a name to me ; yet this heartless behaviour has hurt me in a way that I can never forget. I've said nothing, nor have I written anything to Richard about it, but it takes great self-control on my part to write him in a friendly way ; affectionately—that of course is now out of the question.

" During the past four years my husband has announced to me so often that I must go away, that he was passionately in love with the Wesendonck, that they loved each other, that she couldn't stand me, was jealous of me—in short, wouldn't tolerate our remaining together, etc. And during the latter part of my stay in Paris when I said—in reply to his brutality—' How can you treat a person you once loved in such a way ? ' he replied : ' I only married you in a fit of amorousness. A person as young as I was at that time doesn't know what love is. This I only learned when I got older.' I don't know whether he was referring to the old Bordeaux affair, or to the last one with the Wesendonck.

" Such fine statements disgust me, so that I said nothing and marched off to my little room with my dog and my bird, where I stayed till he came home for dinner, and did not put in an appearance till the soup was on the table ; and then only talked of the most ordinary commonplace matters.

" I'm without a home, and that's no small matter when one has been married twenty-five years and is old and ailing. My husband can't give me a home ; but I don't feel badly about this. On the contrary, I hope that circumstances will keep him away from me for a long time yet. I'm only afraid of him, and if I decide to join him in the future it will only be because of what people say, and with the prospect that he'll be away from home a lot. But where that is to be is as much a mystery to me as to you, my dear Caecilie.

" After Richard's last fine declarations, my only wish is not to have to spend our twenty-fifth anniversary with him. It would be too bitter a day for me and I could hardly live through it. I will pass the day sadly alone. The Wesendoncks were both invited to the ' Tristan ' performance. She couldn't go to Vienna by herself. The whole affair also means nothing to her. It only amuses this cold woman to have Richard dangling after her. She certainly doesn't hide the truth from her husband, the good soul. He puts up the money, not she. But if this man knew what I had had to endure both verbally and in letters, he would have put his money to better use.

" But enough of all this heartlessness and vulgarity. I'll never trouble you again with the matter. One reverts to the subject involuntarily. But it does me good to be able to talk it over with you and Klaerchen. Keep it to yourselves—as I do—and don't love Richard any the less for it. Don't hold it against him that he didn't come to Berlin. Here everything was bustle and confusion and he had to play puss in the corner a lot, for which he was criticized.

" If I wanted to, I could go out to some social affair every day. But I can't abide them. It all means nothing to me. I only associate with people who go with me for myself alone, and not because I'm the wife of the famous Richard Wagner. I'm quite content to live modestly on his money, but not on his fame, to which I once contributed—even if only indirectly. In Dresden I shall probably stop with the Tichatscheks. She has proved herself a loyal friend to me. She also has her own troubles with her husband. But he doesn't treat her badly and brutally, and that is what I also would like. I don't ask for more, and can't ask for less. I send respectful greetings to your husband, because he is certainly the finest of all. With a kiss from your devoted Minna."

Minna accompanied Wagner to Frankfort and from there he went to a meeting of the German Association of Musicians in Weimar, as he had promised Liszt. Here among the large gathering of music-lovers from all over Europe he also met his old friend Alwine Fromann, who had never wavered in her allegiance to him. After a few days Blandine Ollivier and her husband also arrived from Paris to " become his neighbours at the Altenburg " (as Wagner said), and the days, which were lively enough to begin with, now became boisterously gay. During the entire time Blandine never left Wagner's side, and he let himself be persuaded to travel with them to Vienna via Nuremberg and Munich.

" They had decided to visit Cosima at Reichenhall where she was taking a cure (he wrote in *Mein Leben*). When we took leave of Liszt at the station we also thought of Buelow, who had distinguished himself so greatly during the past few days and had left the day before. We showered praises on him, but I remarked in a friendly bantering way : ' He didn't need to marry Cosima ! ' whereupon Liszt added with a slight bow : ' *That* was a luxury ! ' We travellers, especially Blandine and myself, now got very hilarious and this was only intensified by Ollivier's ' *Qu'est-ce qu'il dit ?* ' which followed every outburst of laughter on our part. He had to submit good-humouredly to our constant joking in German."

They were met at Reichenhall by Cosima, whose health, fortunately, had greatly improved. It was feared for a time that she might develop tuberculosis like her brother Daniel, who had recently succumbed to it.

" However, Ollivier and I were usually excluded from the general gaiety which here too immediately marked our intercourse (Wagner continued) as the two sisters usually shut themselves up in their room to secure more privacy for their talks, which could be heard a long way off owing to their incessant laughter. So French conversation with my political friend was almost my only recourse. Yet I managed to gain access to the sisters a couple of times by announcing among other things that I proposed to adopt them since their father did not bother about them any more ; which was received with more mirth than confidence. . . . After a few days I finally had to think of continuing my journey which had been so delightfully interrupted. I took leave of them in the vestibule and here caught an almost shy questioning glance from Cosima."

" I was delighted with Cosima in Reichenhall (he wrote in a letter to Hans von Buelow). If only the naughty child would only take care of herself properly ! I hear she has gone to stay with her father again. If she only doesn't give way again there to the little excesses that are so bad for her. She's a wild creature and no mistake. But she has great distinction. You must look to this to induce her to make any sacrifice, even that of little harmful habits, for it's pride that must make her even-tempered and calm. My kindest regards to her. The sisters were both so gracious, unusual, brilliant and charming that I managed to swallow Ollivier quite famously."

Wagner finally reached Vienna on 14th August (1861).[1] Here for the time being his friend Standhartner (who was on the point of leaving with his family) placed his flat at Wagner's disposal. " A pretty niece who lived with her mother and sister in the same house " was to look after him, prepare his breakfast, etc., while he would be permitted " to make use of the whole place with the greatest freedom." This charming house fairy, whom chance had brought in his way, was the lovely Seraphine Mauro, who had Italian blood in her veins and a " face (according to Wagner's friend Weissheimer) as pale as marble, framed in the blackest curls imaginable which fell to her rounded bosom." Wagner was not insensitive to so much beauty in his immediate vicinity, and his " sweet doll " (as he always called her) did not allow him to languish in vain. Unfortunately she destroyed all his letters later on. The real sufferer in this case was Wagner's friend, Peter Cornelius, who, in availing himself of the privilege of all lyrical temperaments to be unhappy in love, had long before lost his heart to pretty little Seraphine.

The artistic results of his stay in Vienna were less happy for Wagner. The prospects for the promised " Tristan " performance at the Royal Opera were anything but good, as the only suitable

[1] Exhibit 385A-D of the Burrell Collection comprises four hitherto unpublished letters to Minna dating from this period, reflecting Wagner's reaction to incidents and persons. The letters are dated 10th May, 9th August, 3rd October and 4th November. In Appendix A the letter of 9th August is dated " Vienna," which is obviously an error for Weimar, as he speaks of having to " fight tooth and nail " to avoid the torchlight procession planned " by the townsmen of the Residency " to celebrate his presence at the music festival.

tenor (Aloys Ander) was suffering from a voice complaint which prevented him studying a part which in any event was beyond his powers. Frau Meyer-Dustmann, the Isolde, was the only one who went to work with enthusiasm and great success.

"With Dustmann, the case is fortunately different (he wrote Minna). She sang the first act so well for me yesterday that I thoroughly enjoyed it. She will sing the part to perfection—she is indeed the most talented of the lot."

In her he soon had a devoted admirer and a valuable helper in his discouraging negotiations with the management, who for fear of the anti-Wagner press soon began to dilly-dally with the "Tristan" affair, using Ander's illness as an excuse. At first there was nothing to be done. As Wagner's stay in Vienna now had no further purpose he was glad to accept an invitation from the Wesendoncks to join them for a few days in Venice, especially as he had had to give up his pleasant quarters owing to Standhartner's return. Yet even this meeting with his beloved, which seemed like a dream of other days, filled his soul with bitterness and destroyed his last illusions.

"Now at last I'm quite resigned (he confessed to the woman he had lost for ever). One thing I had never given up, and thought I had won it—with difficulty : the refinding of my Asyl, the possibility of living near you. But an hour's meeting in Venice sufficed to destroy for me this last fond delusion ! I soon had to recognize that you cannot maintain the freedom which is essential to you and to which you must hold fast for your existence's sake, as long as I am near you ; only my being at a distance can give you the power to move freely as you will. Only when there is nothing to buy are you exempted from conceding a price. I can't bear to see you restricted and oppressed, domineered over and dependent—as the price of my proximity. For I can't compensate you for this sacrifice because my presence can no longer offer you anything, and the thought that the paltry little that I can be to you under such circumstances is purchased at the expense of all freedom, and practically of all human dignity, makes my presence a torture to myself. . . . The horrible last stage has been surmounted ; Venice, the return journey and the three weeks that followed—terrible !—are behind me."

The true ground for this inner break was that Wagner had found his friends (as he says in *Mein Leben*) "on very happy terms." Wesendonck had succeeded in guiding his wife with a firm hand through all the reefs of the "Tristan" episode, and now in leading her back to himself had won her anew. On 16th June 1862, after several years of estrangement, she again bore him a son! This completely changed Wagner's inward relationship to her. She now became for him *only* a friend.

" Since our last meeting in Venice (he confessed to his friend Peter Cornelius) the correspondence between me and my friend Mathilde Wesendonck was involuntarily interrupted for a considerable time. Everything is so agreed between us, and arranged on the basis of such perfect resignation, that I only write her in a happy friendly tone ; also on the other hand because intercourse with her highly upright but for me (quite apart from personal considerations) tedious husband has become so intolerable to me that I've given up all permanent personal intercourse with both of them, and now limit myself to superficial correspondence."

But even this was interrupted for long intervals.

" I'm now finally going to write the Wesendoncks again (he wrote Frau Wille). But I can only write to *him*. I love her too much. My heart overflows so when I think of her that it is impossible for me to approach her in the form that is now more than ever enjoined on me. I cannot write her how I really feel without disloyalty towards her husband whom I sincerely admire and esteem. What's to be done ? How can I speak to this woman as I now should—and must ? Impossible! Indeed I even feel I should never see her again. *Ach!* Even in Venice, this seeing her again made me thoroughly unhappy. Only when this memory had entirely faded did this woman become to me all that she had been. I feel that she will always remain beautiful for me and my love for her will never grow cold—but I must never meet her again—not under this cruel compulsion—as necessary as I recognize it to be—which must nevertheless mean the death of our love. Since I left Zürich I'm really living in exile. I can never tell you all I have sacrificed! O dearest friend, one really loves only once—whatever intoxications and flattery life may still offer us. Indeed only now do I know for a certainty that she will never cease to be my only love."

As bitter as was the disillusionment of those few days in Venice for Wagner, the world has to thank it for an immortal treasure —the " Meistersinger." It was Mathilde Wesendonck who in her effort to make him forget the " Tristan " disappointment in Vienna, spurred him to new creative work and interested him again in an early draft of the " Meistersinger," which he had hastily sketched in Marienbad in 1845, and was now in her possession. And what more fertile soil could be found for a lyrical hero like Hans Sachs than Wagner's own melancholy resignation at that time? He threw himself ardently into the work, the tension relaxed, and Tristan was healed by Hans Sachs.

Immediately on his return to Vienna, Wagner went to work on a detailed scenic plan of the opera. During this work

" A new and apparently favourable diversion set in for me through the arrival of Prince and Princess Metternich in Vienna (he wrote in the story of his life). The concern of my Paris friends about me and my situation was unmistakably real. By way of showing them some friendly attention I persuaded the opera management to allow me to invite the excellent orchestra to the theatre for a few hours one morning to play through some selections from ' Tristan ' by way of a rehearsal, as it were. The orchestra, as well as Frau Dustmann, were so kind as to comply with my wish. Princess Metternich and some of her friends were invited to this audition at which I conducted three long excerpts, which went so brilliantly that I felt sure I had made a most excellent impression—and no mistake. My aristocratic friends and also —strange to say—Fräulein Couqui, the *première danseuse*, who had attended the rehearsal on the sly, overwhelmed me with evidences of their enthusiasm."

In an anonymous newspaper notice a few days previous to this Wagner had praised the " talented Couqui " as " one of the most important coryphæi of her gracious art." Her attitude was therefore hardly so " strange " after all.

" One day the Metternichs (he went on), hearing of my desire to find undisturbed seclusion for the creation of a new work, informed me that they were in a position to offer me just such a quiet retreat in Paris. The Prince had recently furnished a very spacious Embassy, and could place at my disposal a pleasant suite overlooking a quiet garden. My Erard was still in Paris, and if I could go there the end of the year I should find everything ready for me to begin my work. I gratefully accepted this very kind invitation with undisguised delight, and my only concern now was to put my affairs so far in order as to be able to leave Vienna and move to Paris with some degree of decency."

But there was no question at this time of settling down with Minna.

" The experiences of my last stay in Paris showed me how little I can count on myself and on my best and calmest resolutions as soon as the hidden inner dissension comes into contact with the boundless agitations of a stormy and often desperately troubled material existence. Fully conscious of my best intentions of always treating you with calmness and kindness, I can still distinctly imagine our getting on excellently together in the course of time and of being able to enjoy a comfortable life, relatively speaking. But this only on the condition that my position is absolutely assured and that I am offered once and for all a definite home in some pleasant place where I have suitable employment and a really adequate income. If I achieve this, and it's what I'm working for with all my might—for this is also essential for my own well-being—I should be the most heartless of men if I didn't offer to share the longed-for sanctuary with you, my poor, sorely tried wife, after so many storms and tribulations. Then with certainly the deepest joy I would send you the summons : ' Come along, dearest. Now at last we'll enjoy a little comfort for once.' "

But this was still mere castles in the air. At the moment he had only poverty, failure, and plans to report to Minna, and he accordingly had to request her to abandon the idea of joining him for the time being and to go ahead and settle down in Dresden where after all she felt most at home. Although Minna, after her recent experiences, certainly had no desire to repeat the Paris venture, it was inevitable that this news from her husband —just on the eve of their silver wedding—should embitter her.

" On the twenty-fifth anniversary of my wedding, which I passed very sadly (solo), I received as a present from my husband, a gold bracelet and my *congé* for a whole year (she wrote Emma Herwegh on 15th December 1861)[1]. Then, he says, maybe we'll see each other once in Munich or on the Rhine. Meanwhile I'm to settle down here permanently. . . .

" If I could only wipe these twenty-five years out of my life, I might possibly also be light-hearted again. But one must do no wrong and always be thankful not to have been flayed alive. I shall remain here until next April ; only the gods know where I'm to go then ! That's what one owes to the Tristans ! "

As Vienna had definitely abandoned the idea of giving " Tristan " for the time being, Wagner left for Mainz the middle of December in order to wind up the negotiations for " Meistersinger " with his publisher Schott. He succeeded in obtaining from the latter the necessary advance so that he could finish his work in peace, but just as he was about to leave for Paris he received a letter from Princess Metternich in which she informed him that to her great regret she was obliged to cancel the invitation extended to him in Vienna, since owing to a death in her family the suite destined for him was now occupied by a

---

[1] On the day before, that is, 14th December, Minna wrote Wagner's friend Kietz in Paris in the same vein and in practically the same words. Exhibit 393, Burrell Collection.

relative of the deceased. Wagner, who at that time was absolutely forsaken and homeless, held staunchly to his Paris plans, especially as he hoped to put up temporarily at the Olliviers ; but here he met with a very cool reception. His reappearance on the Paris scene, and especially in Ollivier's own house so soon after the " Tannhäuser " fiasco, seemed to embarrass the latter, whose manner (as Wagner said) was " dry and casual."

" Blandine (he continued) seemed to have changed remarkably since the summer and had an air of melancholy seriousness. It looked to me as if she were pregnant. . . . I made up my mind, anxious as I was, not to trouble Ollivier any longer. Blandine took leave of me with a look of ineffable sadness."

Wagner was not to see her again. She died in childbirth the following summer.

Since the Metternichs could not extend Wagner the anticipated hospitality, even at the beginning of the new year, the " Meistersinger " text was born in a little hotel room on the Quai Voltaire. But the nearer he approached the end of his task the more he worried about his future home. He turned in vain to his friends. Agnes Street-Klindworth in Brussels and the Buelows in Berlin replied evasively. He even sent an appeal to Mathilde Wesendonck,[1] in spite of his resolve to renounce her. To this she replied with great delicacy, exhorting him to stand firm in his renunciation, and expressing her reaction symbolically by sending him a little bronze cast of the Lion of St. Mark's. He then thought of setting up a bachelor establishment somewhere along the Rhine with Peter Cornelius.

" *Gott!* (he wrote him). How I should also like to have the poor ' Doll '[2] there, too ! In such things I have an ineradicable, naïve morality. I should see positively nothing wrong in the girl's coming to me and being to me all that her sweet little nature fits her to be. Yet how to find the *terminus socialis* for it ! *Ach Himmel!* I'm laughably sorry about it ! "

In the end he preferred to look for a quiet spot in the neighbourhood of Mainz, where he would be under Schott's financial protection. He had his Paris furniture (which had been in storage for the past year) sent to Schott's address, and early in February (1861) he, too, left for Mainz with the finished text of

---

[1] Not included in the published Wagner-Wesendonck correspondence.
[2] Seraphine Mauro.

" Meistersinger," and took up quarters in the house of his publisher. At a party given in his honour by Schott he read his poem for the first time to a large company.

After a wearisome search in the environs of Mainz he at last found the longed-for nest for the " Meistersinger " in a fair-sized summer cottage close to the Rhine in Biebrich. As the place was not very roomy it could only accommodate a small portion of his Paris furniture, so the remainder had to be stored in a shed close by. While he was still busy getting his place in order Minna suddenly and unexpectedly appeared on the scene in order to help him get settled, as she knew how unpractical and helpless he was in such matters. In a letter to his friend Cornelius he bemoaned the malignant star that again hovered over this brief association.

" You know how much I longed for a regular home again and how I felt I should achieve this by a reunion with my wife. While I was gloomily trying to set up winter quarters here at Biebrich, my wife—moved by my predicament[1] took the sudden notion of following in your footsteps more or less, and instead of answering my letter[2] she appeared here in my rooms just as I had finished rigging things up as best I could.

" My heart rejoiced to see her, and she must easily have seen from my great emotion and delight how I felt. I scolded her for not bringing her parrot straight away and settling down for good, instead of only coming for a week to help me get settled. But we began at once to talk over the question of permanent quarters in Wiesbaden. She looked fresh and well, which convinced me that she invariably recovers when she is left to herself to follow her own inclinations as regards her associates and manner of living and doesn't have me to interfere in any way. How hard I tried, in spite of our completely divergent tastes, characters and viewpoints, to work out a permanent and endurable life together by means of all kinds of sensible conventions and concessions ! The dreadful misfortune of having no children to act as a bridge between us and the fact that owing to my love of seclusion we are thrown on our own society and necessarily get constantly on each other's nerves, became very evident to me again on the very first day ; but I was still so very well-disposed that I gladly fell again into the curious language of make-believe that one uses to a child and listened

[1] And not by selfish avarice, the motive unchivalrously imputed to her in the Autobiography.

[2] Exhibit 396A in the Burrell Collection is Wagner's letter to Minna, dated 14th February 1862, in which he " left the decision (to come, or stay) entirely in her hands " and to which she reacted immediately by setting off for Biebrich without waiting to reply.

K

with apparent interest to things that are entirely foreign, and often even repugnant, to me. Next morning fate intervened in an extraordinary way. Indeed this time I was actually amazed at so obvious a demonstration."

A Christmas parcel and letter that Mathilde Wesendonck had sent him from Vienna arrived just at this moment in Biebrich after numerous wanderings.[1]

" This letter arrived on the second (he continued), the little box on the third day of my wife's visit; and both fell immediately into the poor woman's hands. Incapable of viewing my relations with that woman in any but an odious frivolous light, she refuses to understand any of my explanations, but lets herself go in that common way that makes me perfectly wild. She attributes my irritability to my being subjected continually to this woman's exciting influence, and the whole crazy fabric is there again—in all its old-time glory ! I felt I should go out of my mind.

" This woman was exactly where she was four years ago ! The same outbursts, word for word—the same vulgar tone ! These tempests over, I pulled myself together again. I tried to regard it as a final thunderstorm—to go on hoping and not gainsay the possibility. But now the misery set in again in earnest : suspicion—mistrust—a false interpretation put on every word ! And in addition—completely alone here—alone during the long winter evenings with a creature who hasn't the faintest comprehension of my real nature, who as soon as I pick up a book, can't even follow suit—who is incapable of occupying herself.

" So there I was—bent on nothing but quiet and a peaceful mind, longing to get on with my work ; always contending (at terrible odds) with lack of means, my general situation, upset by every communication from outside, gossip and the like. And finally my wife's heart ailment growing worse again. They were ten days of hell. But these ghastly ten days were at least a good thing to the extent that they brought me a last warning. And I had to marvel that this serious warning should come in all innocence from my friend. . . .

" It is now certain that I can't possibly live with my wife any longer ! You can't know what lies in these few words. My heart bleeds, and yet I realize I must forcibly combat all soft-heartedness, for my only salvation lies in firmness and frankness. . . . My wife can take care of herself, for I shall always leave her the cloak of pretence ! To really divorce her is, and remains, impossible for me. It's too late for

[1] Minna's version of this unfortunate contretemps contained in a letter to Nathalie dated 6th March and stating that she " was so furious that she almost had a stroke," is contained in the Burrell Collection (Exhibit 361H). Allowing for the informality of intimate family intercourse, this communication does not differ greatly from the account given to Caecilie Avenarius two years later.

that and the cruelty of such a procedure revolts me. I've now decided on the following solution.

" From next autumn my wife is to settle down in Dresden, taking with her all our belongings except the few I'm keeping here ; and she will reserve a room ' for me ' there. On the plea (valid, of course) of a quiet sanctuary in which to work, I shall always keep a permanent little corner for myself like the one I now have and—perhaps—pay my wife a fortnight's visit now and then. That's the way it's to look, so as to look quite harmless. . . .

" I've been worried ever since I parted from the unhappy woman in Frankfort yesterday—always angrily fretting about herself. And it's only the definite consciousness that soft-heartedness will only prolong the agony for both of us that can finally bring me—to the point of resignation. O God ! then the tears well up in me and I say—O for a kindly woman to wrap me in her sustaining arms ! But I'm putting all that out of mind. And thus, it seems to me, all my wife's sufferings are avenged ! "

Minna also left a description of these Biebrich days from which it can be seen that the two old comrades had already drifted so far apart that any attempt to come together again could only lead to suicidal desperation.

" Next month it will be two years since I parted from Richard in Biebrich (she wrote Caecilie Avenarius, 25th January 1863). He wrote me that it was a lot of trouble getting settled. On the other hand if there were only a woman about, things would be entirely different. I set off at once to go to him to help him out as best I could. He was delighted beyond words when he saw me. He almost tore my head off, and even wept. God ! I already began to look round to see where I should live. But my unhappy illusion was very short-lived. The very first morning while we were at breakfast and my good husband was telling me his immediate plans he received a letter from Frau Wesendonck. I was then in the way. The game was up ! The intimate confidences were transformed in a twinkling into rantings and shouting so that it absolutely seemed to me as though I had done something awful, and I scarcely dared to raise my eyes from the needlework I'd sought out. *Ach!* and how indifferent I really was to this correspondence. If I had only had to suffer a little less under it. . . .

" The second day, after we got back from Darmstadt, as we were at breakfast, another letter arrived from her. I was dreadfully scared because I knew what was in store for me. It was terrible. He went at me in spite of my protestations that it was all immaterial to me—he should go ahead and read it—answer it if he wanted to ; but he should have a little pity on me as I wasn't to blame for it. It was all no use. The rage and blusterings kept up. A third letter arrived, to my astonishment, and a few days later a little parcel containing an embroidered pillow, toilet water, etc.

" O God ! I was so done up with all this senseless shouting that on the tenth day I began to pack my things, in which Richard gladly concurred. Deeply troubled, but with dry eyes, and sharp pains, I set off again and arrived with a bad cold, and again badly hurt, in my peaceful cell where I cried my heart out undisturbed ! "

Wagner's longing for the Eternal Feminine was soon to be fulfilled, and this in twofold guise : in love of a more ideal description for a beautiful and very sensitive girl whom this very volatile lover wooed with due propriety ; and in a more realistic love affair with a temperamental artist, whose reputation, how-ever, was none of the best. Wagner met the lovely girl, Mathilde Maier (whose innocent charm he sought to capture in the figure of Eva) at a party at Schott's, where his hostess had chosen her as his dinner partner on account of her cleverness.

" Her very sensible and sincere character, which was a peculiarly suitable vehicle of expression for the Mainz dialect, made her stand out very advantageously from the rest of the company without being in any way conspicuous (he wrote in *Mein Leben*). I promised to call on her in her home, and now came into contact with a town idyll to which hitherto I had scarcely paid any attention. Mathilde, the daughter of a notary who had died leaving a modest legacy, lived with her mother, two aunts and a sister in a small but well-kept house ; while her brother, who was taking a business course in Paris, was a perpetual worry to her. For it was her thoroughly practical mind that ran the affairs of the entire family, seemingly to the great satisfaction of everybody.

" They received me with remarkable warmth whenever my own affairs took me to Mainz—which was usually once a week—and I was always pressed to have some light refreshment. Moreover, as they had a very large circle of acquaintances (among them Schopenhauer's only friend, an old gentleman living in Mainz) I also frequently met Mathilde elsewhere ; for instance at the Raffs' in Wiesbaden from where she would sometimes walk home with me in company with an elderly friend, just as I also sometimes went on with her to Mainz."

They met more and more often and Mathilde did her utmost (as far as consideration for her reputation in the little town permitted) to supply the missing touch in the artist's home. At a little party in Wagner's " Beaver's Nest " in celebration of his birthday she took charge of the preparations very efficiently and played the part of hostess with dignity and much charm. Her present to him on this occasion, as on all future anniversaries, was six standard rose trees in full bloom.

The friendship between the two became more and more intimate and the society of this fresh young girl, with her alert mind, soon became indispensable to him. He even considered making a permanent tie of this affectionate attachment.

During these weeks, the correspondence with Minna became more and more atrabilious on both sides. In Dresden she had taken renewed steps with Lüttichau (Intendant of the theatre) and with the King's minister, Herr von Beust, to effect Wagner's amnesty, and Wagner was required to submit a final petition for clemency, to which Pusinelli appended a medical certificate concerning Minna, in which he certified that the separation from her husband resulting from the decree of banishment was wrecking her health.

" During the years 1843-9 (read Pusinelli's ' true and conscientious ' report) I had occasion, as family physician to the Wagners, to observe the excellent health and strong constitution of Frau Wagner up to the time of her departure from Dresden. During her following sojourn in Zürich I received from time to time indefinite rumours of her ill health ; but I could only confirm the truth of these reports in the year 1858 during her temporary visit to Dresden, where she had come to recover her health.

" I admit that the appearance of this otherwise so healthy and rugged woman shocked me deeply. I had not expected such a noticeable change in her whole outward appearance, such a poignant expression of deep inward suffering. My examination unfortunately confirmed the truth of the disorder which I suspected at the first glance. I found an organic heart affection, a highly advanced enlargement of the heart, particularly on the left side, with simultaneous thickening of the walls. The curvature of the chest in the proximity of the heart, the chest vibrating under the force of the heart-beat, the violent, hard and very irregular pulse, the constant difficulty in breathing, the tremulous, quaking voice, the anxious, almost frightened, expression of her pallid face, the constant and very evident anxiety, these and other things confirmed the diagnosis. In addition, there are stoppages in the portal vein system, œdematic swelling of the lower limbs, night sweats, etc., so that the present condition seems an almost hopeless one.

" I was therefore greatly perturbed and reluctant to see the invalid leave here again in the autumn of 1859, in response to her husband's summons, and exchange the salutary quiet of her home here for the excitements of Paris life. And the results were all that were feared. The reports that I received were not reassuring and gave every indication of great homesickness. After two miserable summers the invalid finally returned here in the autumn of 1861. The good effects of the earlier sojourn in Dresden were almost entirely eradicated and speedy action and the strictest treatment were necessary to re-establish the condition of 1858.

" Since then the evil has been checked. The enlargement of the heart has not increased and all has now been achieved that can be achieved, that is, the malady has been arrested. For there can be no hope of a definite cure. But in order that this condition may be permanent the patient must live under conditions conducive to such end and avoid all the pernicious factors that induced the malady. Among the latter, emotional excitement holds first place."

This time Minna's efforts were successful. A few days later she was formally notified of Wagner's full amnesty. She now definitely assumed that he would return to Dresden and celebrate his birthday with her. When a few days before that date she received a telegram to the effect that he would be unable to come,[1] and friendly busybodies in the meantime had whispered to her that quite other reasons were keeping him in Biebrich, her anger knew no bounds !

She became more and more aggressive in her letters, and gave increasing space to the unfortunate incidents of her Biebrich visit. Wagner's attempts to pacify her only led to silly new suspicions. It finally got to the point where the mere sight of a letter from her filled Wagner with horror, even before he had read it, and for days afterwards robbed him of any desire to work.[2] On 14th June (1862) he turned to Pusinelli in his desperation and begged him to intercede, since the situation was unbearable for both. It is not clear whether—as he writes in his autobiography— he really proposed to Pusinelli to persuade Minna to agree to a divorce or whether his friend, after discussing the matter with Wagner's sister, Frau Brockhaus, took it upon himself to propose this to Minna. At all events her reaction was an abrupt rejection.[3]

" If he wants an absolute divorce (she wrote Pusinelli in June 1862) then I say No ! He should have patience till God divorces us. Separation ? He has already separated from me, for I have knocked about the world alone for years. He can come to Dresden whenever he likes ; he will then always find a sanctuary. I've shown that I put up with everything patiently, and never say a word during his angry outbursts.

[1] This telegram (dated 20th May) is in the Burrell Collection, Exhibit 400A.

[2] The Burrell Collection contains Wagner's letter of 5th October 1865 (Exhibit 435), in which he conveys to Minna this unfortunate fact and directs her to communicate with him in future via his friend Dr. Pusinelli.

[3] There is a letter from Wagner to Minna, dated Biebrich, 27th June 1862, in the Burrell Collection (Exhibit 402), in which he explains his action in writing to Pusinelli who is represented as having gone farther in his zeal than he was authorized.

As a result we'll keep to the agreement that he should come to me in Dresden from time to time. He can do that whenever he likes. . . .

" I simply can't understand how my sister-in-law Brockhaus could second the divorce with such irresponsible readiness, for she can't have forgotten the circumstances under which I—then very happily situated—gave my hand to her brother, who had been cast off by his entire family as a person without talent, frivolous, etc. I brought Richard back to her as the composer of ' Rienzi ' and the ' Dutchman,' and they all thanked me for it. Even all fate's various blows were unable to separate me from Richard. I worked, helped him to the best of my ability, when I might have been riding comfortably in my own carriage. Poverty and misery only served to bind me even closer to the man who at that time couldn't live without me. Since then twenty-six years have gone by—twenty-six very agitated years. Almost a whole lifetime. And haven't I really deserved a better end to all this than a shameful divorce at the last ? No, I could never bear that ! I would rather die."

Wagner's sincere confession to his sister Klära shows how clearly he understood the untenable situation at that time.

" I have hitherto abstained from dragging anyone else into it (he wrote on 11th July 1862) and have tried all alone to get along with the unhappy woman who is uselessly torturing herself and me to death. But there is absolutely no end to be found to the madness. . . .

" It was solely Minna's painful malady that imposed forbearance on me. Her wretched character which pursues with envy and hatred all who are attached to me has long been incapable of this. But I now see that I also am never the person to have a beneficent effect on her heart trouble. So the continuance, or resumption, of our life together is the silliest and most preposterous thing that could happen. Therefore the only question now is the *manner* in which it is dissolved. And this all depends in the last analysis on how far Minna's good sense prevails.

" I've offered her a little home in Dresden. She is to keep a room in readiness for me. I'll try to see her there. If she acts sensibly (which I very much doubt) then I can often visit her and can also hide the break from the world without too great embarrassment for her, particularly as I have a quiet sanctuary somewhere also where I can work.

" This is the last effort of my good will. But I still doubt whether it will be successful. The idea of a divorce didn't originate with me, as sympathetic as it is to me, and as excusable as it must also be for me to indulge the wish to spend my remaining years in the company of a sympathetic person, with its fruitful effect on my work. But I'm not seeking happiness—only liberation from a burden that is making me miserable. We missed the right moment for this long ago. My good nature, as well as my sense of fair play, have induced me to let an incurable evil grow until it has become intolerable. Now from the human point of view I can offer nothing else as ground for divorce than the mutual advantage deriving from a complete separation."

After Minna's sharp rejection the question of a divorce (perhaps prompted by Wagner's interest in Mathilde Maier) remained open, as Wagner also met with opposition on the part of " Schöne Tilde " herself. Her provincial background and consideration for her mother and aunts made her evade a divorce in view of Wagner's " uncertain situation."

In addition Mathilde suffered from a hereditary disease of the ear, which grew worse just at this time, and the feeling that with such an infirmity she was not fitted to be the life companion of a genius whose kingdom was the world of music made her finally decide to give him up.

Wagner found comfort and oblivion for his unhappy affair with Mathilde Maier in his liaison with Frederike Meyer which, far divorced from the sphere of the ideal, was definitely dedicated to an enjoyment of life, even though here, too, he was not spared bitter experiences. She was a sister of Frau Dustmann (Luise Meyer), his Vienna Isolde, and was herself an actress at the Frankfort theatre. During a brief stay in that city he attended a theatrical performance where he was impressed by " her fine and sensitive acting," and wrote her at once to express his admiration. Soon after this he made her personal acquaintance when he went to Frankfort expressly to see her in a Calderon tragedy.

" She told me (he wrote) that she often visited some friends in Mainz and I thereupon suggested that she should also include Biebrich on one of these occasions. She promised me that she would do so sometime."

He did not have to wait long for the fulfilment of this promise. But as bad luck would have it Frederike fell seriously ill during her visit to Biebrich, and was unable to return home. To Wagner's no little surprise, Herr von Guaita, director of the Frankfort Theatre, turned up in Biebrich next day, and his nervous excitement over the invalid made the relationship between the two fairly clear. Frederike then returned to Frankfort under her lover's tender care. Soon after this incident Wagner learned that she was generally assumed to be Guaita's mistress, as he had furnished a beautiful house for her there ; but this rival attachment was by no means calculated to dampen his ardour for Frederike. On the contrary, he went to see her on her recovery, and persuaded her to take an extended holiday for the sake of her health and stay near him on the Rhine. In the " Beaver's Nest " life now began to be very lively and gay during the summer months. The first visitors to arrive were Hans and Cosima von Buelow, who stayed two months.

" Of all the expected guests, Buelow came first by himself (he wrote in June 1862 to Mathilde Maier, who had gone to Cannstadt on a visit). Sweetheart, that man is pure gold ; a rarely loyal heart, and from his early youth on devoted to me with such tenderness and sincerity as to make his wife actually jealous of me."

Buelow was rather worn out by his gruelling work in Berlin, and had frequent fits of despondency, particularly since in addition to the perpetual attacks to which he was subjected in Berlin as a single-handed, courageous champion of the " music of the future," he also had worries of his own on account of his far from happy marriage with Cosima. No ardent passionate attachment had brought these two together ; as Cornelius wrote :

" Buelow's marriage was a friend's sacrifice to his master Liszt so as to give the illegitimate child a brilliant, honourable name and thus ensure the father deep satisfaction and relief. That was his aim ; it was an act of gratitude."

Cosima on the other hand was a cool, highly intellectual nature who was drawn to Hans by a certain feeling of sympathy—pity in fact for the friend who, forgetting himself, fought for the works of Liszt and Wagner. It is significant that the first real intimate approach between them took place on the evening of a Berlin concert when the " Tannhäuser " Overture was hissed. Coming home very late in a state of profound despair, Buelow found Cosima sitting up alone to comfort him. She sensed the great artist in him and thought herself able, as his mentor and his muse, to raise him above the battles and storms to great creative effort of his own. It was less as a lover than as an ambitious comrade and fellow champion that she linked her life to his. " My wife is such a perfect friend to me that nothing more ideal could be imagined," he remarked on their wedding day.

At first their married life was one long harmony. Skilfully and ever more and more deliberately Cosima urged her husband to turn his thoughts to creative work of his own. She constantly drew up new artistic projects to spur him on to creative work, and even surprised him with an opera libretto that she had written for him. But Buelow could never make up his mind in this direction and could not summon the necessary self-confidence to undertake the work. The great creations of Liszt and Wagner, which were the lodestars of his youth and of which he was still the fanatic champion, shackled his own pinions.

" I'm a dead Hamlet (he once said of himself) who after all is not up to his task and who is suffocated by the flood of bagatelles over which he is forced to slave his life out."

When Cosima came to fear that she might have been mistaken in this very vital point in her husband, that her ambition to see the man at her side in the foremost ranks of the creative artists was going to prove a vain one, she was overcome with bitter disappointment. During their stay at Biebrich her fear became a cruel certainty. Wagner's proximity, the enchanted world of " Tristan " and " Meistersinger " that opened up before Buelow as he lived through their creation, brought him the tragic realization of his own inadequacy. He now definitely buried all hope of achievement on this path and brought to a conclusion all individual effort as a composer.

" With Wagner as neighbour, everything else shrinks up so miserably and becomes so childish, empty, and futile (he wrote). All my own stuff strikes me as so wretched, so shoddy, that I can't even look at it. . . . I wish it were bedtime and everything were over. I've lost all self-assurance, and with it all joy in life. What can one do with an impotent piety ? "

This artistic resignation on the part of her husband robbed Cosima's marriage of its most important meaning. The inner breach in their relationship really dates from this time, especially as Wagner's genius (the " Meistersinger " sent her into veritable ecstasies !) represented for her the highest perfection of all those qualities and abilities that she had vainly hoped to find in her husband.

" Cosima seemed to have lost—and in the pleasantest sense—that shyness that I had noticed on my visit to Reichenhall the year before. One day after I had sung Wotan's ' Farewell ' in my fashion to my friends I noticed the same expression on her face that she had shown me, to my astonishment, when we parted at Zürich, only now the ecstatic element in it had been resolved into a serene transfiguration.

Here all was silence and mystery ; but the feeling that she belonged to me took hold of me with such certainty that, already strangely excited, I went so far as to indulge in the most extravagant boisterousness. When I accompanied Cosima across an open square to the hotel in Frankfort, the notion struck me to ask her to get into an empty wheel-barrow that was standing nearby so that I could trundle her to the hotel. She agreed instantly, while I (through sheer astonishment) lost the courage to put my crazy project into action. Buelow, following behind, had witnessed the incident. Cosima, without the slightest embarrassment, explained the matter to him and I could not say, unfortunately, that his mood was on a level with our own, as he cautioned his wife to mind what she was about."[1]

The singer Schnorr von Carolsfeld and his wife Malwine arrived soon after the Buelows. Wagner had heard them both in a " Lohengrin " performance at Karlsruhe,[2] and admiring them greatly, intended to engage them for a " Tristan " performance later on. Unforgettable hours of music now alternated with gay parties and jolly excursions on the Rhine, when they engaged in all sorts of merry pranks. Frederike Meyer was always in the party, and the free and easy manners of the " merry theatre crowd " with their boisterous gaiety aroused no little scandal among the local Philistines. One day the painter, Caesar Willich, arrived in Biebrich with a commission from Mathilde Wesendonck to paint Wagner's portrait.

" In his delight over the recent happy confinement of his wife, Wesendonck had taken the notion of giving her a very expressive gift in the form of my portrait " (wrote Wagner in *Mein Leben*—a passage that was deleted later on).

But to sit patiently for his portrait was torture to this volatile, restless man, and it was only through Cosima's helpful interven-tion that the painting was completed. She forced Wagner to sit still by reading aloud to him for hours. There is a certain irony to this picture, for here we find Cosima voluntarily sacrificing herself for a whim of Mathilde Wesendonck's ! Though Wagner considered the " sharp profile " " a horrible picture " he had Willich make a copy for him which he gave to Minna as a birthday present when she was fitting up her new flat in Dresden. And

---

[1] The wheelbarrow episode was deleted from *Mein Leben*.
[2] See Wagner's *Recollections of Ludwig Schnorr von Carolsfeld*. The Burrell Collection contains an interesting telegram from Wagner to Schnorr von Carolsfeld (Exhibit 408A), dated 25th May 1862, ordering a seat " incognito " for this performance.

later on he asked her to lend the oil portrait—" still the best one of him "—to Weber, his Leipzig publisher, who wanted to make a copperplate engraving of it as frontispiece for the "Nibelungen" poem. So he could not have found the portrait so " horrible " as his account in *Mein Leben* would lead one to believe.

Under these conditions work on the " Meistersinger " made slow progress, and when Schott's bulldog Leo bit Wagner on the thumb of his right hand, which made writing impossible for some weeks, Schott lost his patience and refused to hand out any more advances till the long overdue manuscript had been delivered. All Wagner's efforts to move him failed, one reason being that Frau Betty Schott, who heretofore (as a genuinely enthusiastic friend) had always put in a word for Wagner with her often uncomprehending husband, was now jealous and indignant over Wagner's liaison with Frederike Meyer, and therefore threw all the weight of her influence against him. When news reached him from Vienna that the rehearsals for " Tristan " were about to be resumed and that (Ander having recovered) there were now no obstacles to the performance, he decided to suspend work on the " Meistersinger " and accept the invitation to Vienna.

Before proceeding there, however, he betook himself to Leipzig, his birthplace, in accordance with a promise given to his Biebrich friend, Wendelin Weissheimer, to conduct the first performance of excerpts from his " Meistersinger " at the latter's concert, which the Buelows also attended.[1] From there he went to Dresden for a few days in order (as he modestly expresses it in his autobiography) " to honour Minna with one of the visits deemed necessary to support her in her difficult situation," and also to call on, and express his appreciation to, the leading officials, through whom Minna had at last secured his amnesty in Saxony.

" Minna accompanied me from the station to the flat which she had rented and furnished in the Walpurgisstrasse (he wrote in *Mein Leben*). At the entrance I found a small doormat on which she had embroidered ' Salve.' I recognized our Paris drawing-room again in the red silk curtains and furniture ; a handsome bedroom for me with—on the other side—a most comfortable study, these together with the drawing-

[1] An original programme of this concert (1st November 1862) is in the Burrell Collection, Exhibit 409.

room were to be at my entire disposal while she had fixed up for herself one little room with alcoves that looked on to the courtyard.

" Dreading the embarrassment of being alone with me, she had invited my sister Klära in Chemnitz to visit her and was now sharing her little room with her. Klära showed herself extraordinarily clever and sympathetic. She was undoubtedly sorry for Minna and anxious to help her over this difficult time, but all the while with the intention of strengthening her in the conviction that our continued separation was necessary. . . . Moreover, I succeeded in avoiding all discussions with her, this being all the easier since we spent most of the time in the society of others. . . . We also had a party in Minna's drawing-room where I again read the ' Meistersinger ' to those who had not yet heard it.

" After I had again supplied her with money to last some time, the fourth day she brought me back to the station where she took a very anguished farewell of me, filled with the most anxious forebodings that she would never see me again."

And she was not deceived in this, for the paths of the two comrades, once so closely united but now for so long a time held together solely by purely outward ties, had here converged for the last time.

On returning to Biebrich, Wagner settled his most pressing debts with the aid of a large sum that had been placed at his disposition by the Grand Duke of Weimar through Cosima's appeal to Liszt. On 15th November 1862 he then set out for Vienna accompanied by Frederike Meyer, who had thrown up her engagement in Frankfort on his account. In Vienna she also spent all her time with him.

" We were at Wagner's (wrote Peter Cornelius). He gave a musical soirée for his Fräulein Frederike Meyer. Her maid stayed in the room as chaperone. This business with Frederike is not so bad as they make it out in Mainz. She is quite a nice girl, so far as one can judge. She is intelligent, without putting on any airs. She isn't very good-looking, but she has a lively expression. Wagner behaves very nicely and decently in her presence. If he absolutely must have such a liaison then this one seems to suit him very well."

An attempt on Frederike's part to secure an engagement at the Burg Theatre in Vienna fell through as her guest performance was not as successful as it should have been. But here, too, her sister Frau Dustmann was not altogether blameless. The latter felt herself compromised by her sister's arrival in Vienna as the latter had been cast off by her family on account of her conduct. So

Frau Dustmann did everything in her power to prevent the engagement. The full force of her wrath, however, was directed against Wagner, whom she blamed for this painful situation and who (she claimed) " exploited her sister in a twofold manner," meaning no doubt that he not only had a liaison with her but took money from her as well.[1] Her interest in " Tristan " visibly cooled, and behind the scenes she went squarely over to the enemy's camp. Wagner tried to exorcise the evil by removing Frederike from Vienna. He persuaded her to go to Italy for the sake of her health, but it was then already too late, and the real reason for the ultimate fiasco of the Vienna " Tristan " plans, which was caused not by Ander but by Frau Dustmann, must be sought in Wagner's quarrel with his Isolde.

Since the anticipated receipts from the " Tristan " performances now proved elusive, he saw himself obliged to make up the loss to a certain extent by giving concerts. Three big concerts in Vienna opened the series, but they too ended in a deficit. A donation of a thousand *gulden* from the Empress Elizabeth, made at the instigation of Frau Kalergis, and large sums collected by this devoted friend at the instance of Cosima on Wagner's behalf, covered the losses. A concert in Prague followed. Here he met his old friend Marie Löw again, who by that time had given up her singing and was now playing the harp in the orchestra. " We were often at Wagner's (she wrote) ; he is very kind to us and would have liked to have adopted Lilli as his daughter."

" I only remember that Wagner hugged me impetuously (wrote Lilli Lehmann of her first meeting with the Master, whom she later admired so greatly) and kissed me till I was thoroughly frightened and declared tearfully on our return that I would never go there any more. Mamma quieted me and finally I did go again. He insisted that I sing something for him, and the result was that he wanted to adopt me because I was to sing all his works for him ! But Mamma said— making light of his ardour—'Never mind, Richard, perhaps she'll sing all your works later on. Now Lilli is too young ; and you, too, are far too young a father.'

" It is not astonishing that Wagner made a very strange impression on me at that time. A yellow damask dressing-gown, a red or pink tie, a wide, sleeveless cape of black velvet, lined with rose-coloured satin (he even wore this costume to the rehearsals !) ; one did not wear such things in Prague ! I stared in open-mouthed astonishment ! But the

[1] See Istel's *Wagner im Lichte eines zeitgenössischen Briefwechsels.*

impression he made on me then as a man never changed. His eyes, his voice, struck me at that time and I never forgot them from that moment. What he then gave me with his music, his words, made a deeply moving and ineradicable impression on me. All that I heard remained with me always, since everything had engraved itself so deeply on my youthful memory and consciousness."

The Prague concert was followed by an extensive Russian tour which took him to Petersburg and Moscow. The by no means insignificant sums gained on this excursion (close to 7,000 *thalers* clear profit) were to provide a new home for him and support him while he was working on the " Meistersinger," since he had had to give up his place in Biebrich when he paid a flying visit there on his way to Russia, the owner wanting it for himself. His bold original plan of building a house of his own on the Rhine also had to be abandoned owing to the uncertain state of his finances. The difficulty of deciding where he was to go was solved by chance.

Carl Taussig reported from Vienna that he had found the very thing for him in a pleasant little house with a large shady garden in the suburb of Penzing. As caretakers there Wagner found Franz Mrazek (" a very obliging individual ") and his wife Anna (" a very clever and ingratiating person ") and engaged the two faithful souls at once. A maid, Prucha, completed the household. He next proceeded to furnish the Penzing house with all the exaggerated luxury and loud colour schemes which provided the indispensable stimulus for his work. Two upholsterers and the dressmaker, Bertha Goldwag (who later became famous through the publication of Wagner's letters to her, which were filled with sketches and the most detailed descriptions)[1] worked tirelessly to carry out his wishes. It was no simple matter, because this reveller in silk and velvet was continually changing his mind as new colour combinations occurred to him. Very revealing is this extract from a little-known letter to one of the two decorators:

" Please give my man all of the red plush (he wrote Herr Schweikhart). Only keep out enough for the mirror and the big upholstered easy chair for the bedroom. Don't cut any more carpets either. I've decided on a different one for the spare room. I now expect the following jobs from you :

[1] The majority of this correspondence is now in the Congressional Library, Washington.

(1) The two brown armchairs for the music room.
(2) The corner behind the sofa.
(3) The two armchairs for the green corner room that are to be re-covered (violet silk).
(4) The high armchair in violet velvet.
(5) The large, red velvet easy chair for the bedroom.
(6) The large mirror.
(7) The violet velvet covers and the mahogany chest of drawers and the pier cupboard.
(8) All the curtains for the green room, as well as hanging the white ones already on hand.
(9) Blue woollen blinds for the writing-room.
(10) Lilac ditto for the green room.
(11) Blue silk blind for the bedroom.
(12) White quilted cover behind the bed, as well as the violet *passementerie* which is still wanting for the bed.

" Besides these items you were also to put up curtains in the dining-room for me as well as small white window curtains. . . . I think that at this rate you will have more to do than you have time for. But as I must finally get through with the job, I hope you will consider it fair if I give the work in the red study and the spare room to someone else who can be working at the same time. This can't be changed now as I have already made my arrangements. . . .

" I must ask you to return to the shop the second divan bed for the spare room. I've decided on a different piece of furniture. The silk material with bunches of flowers (white and blue) for a chair and hassock for the study, I don't intend to use now for this purpose, so I must ask you to return them also to my servant."

The dressmaker, on the other hand, was entrusted with the interior decoration of the Holy of Holies, the study. She described it as follows :

" The walls were covered with silk with festoons all round. From the ceiling hung a wonderful lamp with a subdued light. The whole floor was covered with heavy and unusually soft carpets into which your feet literally sank. The furniture consisted of a small sofa, some armchairs and a small table. All these seats were covered with costly rugs and cushions which he used chiefly to rest his elbows on. I made them all ! "

His personal wardrobe was also entrusted to Bertha. Coloured satin trousers with jackets and slippers to match, all lined with padding and fur, were provided by her diligent fingers, including twenty-four dressing-gowns of different colours.

But the important leading lady was missing from this fairyland conjured up out of nothing—the queen in other words. Minna, of course, was no longer considered. In a letter to Nathalie of 20th June 1863[1] he wrote that he now clearly realized that he could no longer live with Minna but she " would always remain his wife." He " would never consider divorcing her," but would stay by himself and no one would take her place. " My lot is loneliness (he wrote), my life—work ! "

" You cannot realize (he wrote Buelow two days later) how this question of my wife still torments me ! She writes me very seldom, but when she does it always brings down trouble galore. The slightest contact tells me how criminally foolish it is not to break off completely instead of always leaving a loophole where a tormenting hope can come in or out for the poor soul. Things have come to such a pass ! And now I'm tortured and worried again by a thousand fancies. . . . I realize that all this can only be changed (since they are only processes within myself) by bringing suitable counter-pressure to bear. But once again, where am I to find it without committing theft ? Nothing in the world can induce me to expose my poor wife to the horrors of a middle-class divorce. And so the distress goes on ! and my life is perfectly miserable, believe me ! "

" How much I needed a certain feminine care and management of my household just at this time was borne in on me when I expressed to Mathilde Maier in Mainz the ingenious wish that she come and supply the deficiency in a becoming manner (he wrote in *Mein Leben*). I had certainly thought that my good friend was sensible enough to interpret my meaning without feeling ashamed in any way. And I really do not believe I was mistaken ; only I had failed to take into account her mother and her Philistine surroundings. On the whole, my invitation seemed to have caused her the very greatest agitation."

He had made the following proposal to Mathilde, " at first purely theoretically, like a moral problem."

" I need a home, not in the local sense but the personal. I cannot marry as long as my wife is alive. To divorce her now in the present condition of her health (an enlargement of the heart in the most acute stage) when the slightest shock might kill her—I cannot deal her this possible death-blow !

" On the other hand, she will support anything as long as the legal semblance is there. You'll see ! These conditions, this condition of affairs, will be the death of me ! I need a woman who can decide in spite of everything and everybody to be to me what under such miserable circumstances a woman can, and must be, to me if (I say to myself) I am to continue to get along in life. Perhaps self-presumption

---

[1] Now a part of the Burrell Collection, Exhibit 419.

now blinds me when I venture to assume that a woman who would decide to dedicate herself to me under such precarious circumstances would be willing to withdraw from all purely human relationships that have no rational application in the existence and activities of a man like myself.

" It shouldn't even be necessary to set her mind at rest by the fact that in other countries and in other social circles the situation in which she would be placing herself would not be at all shocking. But she must understand that she stands far above all ordinary customs and conceptions. I want a dear woman at my side, even if she's nothing more than a child !

" Then—I think to myself—she who loves you enough for that must be happy and contented. . . . Let's assume that I rent a sitting-room and bedroom somewhere in the centre of town—good, decent ; and furnish it modestly. Here I shall live. I shall be found there in the afternoon during fixed reception hours. Once for all, no one is to be admitted during the forenoon, and only on very rare occasions in the evening. But—where am I to work then ? Where am I really at home ? For that I also have an answer.

" There's a pleasant flat in an attractive open suburb. But *I* won't live there ; instead a dear child (or woman, just as you care to call her). My Biebrich furniture will also be there, and the Érard grand piano. This loyal soul will look after everything for me carefully. And there in the morning I shall wake up refreshed. The child comes to my bed, brings me my breakfast, and then I go to work, where no one can disturb me but the friend who looks in to see if everything is in order. Then she also prepares a simple lunch for me. Next I must go to town, give interviews, pay calls, and if all goes off well, then in the evening, in good time, I shall be back home again where I belong.

" There's no question of the feasibility of this plan in a big city— it goes without saying. But who is she, who lives out there ? Richard Wagner's last Asyl—his angel—his wife, if the unhappy creature whom he married in his blind youth should some day die before him. See ! these are the New Year's Eve and New Year's Day thoughts of a—distracted person ! God knows what you'll think of it ! Nevertheless I shouldn't hide the fact from you that I'm hatching such things in my mind. How will you take it ? "

Mathilde, out of regard for her family, naturally never seriously considered this very audacious plan of Wagner's. He, however, did not want to send for Frederike Meyer after the unpleasant consequences of her first stay in Vienna.

" The unfortunate Frederike would like so much to come to me (he wrote Buelow), but think into what an abyss of difficulties and worries this would plunge me afresh ! "

He accordingly postponed for the time being the fulfilment of her oft-expressed wish to " come to him again for a short time," after which, she assured him, " she would leave him in peace for all time." He suggested that they meet in Karlsruhe, where he was giving a concert in the near future, but this time she let him down, being unwilling to wait so long. He subsequently learned that in the meantime she had become reconciled to her former lover, Herr von Guaita, and had penitently returned to him.

Wagner therefore had to look round for another of her sex who would not only manage his house for him but render his hours of relaxation agreeable. However, the first person he selected for this rôle—Lisbeth, the daughter of a pork butcher in the Josefstadt—proved to have little talent for the task.

" A young girl of seventeen, of irreproachable family (he wrote Frau Wesendonck) was recently recommended to me as being docile, willing, and thoroughly unspoilt. I took her into the house on the understanding that she should prepare my tea, keep my things in order, and lend me her society at table and in the evening. Heavens, what it cost me to get the poor child out of the house again without visibly hurting her feelings ! She was frightfully bored, was homesick for town, but made every possible effort to hide the fact so that I could only ensure relative happiness for myself again by getting rid of her. But it took a journey to accomplish it ! Recently the elder sister of the girl I dismissed came to see me. She is more experienced, sedate, seems gentle, and is not unpleasing. I'm now thinking of trying it out again with her."

That this young woman understood better what was required of her and quite fulfilled Wagner's wishes is shown by a love letter he wrote her after a long absence from Penzing on concert tours.

" Dearest little Marie : I shall be back home again next Wednesday. I shall arrive at the North Station in Vienna at seven-thirty in the evening. Franz should be there punctually with the carriage. He should also see to looking after my trunk. And now, my sweetheart, have the house in shipshape order for me so that I can rest in comfort, as I long to do. Everything must be thoroughly clean and well heated. See that my pretty study is in apple-pie order ; when the stove is once going, open the door wide so as to heat the study. Perfume it nicely, too. *Buy the best perfumes so that it will really be fragrant. Ach Gott!* how I look forward to resting there again with you.

" (The little pink drawers are also ready, I hope ???) Yes, yes, look very pretty and charming. I deserve to have a really good time again. On Christmas Eve I'll light the tree. There'll be presents for everybody, including you, my treasure. You needn't tell everybody of my arrival. Only have Franz order the barber and hairdresser for Thursday morning at half-past eight. Till Wednesday then—half-past seven in Vienna, and shortly after at Penzing. I leave it entirely up to you whether you meet me at the station. Perhaps it's even nicer if you greet me first at home in the warm rooms. I shall probably only require the coupé. So remember me to Franz and Anna. They're to make everything very nice. Many kisses to my sweetheart. *Auf Wiedersehn.*"

But the Penzing idyll did not remain undisturbed for long.[1] The profits of the Russian tour had, of course, been far from sufficient to cover the extravagant *mise en scène* of the new home ; and money now had to be found somewhere to keep it going. After Wagner (who was a genius in exploiting new sources of revenue) had exhausted every resource, there was no other alternative but a concert tour. This took up the entire month of November 1863, two big concerts having been given at Pest in the previous July. Here, as he informed Mathilde Wesendonck (not altogether without ulterior motive), a lovely, fleeting apparition had crossed his path.

" A very lovely young singer with a thrilling naïve voice. A Hungarian speaking German with charming correctness who probably in all her life had never known much about music. I was really touched to find something so pure and unspoilt for my music and the dear child seemed so moved by me, and my music, that she really felt what she was singing for the first time in her life. The outbreak of this emotion was indescribably charming and moving, and to many it must have seemed as though the girl had fallen madly in love with me. Here's another one for me to write to ! "[2]

The new tour took him to Karlsruhe via Prague. All his friends and acquaintances from the neighbouring towns (Mainz, Biebrich, Frankfort, etc.) had foregathered there for the concert, among them Mathilde Maier and Betty Schott. The concert took place in the presence of the Court, and by order of the Grand Duke was to be repeated a week later in honour of the visit of Queen Augusta of Prussia.

[1] The Burrell Collection contains two letters written to Minna from Penzing, one (Exhibit 417D) dated 4th July 1863 in which he endeavours to impress upon her that any further correspondence between them is useless and undesirable ; and another (Exhibit 422A) dated 15th February 1864, written after he had learned of the death of her sister Charlotte. " Fate had linked her to one of the strangest of men," he confessed.

[2] She sang some of the Elsa arias at the concert.

" It was especially boring to have to spend all this time alone in my Karlsruhe hotel (he wrote in *Mein Leben*), but then Marie Kalergis— now recently become Mme. Moukanoff—who had also been present at the concert, to my great joy, invited me to Baden Baden where she is now living. My friend was already at the station to meet me and offered to go into town with me, but I felt obliged to decline as I did not feel properly dressed for this, in my robber's hat. However, assuring me that ' we all wear such robber's hats here ' she took my arm and we arrived at the villa of Pauline Viardot where we were to dine, as my friend was not yet sufficiently settled in her own house."

Wagner utilized the rest of the week to make a flying trip to Zürich in order to see the Wesendoncks, and, if possible, raise a little ready money.

" The idea of assisting me did not seem even to dawn on these friends of mine, though I frankly discussed my situation with them."

They had finally realized the uselessness of any further help, which after all would only be a drop in the bucket. So they felt obliged to leave the " joyless, helpless man " to his fate. For even Otto Wesendonck's ample means could not stand such a strain indefinitely.

From Karlsruhe Wagner's route lay through Mainz and Berlin to Loewenberg, in which town the Prince of Hohenzollern (who was much interested in the " music of the future ") had invited him to give a concert. In Berlin he naturally stayed with the Buelows, and this meeting between the friends proved fateful for all three of them.

" As Buelow had to make some preparations for his concert (wrote Wagner) I again went for a drive on the promenade with Cosima in a nice carriage. This time there was no jesting. We gazed mutely into each other's eyes and an intense longing for the fullest avowal of the truth forced us to a confession—that required no words—of the incommensurable misfortune that weighed upon us. To the accompaniment of tears and sobs we sealed a vow to belong to each other alone. It lifted a weight from our hearts. After a night at the Buelows I continued my journey, and our farewell reminded me so vividly of that first wonderfully moving parting from Cosima in Zürich that the intervening years vanished like a confused dream separating two of life's most momentous days. If what then was so ominously incomprehensible had compelled silence, it was now no less impossible to express in words what was tacitly acknowledged."

In Loewenberg he also met a friend of his Zürich days, Henriette von Bissing, a recently widowed sister of Frau Wille.

" Owning an estate near Loewenberg, she too had been invited by the Prince, and now proved to be the same enthusiastic admirer as of old. Very intelligent and witty, she at once became my chosen companion . . . and she also promised me to come to the Breslau concert. Here she put up at the same hotel. My sickly appearance also seemed to inspire her with great sympathy for me and my situation. I told her quite frankly of the latter, and described to her the interruption of that even course of life which is so absolutely necessary to me and my work, which dated from my departure from Zürich in 1858, as well as of my repeated but hitherto vain struggles to bring permanent order into my financial affairs.

" My friend did not hesitate to blame what she called Frau Wesendonck's childish and impulsive behaviour towards my wife, which she herself now felt called upon to expiate. She approved of my settling down in Penzing and only wished that no outside enterprise might prejudice its beneficial effect on me. She absolutely would not hear of my plan of touring Russia perforce during the coming winter, for the sake of money, but undertook to provide me out of her own very substantial income with the not inconsiderable sum needed to make me independent for a long time."

With this comfortable assurance he returned to Penzing after having previously announced his arrival to Marie in the letter quoted above.

The following spring (28th March 1864) Minna wrote to Wagner's friend Kietz that she hadn't seen her husband for almost two and a half years ; that he was living in luxury and that he had become heartless and mean towards " his stupid, faithful, old comrade."[1] But his situation at that time was far from " luxurious." Since the receipts of the concert tour did not come up to his expectations, he was soon forced to negotiate some loans at a " terrific sacrifice." And then the unexpected happened —a contretemps that could hardly have been foreseen. Frau von Bissing, who was probably more interested in Wagner the man than in coming to his financial assistance, cancelled her offer " out of jealousy " (as he wrote Cornelius) when she heard, through a third person, that there was hardly any hope of achieving her desires.

" For this, at the time, wholly inexplicable action, which was alone attributable to the weakness of her irresolute character, I received a very surprising explanation through her sister a short time later. Frau Wille, greatly embarrassed at my question, admitted to me in the

[1] Now in the Burrell Collection, Exhibit 423.

greatest excitement that her sister had said : 'and even if I save Wagner, he will still only love Frau Wesendonck.' "[1]

The Russian expedition also fell through. How then was he to satisfy the growing impatience and anger of his creditors and pay the interest on his loan, which amounted to nearly 30,000 crowns ? He was in danger of falling a victim to usurers, and as his personal liberty seemed to be menaced, he took the urgent advice of his friends and fled secretly from his house, though not without first having transferred all the furniture to Marie (who remained behind) by written deed of gift. A few days before this he had made inquiries through Frau Wille to ascertain if the Wesendoncks would put him up for a few weeks. But this time his friends refused him point blank, reports from Vienna regarding his mode of life there having convinced them that he himself was largely responsible for his difficulties. Moreover, Otto Wesendonck was not inclined to jeopardize his newly won domestic peace a second time after the unspeakable sorrow and renunciations that he had been through. Wagner could not (as he characteristically stated in *Mein Leben*) resist " sending him a reply to point out his great meanness." Making up his mind very quickly he next announced his arrival at Mariafelde to Wille.

" I had a striking spiritual experience in connection with my recent flight from Penzing (he wrote Cornelius). On comparing my feeling on this occasion with the cold and bitterly indifferent mood in which I gave up and left my homes in Dresden, in Zürich and in Paris, I discovered that this time everything happened in a gentler, more friendly and melancholy way. I therefore realized that great as were the misery and anxiety I had gone through in this Penzing house, I had carried away only kindly, mild, and gentle impressions of every place, person, or animal there ; whereas formerly I was invariably so embittered with everything—owing to the tortures of my marital difficulties—that I was always glad to get away."

On arrival at Mariafelde he found that the master of the house had just left for Constantinople, and would only return in five weeks, but Frau Wille gave him a warm welcome.

" She is predestined to be the agent of my destiny (he wrote Cornelius). She is loyal and true as gold, the staunchest of friends. She understands me absolutely and sees that all I need is peace and tranquillity, and not any excitement. From every point of view I have found in her a truly estimable mediator. . . . This woman is beyond

[1] This passage was deleted from *Mein Leben*.

all praise, quite incomparable, positively unique. Everything that can be done to provide me with a sanctuary at once pleasant and suitable for work, she has carried out to perfection. She is even trying to raise at least enough money so that I can still hope to pay something shortly to my local creditors and thus wipe out to some extent the painful impressions made by my departure from Penzing."

" Frau Wille (he wrote Mathilde Maier in Mainz) who though very homely has a unique mind and the warmest of hearts, is one of Frau Wesendonck's most intimate friends. The present plan is for them to allocate a completely independent wing of their spacious house for my exclusive use. But it devolves on Frau Wesendonck to furnish the necessary rooms comfortably for me ; engage a special maid, and defray the costs of my very small household so that first of all I shall have no other contact with the Wille family than that of a neighbour. And, secondly, that I have absolutely no expenses for housekeeping.

" There is no obstacle in the way of arranging this set-up exactly as I wish. The immediate object is to enable me to go on with the ' Meistersinger' again and complete it, if possible, by the autumn. This recent necessity to sneak away like a thief from my servants, my dog, my little home, has broken me, I believe. God knows, if I now only wanted to vegetate, the little room in the Karlstrasse[1] would be a perfect heaven. I ask for nothing more.

" But the main thing is to complete this unhappy work. I wanted to finish it at once without any further interruptions. I fear now that it is all up with it. Life weighs too heavily upon me. Do you imagine that things are easy for me here ? Believe me, the Zürich neighbours, in particular, were rather an obstacle to my flight here. Every contact with them is unspeakably painful, and now I'm faced again with a troublesome task just when I need nothing so much as tranquillity— my time absolutely for myself. Here in the environs of Zürich the important consideration is to avoid giving a false impression—as though we were again estranged. Otherwise I would gladly forgo all contact with the house. My future ! Much could be said on that subject, especially as I must lay down a law for myself to look on any kind of hope as sinful.

" I'm advised by everybody to get a divorce and marry a rich woman. That sounds very sensible, particularly when it's a question of a real *mariage de raison*, except that it strikes me more or less as though you had suddenly got the happy idea of hurrying up and marrying a rich man just to help me out. . . . Yes, such things are easy to say ; but they are scarcely worth talking about.

" Listen, my child, to one thing. If it entailed no sacrifice for *you all*, your mother in particular, to leave Mainz and its narrow streets, and to take a pleasant flat somewhere else (on the Rhine or near Darmstadt,

[1] The Maiers' house in Mainz.

or wherever you like), and if there was a quiet, favourably situated room for me in this flat, for which I paid you an annual rental of 1,000 florins, if therefore all this could be arranged without entailing any sacrifice, without any regrets on the part of your family, then I should most warmly and urgently bid you to arrange matters in this way. This room with you should be a real home for me for my lifetime and under all circumstances, to enjoy which would be one of my dearest refreshments and comforts. This I can state positively and in all truth ! If you can do it, then go ahead and ask me no further questions."

The Maiers actually considered the suggestion. But events then happened so quickly that it could not be carried out. Wagner discussed with Frau Wille every conceivable plan for dealing with the situation in which he had been placed by the friends entrusted with the settlement of his affairs in Penzing, who had caused a public scandal by selling his possessions by public auction. In the course of these discussions he seriously considered the idea of obtaining a divorce from Minna in order to make a wealthy marriage.

" As all things seemed expedient to me and nothing inexpedient, I actually wrote to my sister Luise Brockhaus, asking whether she could not talk reasonably to Minna and persuade her to be content from now on with her yearly allowance and relinquish her claim to my person. Whereupon I was exhorted with great pathos to turn my attention for the present to establishing my reputation and compose a new work, which would be to my benefit without my having to take eccentric measures ; at all events it would be well for me to apply for the post of conductor in Darmstadt, which had just then become vacant."

Dr. Wille's return then set a limit to Wagner's stay at Mariafelde.

" I could see at once that my presence alarmed him ; presumably he was afraid that he would have to come to my financial assistance. ' A man *does* like to be something more than a cipher in his own house and not have to serve as a mere foil for others.' Frau Wille, foreseeing this attitude on the part of her husband, had made an arrangement with the Wesendoncks to send me an allowance of 100 francs during my stay at Mariafelde. When I heard of this I had no choice but to inform Frau Wesendonck that I was leaving Switzerland immediately, begging her in the most friendly way not to bother about me any more, as I had arranged my affairs quite to my satisfaction. I heard later that she had returned the letter—which she possibly considered compromising —to Frau Wille unopened."

From Zürich he went to Stuttgart, where he pinned a faint hope on his friend Kapellmeister Eckert. But this also proved vain. What was he to do next? His home had been broken up against his will and his property was held in pawn. Entirely alone, without any money, pursued by his hard-hearted creditors, he seemed to be heading straight for ruin. He would have preferred to put an end to it all and to his life, which he had come to loathe. Yet some undefined feeling held him back and a firm belief came over him that just when his distress was greatest " the curtain was bound to go up and reveal some marvellous good fortune." And the miracle came to pass. A summons from the young King of Bavaria, whose messenger had only just succeeded in locating Wagner in Stuttgart after a long and fruitless search, rent the ominous clouds and let fortune's rays pour down more brightly than ever before on the almost dazzled composer. Profoundly moved, he sent his saviour his first homage.

" Dear noble King ! I am sending you these tears of heavenliest emotion to tell you that the marvels of poetry have now entered my poor love-starved life like a divine reality ! And this life, its last poetry and music, now belongs henceforth to you, my gracious young King. Dispose of it as your own property. In supreme delight, your true and loyal subject, Richard Wagner."

Chapter VI

COSIMA

" Es war dein opfermutig hehrer Wille."

ON the afternoon of 4th May 1864 Wagner stood in the presence of the King. The first person he told of this miracle was Mathilde Maier in Mainz.

" My heart is overflowing. I must pour it out to a loved one. Picture to yourself a wonderful youth whom Fate has destined to be my saviour. He it is whom he expected, who *had* to be ; but to find him so beautiful astonished me beyond expression. Our interview was one great never-ending love scene. He has the deepest understanding of my nature and my needs. He offers me everything that I require for living, for creating, for the presentation of my works. I am only to be his friend ; no position, no official duties. He is the perfect ideal of my dreams. Here—read his letter ; but send it back to me at once. I am jealous of it.

" And all this now—*now*—in this blackest night of my existence ! I am crushed, as it were. I have not assumed one vestige of responsibility. I am to have quiet—freedom from care of all kinds, leisure to work—nothing else. If I wish to put on any of my works, the King will see that I have everything that I require, that's all. But he loves me, and I love him. Our relationship is exactly like a liaison. He is happy to be able to be something to me.

" I'm now reading my poems to him. He earnestly seeks instruction on all points that are not clear to him, with inwardness and a wonderful power of apprehension. His interest is often deeply moving, his wonderfully beautiful countenance reflects deep pain and the greatest joy, all according to how I touch his feelings. Only one thing makes him unhappy—if he senses any doubt on my part that all my artistic projects will really come to fruition. He wants to see the ideal attained and carried out. One thing would make him perfectly unhappy—if I should pretend, or appear, to be different from what I really am.

" He is divine ! If I am Wotan, then he is my Siegfried. You have no idea how sweet, affectionate and deeply inspired the boy is. God ! And this experience is still vouchsafed me ! Master and disciple ! And *what* a disciple ! It is inconceivable what happiness he brings to my life. And how beautiful it is ! My influence on him is infinite, but the slightest misuse of it for anything but that which is necessary to my being would instantly break him—everything about him is so genuine ! "

To begin with, the King banished all his material cares. He returned to Vienna with 15,000 *gulden* in his pocket to satisfy his most importunate creditors, and make arrangements with the others for the months immediately ahead—above all to rescue what he could of his Penzing belongings. He then returned to Munich accompanied by his faithful servants, Anna and Franz Mrazek, and in accordance with the King's wish, took up his residence in a villa near Schloss Berg on Lake Starnberg, the monarch's summer residence.[1]

" The carriage takes me to him in ten minutes (he wrote). He sends for me once or twice every day. Then I always fly as though to my beloved. It is a charming association. This thirst for knowledge, this comprehension, this exaltation and enthusiasm, I have never experienced it in such an unreservedly lovely form. And then this tender solicitude on my behalf, this charming purity of heart, every expression of his countenance when he assures me how happy he is to have met me ! We often sit like that for hours, each lost in contemplation of the other. . . ."

" Dear friend (he wrote jubilantly to Frau Kalergis-Moukanoff), there is no doubt about this ! Every day the wonder proves more beautiful. He has been sent me by Heaven—it is through him that I still exist and create. I love him. . . . Never, never has history chronicled anything so marvellously beautiful, profound, and exquisite as the relation of my King to me ! Perhaps—this could only happen to *me* ! My art lives in this glorious youth as by a visible seminal force. He is my fatherland, my native heath, my happiness ! "

Nevertheless when Wagner returned to his loveless *garçonnière* after such consecrated hours as these, he felt the loneliness all the more bitterly.

" The forlornness of my home (he complained to Frau Wille), the necessity of bothering with things for which I really am not fitted, of still having to do everything myself, puts shackles on my spirit. Now I've had to move again, furnish a home, occupy myself with knives, forks, pots and pans, bed linen, etc. I, the glorifier of woman ! And in return how kindly they leave me to do their jobs. . . . Whether I shall ever be able to renounce the ' feminine ' altogether ? With a deep sigh, I say no—for I almost wish I could ! "

[1] Villa Pellet, later the property of Prince Bariatinsky, known as Villa Seehaus.

He tried in vain to persuade his Penzing Marie to come to
Starnberg. Even a personal invitation written by the King
himself at Wagner's instigation would not move her to change
her mind.[1] There was one person whom he would have liked to
have had beside him, a person whose presence would have
dispelled all his misery and anxieties at one stroke : this was
Cosima von Buelow. But she was the wife of his best friend !
For a long time he was undecided in his mind. For he realised
only too well that if they should meet again Fate would inevitably
take its course, and everything that had remained unexpressed
hitherto must now become sharp importunate reality. Therefore
on 18th May 1864 he wrote Buelow :

" This year I'm not inviting you to come and stay with me, as I have
reached a point when I shrink not only from the exciting but even
from the stimulating."

He looked on a reunion with Mathilde Maier as the only way
to escape the fatal decision that was facing him. He therefore sent
her the following appeal from Starnberg :

" I must have someone with me who will look after the house for
me ! I can't spare you the shock of again disturbing your peace of
mind with the question : will you come to me and run the place for
me ? Must I still always be afraid of upsetting you dreadfully if I ask
you to come to me ? Haven't things changed any ? Is it always the
same old story ? How it pains me to think of you back again in surroundings where you may not let anyone know that you have even
received a letter from me ! Phew ! How ashamed I am ! Can't you
really see that things must change at last ! My need for you cannot be
dismissed. It must be satisfied.

" I speak of *nothing* but this need for a domestic family atmosphere.
If you should marry, wouldn't you also have to leave your mother ?
Didn't you once almost consider accepting a position ? Think of this
in the same way and call it such ! Here as in Munich I occupy two
connecting floors. I could live downstairs, you upstairs.

" *Gott! Gott!* always these miserable small-town considerations,
and that when so much love is involved ! What after all does one
really love most ? You see how it is ! I've been struggling with myself
a long time to write you very tranquilly on the subject. Now my
patience is up, and it is too scandalous that I always have to do everything all by myself ! It simply can't go on any longer ! A decision
must be reached here, and I fear someday you'll lose me altogether if
you don't truly come to my aid. Here talk and letters are no use ! "

[1] This letter was offered for sale in Vienna in the seventies, during Wagner's
lifetime !

To overcome any possible objections on the part of Mathilde's family, Wagner enclosed a letter to Mathilde's mother in which he assured his " dear, kind friend " that

" Only to someone like yourself, whom I already have to thank for so much love and real devotion, can I venture to address a question and request such as I must do to-day. I now have to decide how I'm to go about arranging my household so that the assured material circumstances that I've achieved will also work to my spiritual well-being. You know that I am separated from my wife. The need of having a woman to take charge of my house has recently become so imperative that I again seriously considered whether it would not be better, more advisable, to send for my wife again, rather than to go on alone. Only the conviction, strengthened by long experience and the warnings of all my friends and relatives, that a reunion must give rise to a far worse situation for us both than that of our separation has made me abandon the idea altogether.

" Under such circumstances I had to consider the question of divorcing my wife. But after extensive inquiries I learned that this is impossible, since my wife (who on the other hand had to agree to our separation) is determined never to consent to a legal divorce. Under such circumstances the only way to obtain a divorce would be to resort to the most extreme and repugnant measures. In view of my wife's health (a heart ailment which makes sudden death imminent at any moment) I could never think of committing a cruelty for some reason or other for which I couldn't answer before my conscience and the world. I'm therefore obliged to leave my marital relationship hanging fire.

" Yet the resultant situation is destructive to my peace of mind. I need a woman who first of all will run the house for me, and finally someone who will be sufficiently my equal in education and character that friendly intercourse with her will satisfy my intellectual require-ments in a sociable homelike atmosphere. I've reached an age which fortunately permits me to adopt a young person as my daughter, and I believe that such a relationship would adequately fill my requirements. But one can't go in search of such a relationship. How and where should I look for a girl whom I don't yet know and whom I might choose too hastily and thereby bring new and unbearable suffering down on my head ? That which I need is not to be sought but must be found as a gift of Fate.

" But the friendly, intelligent and sociable creature that I so greatly need I've already found in this way ! You know what your daughter Mathilde means to me. She understands my need and knows what it can only be at my age—from a sensible point of view. If her age is not such as to fit her altogether for the rôle of my daughter, there are still other degrees of relationship, the assumption of which would enable her to live with me quite properly. I myself have nieces of her age who would be glad to come to me and to whose reception in my home no one could raise any objections. Would such a connection be possible even without the ties of blood? I don't know how such a thing must appear to others. In the light of my intentions and my need it appears to *me* so pure and blameless that it is very difficult for me to think (without real bitterness) that such a relationship as I desire could appear to anyone as irregular and blameworthy.

"One thing is sure, I *must* think of some solution. My household has been planned for such an arrangement now and in the future. I occupy two floors—primarily to ensure perfect quietness—only one of which I shall occupy myself, while the other is destined for the housekeeping and the person who will run the place for me. I must take great pains to find a young woman to look after my requirements in this form or another—in which sensuality will play no part whatever. I'm afraid, and quite rightly so, of finding such a person. I cannot and will not decide for any of my nieces—for many reasons! What will now be the result of it all? Would you have the courage before the world, and sufficient confidence in me—to entrust your Mathilde to me? I know what a difficult and probably crushing question this is for you! Yet I must finally put it to you. *My need is pressing and I must have a decision.* Could you persuade yourself (for the world's sake) that Mathilde was assuming an honourable position and would be worthily taken care of for the rest of her life—that this was offered her—and she found it to her advantage to accept it—and you would put nothing in her way, as sorely as you might miss her love?

"I realize how difficult and almost impossible all this must seem to you. Still I *must* finally put the question to you in all seriousness. And my confidence in your wonderful true love gives me the courage to ask it of you without fearing that I will seriously hurt you by so doing. Or, in order to venture the question, are certain assurances necessary on my part? Should I assure you that Mathilde will be well and honourably taken care of by me, protected in the most meticulous and energetic manner from all suspicion, against any stain or spot? Or should it be possible, without thereby giving nourishment to a frivolous wish, to take into consideration the possible death of my wife, and in such an eventuality, to request the hand of your daughter?

"However you may see fit to reply to me, I shall expect a frank and kindly answer even though it may be contrary to my wishes. I care too much for you to imagine any change in our relationships that might lead me to the injustice of undervaluing your love. I have only one excuse to offer you—for such a request. This is so extraordinary that it can only be excused on the score of the extraordinary aspects of my whole existence. But everything is extraordinary with me! For instance, I won a King as the dearest and most charming of sons, and I now long—chastely but profoundly—for a dear woman at my side. In any event, don't be angry with me!"

Since Mathilde, who happened to be again visiting in Cannstadt, wrote Wagner that she did not have the courage to send her mother his letter as it would " crush " her, and called the plan " utterly impossible," he realized that if achievable at all it would only be attended with a tempestuous struggle and much excitement. So he definitely gave up the idea.

" It will not become me after this to call to you again : calm yourself ! (he wrote Mathilde later). My exasperating situation is grave, and my need is great. It would be completely horrible and absolutely unbearable if I should suddenly be involved again in an emotional turmoil that I'm no longer capable of combating. Any salvation that may come to me must come as a gentle, peaceful happiness, without blemish, without passion of any kind, like sun after a storm, as my charming King came to me in the obscure night of my life. I can no longer bear any convulsions of grief, any silent heartache, for I've already suffered more than any man's due and my strength in these things is at an end."

A fortunate destiny frustrated this union of Mathilde and Wagner, for in spite of all her love and self-abnegation, this narrow-minded woman would never have proved the redeeming Senta for the fickle Flying Dutchman that was Wagner. For his redemption he required a woman who, with fanatic faith in his mission, was ready to do battle with the whole world and make the necessary sacrifice without consideration for anybody. Such a woman existed and was ready to follow his call. He knew that ! And after this last attempt to save the situation had failed, he threw all scruples, inhibitions and considerations for his friend to the winds, and sent the following cry for help to Buelow in Berlin.

" Don't take what I'm about to say to you and what I'm going to ask of you as the sudden whim of a passing mood—but as an important paragraph in the last testament of a dying man. *I invite you with your wife and child and maid to come and stay with me this summer for as long as possible.* This is the result of a long communion with myself. Hans, you will find me in good circumstances, my life is completely transformed ! I am sustained by the truest love—the purest intentions. But my home is desolate and I'm now feeling this more acutely than ever. Help me, dear friends, over this first interim period ! People my house for me, at least for a time. This is my real heart's desire. . . .

" There's a whole floor ready for you and your dear family. Cosima will come with both the children. . . . Now, dear Hans, don't be cantankerous ! I beseech you ! No weighing of this and that. If you have anything on your mind, it lies in my power to banish it. *Trust me! Ach*, I need the pleasure of such a noble, dear association with beloved beings—and how I'm looking forward to your children ! Truly, dear friends, you alone are lacking to my happiness !

" I approached this matter very hesitatingly. First one scruple and then another gave me pause. But now all is clear. We simply must have each other, and the moment for it is now, *now* ! "

Wagner followed up his appeal with several telegrams. At last at the end of June 1864 Buelow sent his wife and two children (Daniela aged three and a half years, and Blandine now fifteen months old) to his friend at Starnberg in advance, while he himself was detained ten days longer in Berlin by his professional duties. It was the first meeting between Wagner and Cosima since that significant parting in Berlin a year before. The passion that had been forcibly suppressed at that time now flamed up suddenly and irresistibly. Everything cried out for a decision.

In the meantime, Cosima had come to recognize more and more clearly the overwhelming force of Wagner's genius and the real cause of his sufferings and his militant attitude towards the world. And the conviction grew in her that *she* was destined by Fate to bring him the longed-for happiness. She now knew her real goal, and marched towards it ruthlessly, sweeping all obstacles resolutely aside.

" I understand less and less (she wrote to Lenbach) how a person like Wagner could have been flung into our present world, and I only rejoice that I was able to recognize him for what he is. This recognition has also shown me my course, and I now have no other thought than the fulfilment of the appointed task on which my happiness depends."

On 29th June 1864, when she was again face to face with her friend at Starnberg, the inevitable came to pass and she gave herself to him completely. On 2nd July she wrote her friend, Marie von Buch (later Countess von Schleinitz) that

" to me everything seems remote—as if the whole world forgets—and that I myself forget everything. When I once explain it all to you, then you will not misunderstand my words. I have been here three days, and it seems as though it were already a century, and that it will last— how long—I do not know. So peace has settled on my spirit, and I have an infinite longing never to see or hear a town again ! "

Buelow, who had arrived at Wagner's the beginning of July " completely run down and with strained and shattered nerves," remained ignorant of this turn in the lives of his wife and friend.

M

With the object of dragging him " away from his nerve-racking musical activities in Berlin and securing a nobler field " for him, but mainly to keep near him the woman he loved, Wagner secured from the King an appointment for his friend as " Pianist to His Majesty." At the beginning of September Buelow returned to Berlin with his family for a short time in order to move his household to the city on the Isar.

In a letter to Buelow of 30th September the following remarks by Wagner could scarcely have been comprehensible to Buelow.

" I too am uneasy about Cosima's ailing condition. Everything touching her is extraordinary and unusual. She requires freedom in the noblest sense of the word. She is childlike, and profound—the laws of her being will always lead her only towards the highest. No one, other than she herself, will ever be able to help her ! She belongs to a peculiar world order which we must learn to grasp through her. In the future you will enjoy a more propitious leisure and a far greater personal freedom to take note of this and find your honourable place at her side. And that, too, is a comfort to me."

The highly bombastic verses that he inscribed to Cosima a day later give a much clearer idea of his plans than the above highly cryptic allusions !

To Thee

" *I am beloved," the star shines down its blessing ;*
The bride for whom the wreath shall ne'er be wound.
" *I love ! " the glowing sun is now confessing ;*
The bridegroom will not lead you in the round,
And heavy clouds with midnight wing oppressing
The stars' mild light in cohorts now surround.
It sinks—but lo, the moveless sun is glinting
With its own mighty glow the clouds betinting.

What new world is it that we here see forming ?
The day is done, yet does not fall the night.
You feel the blessed fire forever warming,
Behold here too the workings of its might,
The passion, sacred, innermost, transforming
Is there poured forth in glorious evening light
And if day follows night, then nothing dreaded
My sun shall to your shining star be wedded.

The sunset of my life I saw before me,
The sun already touched the dimming sea,
And now the star of evening rose above me,
While darkness flooded to eternity.
I smiled at the last gleam, prepared to pour me
Into the night and death's solemnity,
To drink of Lethe final consolation
Soon the day's long labour and vexation.

Why does he halt, why will he not surrender
To-night, what keeps the sun from going down?
Instead of paling, see him now engender
A brighter glow in which the shadows drown.
Does he prepare another day in splendour
With his far rays from a more golden crown?
He halts, he shines, wide distances adorning;
Venus becomes the gleaming star of morning.

Oh magic star of love so sweetly beaming
Is't you that stops my life's sun in its place
And holds it there and keeps it fully gleaming
That had to-night already turned his face?
Oh miracle! Is it your smile redeeming
That halts the heavenly bodies there in space?
Stupendous miracle! How am I able
This to explain from new or ancient fable?

My dawn of day was full of dread and dreary,
My star of life unwilling took its course;
Then bent towards me with love that grew not weary,
So chaste, so passionate in its high force,
That star! And yet, unseen by daylight, eerie,
Mysterious, it faded at its source.
Through bitter struggle, woe and pallid sorrow,
Did I sink down towards night that knew no morrow.

But once again the veil of space uncloses,
What dreaded morning then had promised me.
The loveliest of all the stars exposes
That on my gleaming shines so tranquilly.

What had been dream, now blessedly discloses
Its secret, ending every mystery ;
The star has called the sun to halt his going ;
I love, I am beloved ! Oh joy past knowing !

(Translation of Olga Erbsloh Muller.)

For the winter the King had placed at the Master's disposition a superb villa in Munich, so he now had to fit up another home for himself, which, however, he definitely hoped would be the last time. As he required a housekeeper in addition to his own faithful couple and his manservant, he did his best to secure a suitable person. He thought at once of Vrenli, the pretty and efficient maid who had looked after him so devotedly and affectionately during his stay at the Hotel Schweizerhof in Lucerne in 1859 during the dark " Tristan " days.

" But Vrenli is my guardian angel here," he wrote Frau Wesendonck at the time, asking her to select " a nice present for her—a dress, say—woollen or silk—no matter what it costs." He therefore wrote Vrenli, who was still in service at the Schweizerhof.

" Now we can really arrange it if you're still free, and willing. I'm just settling down in Munich for the rest of my life, and am moving into town in the autumn, when I have to furnish my flat. This is just the time for you to break away, and if you're still willing to come to me I shall be very glad if you can come very soon—as soon as possible—in time to relieve me of much of the worry of getting things in order. You'll be comfortable and will have an easy time with me. What matters most to me is to have tried, true and devoted people about me in my house, people who are fond of me and delight in making life pleasant for me.

" You, my good Vrenli, will only have to look after my room—all the dirty work will be done for you. You'll keep my linen and clothes in order and do a little tailoring and sewing, which you do so cleverly ; in short, you're to look after me and make life run smoothly for me, and in return I shall always look after you. All this can be arranged, and I think you may trust me, for you see that even after all this long time, I still think of you and haven't forgotten you. . . .

" For I have no family and now want to make my home as pleasant as possible. To that end I require faithful and sincerely devoted people who entrust themselves to my protection and devote their lives to me in return. I still think of my good Vrenli and say to myself : I must have Vrenli, too ! Do, therefore, respond to my devotion, trust me, and do everything in your power to come to me very soon."

Verena Weitmann responded to his call and with the help of
Bertha, the dressmaker of Penzing fame, whom he had brought
to Munich, his house was furnished with great care and in all the
usual luxury with its strangely exciting effect on the senses. In
the centre of the first floor there was a large room containing his
Erard piano. A door on the right led to the satin-hung room
which Cornelius called " The Grail." This was closed to all
profane eyes. Here Wagner, robed in costly garments and
surrounded with velvet, silk, satin, colour and light, invoked the
mood necessary for creation.

The walls of this room were covered with fine yellow satin
finished off with narrow draperies of the same material. The two
blunt corners of the long wall that faced Count von Schack's
house were broken by iron galleries, making artificial niches.
These niches, which were about 27 inches deep, were covered
with pleated pink satin. Each of the iron galleries was masked
by double portières of white silk tulle trimmed with lace. The
white curtains and their draperies were decorated with tiny
artificial roses. The room was lighted by a window in the narrow
wall to the left of the entrance. The curtains of this window were
of pink satin with draperies of interlaced pink and white satin.

There was a mirror in the middle of the broad wall, and on the
narrow wall opposite the window hung a reproduction of
Murillo's Madonna. The cornice of the window draperies, the
frame of the mirror and that of the picture were of quilted pink
satin, and the draperies were caught back with loops of white
satin. The ceiling was entirely covered with thickly quilted white
satin and intersected diagonally from one corner to the other
with pearl grey satin ruches about six inches wide. The ceiling
was also edged all round with similar pearl grey ruches, decorated
with artificial roses. The centre of the ceiling was adorned with a
large white satin rosette trimmed with narrow silk lace and roses
like those on the ceiling. The floor was covered with a soft
Smyrna carpet and in the middle of the room was a soft springy
sofa covered with flowered white moiré.

On 15th October 1864 Wagner was able to give a small house-
warming party in honour of his willing-hearted assistants.
Through a strange coincidence, Mathilde Maier was also present
on this occasion. Just at that time the papers had printed an

entirely erroneous report to the effect that Wagner was danger-
ously ill with typhus,[1] and Mathilde fearing the lonely man
might not have the proper nursing, had hurried to Munich
with her mother. To their glad surprise they found Wagner in
the best of health, and after a few days—passed chiefly in his
company—they returned home with their minds at rest. Touched
by their sympathy, he called after them : " If I ever have to leave
Munich, I shall come to you ! I can count on *you* ! "

The Buelows arrived in Munich on 20th November.

" Hans is wretched, almost lost, like the moth that must burn itself
in the flame (wrote Wagner to Mathilde Maier on 29th January 1865).
Exceedingly delicate and sickly by nature, highly excitable, and over-
strung in every way, there's danger of complete paralysis some day,
especially if he doesn't give up his piano playing altogether. But he
won't hear of it, and therefore prefers to jeer vehemently at every
doctor, every friend. You may now imagine how Cosima feels in such
an atmosphere and what a turmoil of suffering, torture and vexation
it all is."

In Cosima, Wagner's home in the Briennerstrasse had now
found its mistress. She placed herself wholly at his service. She
ran his household, received his guests, attended to his vast correspondence, in short, tried to spare him all effort and exertion and
relieve him of every tiresome task. Since the " Baroness," as she
was known, was occupied for several hours a day at Wagner's,
a drawing-room and study were permanently set apart for her
use. Buelow acquiesced gallantly in this arrangement and was
more than happy to be able, through his wife, to make things
easier for Wagner the man, even as he had placed himself entirely
in the service of Wagner the artist. He refused to think that his
friend could ever deceive him. And when on 10th April 1865
Cosima gave birth to Wagner's child, Buelow informed his
friends that for the third time he had " become a mother," as
they said in Berlin when the child was a daughter. "*Ma troisième
fille s'appelle* Isolde Ludovica Josepha " (wrote Cosima to a
friend). " Wagner is her godfather." Thus we have what is
probably the unique phenomenon of a father acting as sponsor to
his own child, the explanation being that this was the closest

---

[1] The Burrell Collection (Exhibit 427B) contains the telegram that Wagner
sent to Minna on 9th October 1864 in which he referred to this " false newspaper
rumour " and assured her that he was well, so that she should not worry.

degree of relationship that he was permitted publicly to acknow-
ledge at the time.[1]

Wagner's paternity intoxicated him, more especially as it
coincided with an event that was reckoned among the serenest
and most sacred hours of his life : the preparations for the
production of " Tristan." " There was a brief space in which I
really thought I must be dreaming—I felt so wonderful ! This
was the time of the ' Tristan ' rehearsals." After a jealous fate
had frustrated this ill-fated work for the last time through the
sudden illness of the Isolde, Frau Malwine Schnorr, it finally came
off on 10th June.

" I felt continually in a dream (he wrote Frau Wille). I marvelled
and marvelled how this had ever come to pass ! This was the wonderful
climax, and yet I was embittered by—absences. Yes, really embittered.
How petty you all seem to me to have evaded this excitement."

Precisely those Zürich friends who were most closely bound up
with his creation—the Wesendoncks and Willes—had not attended
the festival. Even Liszt was absent, kept away by " Roman
illusions." Peter Cornelius was also among the absentees.
Nevertheless Mathilde Maier and her brother and sister had
hastened to be present, and waited the entire time in Munich.
But the excitement of these weeks, which left Wagner extraordinarily irritated and touchy, spoiled this friendly association
somewhat and caused Mathilde to sense a certain coolness in his
feelings towards her. Wagner tried to reassure her.

" *Ach !* you can only imagine such a thing if you've failed to understand me the whole past year (he wrote). But even you, my dear, can
only be that to me which you were allowed, and it was possible for
you, to be. If this meant many limitations there was still much left,
as my letters so gladly and gratefully testified. I have neither rejected
nor rescinded anything ; but only recognized what remained of our
relationship without physical desire. And, furthermore, that this was
no little matter, you can see from those letters.

" Nothing sad nor pleasant ever happened to me that I didn't tell
you of it simply and loyally. If anything important happened to me, I

[1] In 1914 the world was treated to the unedifying spectacle of Isolde (who till
then had been designated in the official Wagner circle (Glasenapp) as Wagner's
child) being obliged to go to law to establish her parentage, since Bayreuth found
it more advantageous—for reasons of inheritance—to represent her as Buelow's
daughter. The outbreak of the war left the case unsettled. Her own apologia,
Memories of my Father, Richard Wagner, which was announced for publication, never
appeared after all. She died in February 1919 following a severe illness brought on
by the excitement of the scandal. She was broken in body and in spirit.

invited you to share it with me ; but this time things went badly again. A short visit—entirely taken up with my work and full of meaning and significance—became an intolerably long period of waiting under the most distressing circumstances.

" Keep your affection for me, which gave me such lovely hours as my happiest memories—gentle, peaceful, unclouded. Your heart lives on in me and will only cease to beat with my own. That is indeed a great and significant gain. Do you think this has often happened to me ? Farewell ; be comforted, gentle, and level-headed. You will always remain for me what you are, and gauge this by what you have been to me in the past."

He could find no words to describe the performance of the Schnorrs. " A wonderful pair of artists, sent me by Heaven ; with a profound understanding of their rôles and tenderly devoted to their task. Amazingly gifted ! " Arrangements were initiated for them to leave Dresden and settle in Munich permanently. Daring artistic innovations were about to be realized when a malign fate overtook the gallant hero. Within a week after their return from Munich the incomparable Tristan was dead. Only the King's great affection and the support of the beloved woman at his side could help the cruelly stricken Master through this dark hour.

On 8th August Cosima had to leave with Buelow on a journey of several weeks to attend the first performance of Liszt's " St. Elizabeth," which was to be given in Pest under his direction. Wagner felt he could bear the separation more easily in strange surroundings, and therefore gladly accepted the King's invitation to occupy his hunting lodge in the Bavarian Alps overlooking the Lake of Walchen. Here he confided his yearnings and the spiritual conflict of the first extended separation from his beloved to the " Brown Book," Cosima's personal journal.

" We must never be separated again, do you hear ? This is the main thing, and if we always stay together the rest will follow. I was so moved that though I opened the two letters from you, which arrived together to-day, I had to wait several hours before reading them. I saw at the first glance that I couldn't bear it. You see, that's how things stand with me ! Yet I finally did read them. And now I am silent ! I stare into space and believe that some day I will give up talking altogether. *Ach*, what nonsense ! And this fool—this Hans— who wouldn't let you go to Penzing, but took you on a round of the Vienna shops instead ! Can you believe it ? And yet this man is now

my only friend ! ' *Ach, blöde Herzen! blinde Augen!* '[1]   You alone have
any rights over me. No one else really knows me. O Heavens, how
long must we still endure this existence ! " (15th August.)

" O Cosima, you are the soul of my life ! wholly and utterly ! I
looked out over the lowlands, sought a ' home,' imagined what Munich
would be without you—all a grave ! Nothing, nothing more without
you. You are the soul of everything that is still alive in me." (18th
August.)

" You still draw forth my work from my soul. But, Oh ! give me
peace in addition ! Stay with me, don't go away any more. *Tell poor
Hans quite frankly* that without you it's all up with me. Oh, Heavens !
if you could only be my wife before the world ! This constant coming
and going, coming again, having to go off again, this placing yourself
at the disposal of others—it's horrible ! Peace ! You poor dear ! I
will also be the death of you. We're wearing ourselves out. Should
one now break away ? Break away. . . ? What am I saying ! Madness !
Could tranquillity, lovely gay laughter ever make us happy ? *Ach,*
but then come the sighs ! May God give sight to the blind ! *But you
are my wife!*" (20th August.)

" O, that one could only find the magic word that would reveal you
wholly and absolutely to your family ! How little and how far from
thoroughly they know you ! Now they're dragging you about ! It
humiliates me deeply that they are in a position to do so ! But that you
really don't let yourself be dragged about but only do so in order to
deaden your suffering, your weakness ; that you talk yourself into
believing that this is the best, and that this person and that also have
their rights, and what the eye sees, and what the others tell you ! Then
I couldn't, and cannot, stand it any longer ! Then nothing has any
sense for me any more ! and even my love seems to me to be a weakness.
Then you seem altogether lost, downright unfaithful ! " (2nd
September.)

" Everything in life repeats itself. A year ago I also lived through a
separation with many of its agonies. And I shall go through it again.
A year from now Cosima will have forgotten everything, will have
forgotten what suffering she now causes me, what spiritual tortures
she is preparing for herself. Then she will suddenly find that there is
nothing for her to do but to comply with some new demand of her
father again and—then the same old story all over again ! One just
has to get used to it ! " (10th September.)

[1] Isolde's words to Brangaene in Act I of " Tristan " in reverse order : O blinded
eyes, O foolish hearts !

On 13th September the Buelows, who had accompanied Liszt
from Hungary to Venice, returned to Munich. Wagner breathed
a sigh of relief as though a weight had been lifted from his
shoulders. But the tragic conflict in which these three persons
were so fatally involved (since they all lacked the courage to come
out with the truth immediately) was now past settlement. A
divorce would have made any artistic collaboration between
Wagner and Buelow in Munich out of the question, and would
even have jeopardized Wagner's relationship with the King.
Wagner, who would have preferred a brutal clarification, had to
bow to Cosima's diplomacy. At first she considered such a
solution unwise and impracticable. So in order to preserve the
status quo in Munich the deception had to go on. Here the most
difficult rôle fell to Cosima, who not only had to be the mistress
of Hans's friend but also Hans's wife.[1] But the most tragic rôle
was Buelow's, who—a second King Marke—sacrificed himself
to Wagner's art to the point of self-immolation and finally went to
pieces when he accidentally learned of his friend's treachery.

Cosima stood high in the King's favour on account of her
association with Wagner. She tried to satisfy his keen desire to
acquaint himself with all Wagner's compositions and writings by
compiling for him a Wagner book which was to contain everything that could be unearthed in the way of the Master's early
literary and theoretical articles, albeit now doctored up a trifle
for the benefit of the royal palate. In obtaining, or demanding,
the return of manuscripts that Wagner had previously given his
old friends she did not always show the greatest tact. For
instance, Taussig complained that :

" Wagner has had the extraordinary notion of requesting me
through the Delphic Oracle, and in a highly uncivil manner, to return
the original score of ' Tristan.' I have ignored this demand. Wagner
might at least have written me himself."

Even Mathilde Wesendonck voiced a protest.

" In a letter received to-day (she wrote him) Frau von Buelow
requests me to send her some of your literary manuscripts that are in
my possession. I've gone through the portfolio, but it's impossible to
send anything unless you give the order yourself."

There were also unpleasant discussions with Cornelius and

---

[1] Buelow also considered Isolde (born 10th April 1864) his child.

Brahms on the same subject. Wagner's friends of earlier days watched with concern Cosima's growing influence over him, with its alienating effect as far as they were concerned, especially since they did not view the relationship in such an innocent light as Hans von Buelow.

" Wagner only remembers people as long as he needs them (wrote Cornelius to his fiancée), and he's now losing the elasticity to keep up the semblance at least, and above all the kindness of heart which induces fairness to all and a friendly attitude towards everyone who deserves it.

" Take the Maiers, for instance, and the Wesendoncks ! Then it was Taussig's turn. Cosima says the latter ' has no touch ; that he can't be counted among the great pianists ; that he's a caricature of Liszt ; has no individuality.' These, so to speak, were the four main indictments in the papal edict against Taussig. Wagner tacked about so as not to expose his past relations with the reviled artist.

" But the principal thing is this love affair between Wagner and Cosima. . . . Since it started, Wagner has been wholly and completely under her influence. With or without the two children, she's now with him every day since Buelow has been away on a concert tour. You can no longer speak to him alone. No letter reaches him without her opening and reading it to him. . . .

" But where does Buelow stand in the affair ? Has he really turned his wife over to Wagner on some highly romantic understanding ? The real marriage between Hans and Cosima has been only a sham now for a long time. Otherwise Hans's behaviour would be inexplicable."

Wagner's correspondence with Minna was also unfavourably affected by his relations with Cosima. In February 1865, when Minna hinted at certain rumours that had reached her ears, he immediately sent her a telegram to reassure her.[1] But he answered no more of her letters, and went so far as to send her the following cold-blooded missive on 5th October 1865 :

" I have not yet read your letter. Ever since your letter of last spring, which depressed me so dreadfully, I have decided not to allow anything to embitter my memories unnecessarily."[2]

This was his last message to his old comrade.

If his friends were already voicing such concern, the enemies and envious rivals of the " King's favourite " seized with avidity any incident that might be exploited to his detriment.

[1] This telegram in which he hastened to inform Minna that he was " still enjoying the full favour of his divine protector " is now in the Burrell Collection (Exhibit 434).
[2] Exhibit 435B, Burrell Collection.

The first onslaught of his enemies had been victoriously parried in February 1865, but in the late autumn the opposition returned daringly to the attack and encouraged by certain members of the Cabinet who were concerned for their jobs, bent all efforts to effect Wagner's downfall since he had brusquely refused to exert his influence with the King on their behalf.

The following disgraceful incident shows to what lengths they went to achieve their ends. Wagner had applied to the King in October (1865) for a loan of 40,000 *gulden* to wipe out his debts. The King had granted this request in spite of the opposition of his Cabinet Secretary (Franz von Pfistermeister), and the latter accordingly notified Wagner that he was to come and fetch the money. Cosima went to the Royal Treasury in his stead and was greatly surprised to find the sum—in small silver coins—packed in sacks which had to be driven openly through the streets of Munich !

" Regarding the collection of Your Majesty's present to the Friend (wrote Cosima to the King on 1st January 1866) the circumstances are as follows : My husband was away, the Friend was not feeling well, when word came that the royal gift could not be sent to him. He had no one here whom he could trust. Thinking that it would be a simple matter and that I should only be burdened with a couple of bank-notes, I requested the Friend to allow me to attend to the matter as I also often had to go to my banker.

" In my great naïveté I went calmly to the Royal Treasury with my eldest daughter. My astonishment was indescribable when I was informed there that I would receive no paper money—only silver currency ! I didn't know what to do ! Still I was anxious not to have the Friend enter the unfriendly place ; besides, next day he was leaving for Vienna. I overcame the difficulty. Taking into consideration that no outsider was involved, I depended on discretion and a certain sense of honour which never allows a lady to be made a public spectacle, and carried the sum to the Friend in two cabs. The affair fairly made him shudder ; he thanked me and almost scolded me. Then he admired my courage and said that the fact that my friendship for him had brought me into such a situation weighed on him like a burden. I smiled and said : ' But it's all over now ! ' When my husband returned, he told the latter of my first adventure. My husband smiled and told me to be more prudent next time."

Wagner's account of the incident differed slightly.

" Last October (he wrote the King on 9th June 1866) your Royal Secretary (von Hofmann) wrote me that His Majesty the King had granted me 40,000 *gulden* from the Royal Treasury as a gift. The Friend just happened to be with me at the moment. She noticed the tremendous impression made on me by your love and favour, which now relieved me from a chain of long, sorrowful material cares. She was so childishly delighted over this beautiful gesture on your part that she only regretted that this great happiness was communicated to me through a dry official notification from the Secretariat instead of which she would have liked you, dearest one, to have given me the gift in person.

" I smiled at her naïveté, but she insisted on seeing that the Friend's gift be brought to me, at least. As I was really disinclined to go to the Treasury myself, she begged me to give her an authorization, and with this she actually set out next morning for the Treasury with her eldest daughter, as though for a festive promenade. She then presented her authorization and requested in my name (an indisposition having prevented my coming in person) the sum granted me as a gift.

" The innocent soul must have imagined that she would be received in a friendly and respectful manner by your officials, in whose eyes the royal favour should also have made *me* seem worthy of respect. But this was her first disappointment. She was asked rudely and laconically how she intended to carry the money, if she perhaps was going to transport the sacks of silver coins herself ? When she requested, in astonishment, that she be given paper money, she was told that there was not enough on hand, she must take at least the half in silver.

" Her first consolation at this unfriendliness was the thought that she had been able to spare me such humiliating treatment, and under-took (moved by a gay feeling of friendly ambition) to let nothing intimidate her but to shame the very unsuitable executors of the kind royal favour through her endurance. She had the governess call two cabs, and directed them to draw up to the door of the Treasury, and then with calm indifference, she herself helped to put the heavy money bags in the cabs, during which proceeding she remarked that even the rude behaviour of the Treasury officials finally gave way to a certain respectful sympathy as though they had involuntarily grasped the tender motive underlying the so strangely energetic behaviour of the noble young woman.

" She actually arrived at my house with her two cabs, brought me the royal gift with difficulty, and gaily described to me what effort it had cost her to carry out her project of seeing that I received the gift only from the hand of a friend. I was shocked at this impulsive act which might possibly give rise to mortifying publicity. Immediately recognizing the intention behind her action—the big-hearted, tender impulse—it has been impossible for me up to now to reprove her for it, even to-day when this unusual incident has been branded as a horrible crime."

Through a clever crescendo of slanderous attacks an effort

was made to cast suspicion on Wagner and goad him into some imprudence. One day a report was circulated in all the papers to the effect that he was wallowing in luxury while his poor wife was living in distress and penury in Dresden and having to support herself by taking in washing. When Minna learned of this she immediately sent a public denial to put an end to this " vile lie."

" As a result of a rumour circulated by various Munich and Vienna papers (ran the announcement in the *Munich Volksbote* of 16th January), I hereby truthfully declare that I have so far received adequate support from my absent husband to guarantee me a carefree existence. It gives me great satisfaction to be able by this explanation to silence at least one of the many slanders that are brought against my husband."[1]

It was the last loving service that his wife, now living in comfortable retirement among her Dresden friends, could render him.

In the beginning of November, when an attempt was made by the Queen Mother and the King's grandfather, King Ludwig I, to induce the young monarch to drop Wagner, the sovereign reacted by inviting the latter to his country residence, Hohenschwangau. Wagner accepted the invitation of his royal friend on the 4th November and passed eight " heavenly days " in his company.

" Truly only now have I become aware of the great nobility and beauty of his love (wrote Wagner in Cosima's Brown Book). He surpasses everything imaginable. He is myself in a new youthful regeneration—altogether me, and only so much of himself as to be beautiful and powerful. But that isn't a fault—it is a love that is pure love. It is my last wonderful task in life fully to live up to this wonderful faith in me."

The King was also in ecstasies.

" It is impossible for me to bear this bliss alone (he wrote Cosima on 14th November 1864). I must pour it out to a heart that knows and understands me. He, the great Friend, loved profoundly *bis in den Tod*, and you, dear highly esteemed lady, are the only persons on earth who understand me. This is indeed the truth, as sure as God exists. I am in Heaven! O what beautiful, wonderful days! And He says He is happy—O immeasurable bliss! Let us now solemnly vow to do everything that lies in human power to ensure Him the peace He has won—drive from Him every care—rather take every sorrow upon

---

[1] Minna's draft of this announcement, dated 9th January 1866, is in the Burrell Collection (Exhibit 449). It is described as " written in a wavering hand " and differs slightly from the notice that appeared a week later in the Munich paper.

ourselves if possible—love Him—love Him with all the power God
has imparted to the soul!

"O I know that our love for Him is eternal—eternal—and yet the
thought is clear and treasurable to me to have begged such a loyal
friend of His as yourself to unite with me in being to Him everything
that is possible for a human being to be to an adored one—a saint.

"O He is divine, divine! My task in life is to live for Him, to fight,
to suffer when He needs it for His complete salvation! How happy I
am that the Beloved Friend has found such pleasure in this rock-bound
castle and its surroundings! It was here that I wandered joyfully
through woods and meadows when a boy, always with His picture
in my mind and heart. On the smooth surface of the Alpine lake I read
the 'Ring of the Nibelungs.' And now to have the longed-for One with
me, to be able to spend the day with Him, O undeserved happiness
for me! Now the eyes of the profane world must open at last and
understand our relationship in spite of all scandalous intrigues."

But the King was in error. When Wagner returned to Munich
from Hohenschwangau he found trouble brewing. His adver-
saries had used this visit as a welcome pretext to stir up the public
through all kinds of wild rumours in order to bring about the
downfall of the King's favourite.

Since the attacks in Munich became more and more menacing
Wagner, "egged on by Cosima" (as Cornelius expressed it),
allowed himself to be persuaded to launch the notorious article
in the *Muenchener Neueste Nachrichten* which culminated in an
attack against the Royal Cabinet, and had been written in collaboration with Cosima. He was well aware of the real intriguers,
but had been unable to persuade the King to remove them from
his entourage. This unwise step, which placed powerful weapons
in the hands of the enemy to use against him with the King, who
was being cunningly deceived regarding the real temper of the
public, at last led to his overthrow. For the Cabinet it was a
question of life and death. And Wagner was the loser. On
10th December 1865 he left his Bavarian residence at the request
of his royal friend.

"He went to the station at five in the morning (reported Cornelius),
where we waited some time for Wagner. At last the carriage arrived.
Wagner looked like a ghost, with pale distraught features, and a grey
shimmer over his long limp hair. We went with him to the train.
Franz, his servant, and Pohl, his dog, travelled with him. Wagner was
still engaged in earnest conversation with Cosima, and Heinrich heard
him stress especially the word 'Silence.' Cosima was quite broken.

When the train disappeared behind the pillars, it was like the fading out of a vision.

" We took Cosima back to Wagner's house. Since then she has been in an indescribable state. God bless the pair of them if they really love each other deeply and if poor Wagner has at last found the right person for him in the evening of his life.

" It seems that Wagner really *does* love Cosima. He says the hope of seeing her soon is his only solace ! If he is really *in love* at last, and Cosima apparently loves *him* passionately, then I wish with all my heart that peace and happiness may be in store for both of them. Perhaps Buelow may also find a greater consolation and peace in solitude. I'm convinced he is treading a thorny path, and God know he is a good and honourable fellow who deserves a better fate."

Wagner again turned his steps to Switzerland, and after a short stay at Vevey took a country house, " The Artichokes," in the environs of Geneva. He immediately sent for his little Swiss maid, Vrenli, to come to him from Munich. Although the house was only available for three months, it nevertheless had to be furnished in the usual style and with the most meticulous care, to which end the dressmaker was again summoned from Vienna. Franz was soon sent back to Munich to look after Wagner's house during his absence.[1]

The King, who after Wagner's departure clung more and more closely to Cosima, suffered inexpressibly from the separation after it had become clear to him that he had been made the tool of an anti-Wagner clique.

" I can't stand being separated from him for long ! (he wrote Cosima on 2nd January 1866). I suffer dreadfully ! If I could help him bear the burden of existence in an inhospitable land, if through my presence I could be of any service to him, I would now gladly leave my land and subjects and follow him ! For the voice within me is calling loud and insistently—your first and most sacred duty is to love Him, for whom you were born and destined to all eternity, to help Him as much as you can, to be devoted to Him in steadfast loyalty !

" This is no passing youthful infatuation ; this is the inner impulse which my soul will, and must, obey ! This is indeed the truth, God knows the shattering truth ! O dear Friend, I am suffering, suffering inexpressibly ! I now feel all alone—alone on the throne surrounded by princely glamour, the fire of which fails to warm, not comprehended

[1] The Burrell Collection contains a number of hitherto unpublished letters of Wagner to his servants, Franz and Anna, written during this time, in which he gives them various detailed instructions for looking after, and disposing of, his belongings. See Exhibits 454 and 455, A, B and C.

by my subjects, completely misunderstood in my glowing enthusiasm and loyalty to Him.

" I actually brought myself to send him away ; I had to that day— he wanted it thus ; indeed, I could not do otherwise. Yet now when I long to have him back again within a few months, this is to be made impossible for me ! *That* I will not tolerate ! I will go to Him if I can be anything to Him in a distant land (O please let me partake of this !), yes, go to Him—or die ! Yes, die ! O, don't be frightened at the thought—please don't ! To share His life with him—at his side ; but without Him, life has lost all value and meaning for me ! Then have done with it ! have done with it ! I have never been so miserable ! O, it is comforting to know that there is one soul to whom one can unburden his heart—one among millions ! I am longing for a letter from you. God protect and bless the Friend and you. Good luck and blessings on you both ! "

Since the Prime Minister (von den Pforten) threatened to resign if Wagner should return, the King did not venture to take any action, but for the time being submitted to the " devil that had seized everybody and had made everything so fearfully sad." As the sojourn in Geneva was limited to a short period Wagner began to look round for a suitable site in which he could go on with his work far from the turmoil of the world. He first turned his steps to the French Riviera, and while in Marseilles received an unexpected telegram from his friend, Dr. Pusinelli in Dresden, informing him that " *Ton épouse morte la nuit passée sans maladie précédente, ni agonie. Que faire ?* "

This despatch with its news of Minna's death only caught up with him after a considerable delay, so that it was impossible for him to reach Dresden in time for the funeral even had he wanted to. On 26th January he therefore wired his friend to this effect :

" Your despatch—date unknown—reached me last night in Marseilles, where I was detained on account of illness, and at all events am too far away to help personally in the sad affair. I therefore beg you, as a true noble-hearted friend, to make all necessary arrangements on my behalf. Am writing you and shall expect a letter from you in Geneva where I arrive Tuesday. Please give full expression to my sorrowful feelings in all arrangements you make."

He then confirmed these instructions immediately in a letter.

" Your telegram with its sad message was re-telegraphed me here from Geneva. This couldn't be done in Geneva before last night as I left there last Monday, have changed my address very frequently, and only sent them a temporary Marseilles forwarding address for letters and telegrams yesterday afternoon.

N

" After a troublous night, I cannot describe my condition this morning otherwise than as a complete stupor in which I sit brooding apathetically without a notion of what I should plan to do next! I assume that you have made the same sort of provision for my poor unhappy wife's remains, and have caused the same honour to be shown her in my name as I should have done had she passed away happily at my side.

" Please arrange for her burial *altogether* in this sense. . . . O, she is indeed to be envied that she was finally allowed to break off the struggle painlessly. Peace, peace for the fearfully tortured heart of this pitiable soul."

On 29th January 1866 Pusinelli then wrote him at length, giving him the desired details of Minna's death and burial.

" Your wife was taken rather seriously ill last December with a catarrhal inflammation of the throat which was soon aggravated by an old kidney complaint. The illness was long drawn out, but yielded at last to treatment, that is, she regained her former condition—bearable at all events—to which she was already accustomed.

" Favoured by January's mild weather, she began to go about again the middle of the month. But she looked bad—haggard, livid. I went to see her Wednesday morning, the 24th, without noting any special changes and without her complaining especially. I discussed a little cure with her and she told me that she was going to Tharandt next day in order to make arrangements for a holiday there in the summer.

" All that day and evening, according to her sister Nathalie, who was with her, she was in excellent spirits, even happy. She went to bed at the usual time and no one suspected anything alarming. Next morning the maid went to her room about seven o'clock and found the window open and the bed curtains thrown back, while her mistress —to her great horror—was half out of bed, dressed only in her night-gown, lying on her back across the bed, legs hanging down—dead— and already cold, with foam on her lips.

" She called Nathalie and others, who confirmed the aforesaid. Doctors were immediately summoned, I first of all. I had unfortunately already gone out and only got there later. But I found that death must have occurred in the middle of the night, at least five hours before she was discovered—and at all events it was a fairly rapid one, induced by a stroke—paralysis of the heart, such as I had always feared.

" The next thing to do, since any attempt at resuscitation was out of the question, was to place the lifeless body in a proper position and notify you and her relatives. I assumed responsibility for the first. However, since I didn't know where to reach you, but knew that Frau Schnorr had knowledge of Buelow's address at least, I first got in touch with her and learned Buelow's address, but heard that only Frau Buelow was in Munich. I thereupon telegraphed her, informing

her of your wife's death, and requesting her (assuming that she knew
your whereabouts) to notify you and send me your address. I also
received a telegraphic reply to the effect that she wasn't in a position
to advise you as you were not in Geneva and she didn't know where
you were at the time. But she sent me your Geneva address.

"I next communicated with your sister, Frau Brockhaus, and we
decided to wire you in Geneva, hoping that they would know your
forwarding address there. This is therefore the message that you
received in Marseilles which left you in doubt regarding the date.
True, I didn't mention the date, assuming that the date of the despatch
would also indicate the date of her death. Thereupon I received your
despatch from Marseilles.

"In the meantime I caused an autopsy to be made, with the permission of her relatives. This fully confirmed the diagnosis : enormous
enlargement and hardening of the heart, and as a result, sudden interruption of its activity during that fatal night. Possibly the deceased
had slept until midnight. Then she must have awakened in a terrible
fright owing to a feeling of suffocation, sprang out of bed and hurried
to the window to open it and get some air. But she scarcely had time
to get back into bed again, and no time to ring for help, as the position
in which she was found next morning showed that the fatal stroke
caught her as she was lying down, and she passed away after a short
unconscious struggle.

"The burial—simple, decent, dignified—took place at three o'clock
Sunday afternoon, with a large and creditable attendance. The weather
was beautiful—mild and sunny. Numerous palms and floral offerings
covered the remains and the coffin. Five carriages formed the cortège.
In the first were Pastor Pfeilschmidt of St. Anne's Church, Nathalie,
your sister Frau Brockhaus and myself and son Karl—of whom the
deceased was very fond and to whom she had given a pretty book last
Christmas—her adopted godson since the death of our unforgettable
Erich, her real godson. Friends followed in the other carriages :
Heine, Police Councillor Mueller, the sculptor Kietz, Kummer,
Concertmaster Schubert, Frau Tichatschek, Kriete, Haenel, etc.
Burial took place in St. Anne's Cemetery, the grave lined with sprigs
of green. As the long procession approached, buglers of the Royal
Orchestra played dignified funeral music, and a choral society sang a
chorale. The talented speaker spoke with dignity and not without
inspiration. This was followed by more sacred music and by the men's
chorus, and with the farewell greeting of the sun, with its promise of
spring, we strewed flowers—our last greeting—on the coffin now
resting in the lap of earth.

"I'm now awaiting your instructions as to the next steps. Minna
left a will and deposited it with the authorities. She named you and
her sister as her heirs. Did you know about the will ? and do you agree
with its dispositions ? If you wish a copy I'll send you one. The wishes

of the deceased will certainly be sacred to you. I close this report with the wish that it may ease your mind. Awaiting news from you, I am, etc."

Maintaining the fiction to the last, Minna's will named her " sister Nathalie " her sole heir. Even before the Penzing catastrophe Wagner had legally transferred to Minna all the Dresden household effects (his former Paris furniture) in order to prevent its attachment by his creditors. At first Nathalie continued to occupy Minna's flat, Wagner paying her an annual allowance of 120 *thalers*.[1] She soon married an artisan by the name of Bilz in Leisnig near Chemnitz, and when she became a widow a few years later, Wagner purchased quarters for her in an old ladies' home in Leisnig, where she passed the remainder of her days.

As it was unpleasant to think of his letters to Minna being in the possession of an outsider he requested their return from Nathalie, but the latter, naturally strongly influenced by Minna in her feelings towards him, feared that he would destroy these documents, so she accordingly kept back those letters that bore most important testimony to Minna's character and her tragic marriage, that is, the earliest ones from the Magdeburg and Koenigsberg days, and the most recent ones. She finally sent him 269, with the assurance that this was all she had. The remainder she sold later on to the English collector, the Honourable Mrs. Burrell, and they now form part of the copious Burrell Collection, which was purchased in 1931 by Mrs. Mary Louise Curtis Bok of Philadelphia (Mrs. Efrem Zimbalist), and donated by her to the Curtis Institute of Music in that city, where the 840 documents comprising the collection are now fully available to Wagnerian scholarship.

Minna's grave was always tended by Wagner's friends, and in 1920, when the lease to the burial plot expired, Siegfried Wagner renewed it for a further forty years. In a letter to Nathalie, now in the Burrell Collection, Cosima also stated that having " learned that the grave of her mother had been damaged by the weather " she had seen to its restoration.

After receipt of Pusinelli's telegram on 25th January Cosima

---

[1] These payments were continued by Cosima after Wagner's death as shown by certain letters of Cosima to Nathalie now in the Burrell Collection. (Exhibits 8A, B and C.)

wired Wagner immediately at the Grand Hotel, Marseilles :
" My soul hovers over you in this dark hour. Please send news
if possible." To which he replied on the 28th : " Letter received.
Back in Geneva to-morrow evening. Pusinelli's telegram received.
Everything arranged telegraphically and by letter. Not upset.
Am composed. Only need quiet. Yesterday's letter expresses my
mood. Will be with you shortly. Everything is clearing up.
Only stupefied, and greatly so."

Since it was impossible to find suitable quarters in the south of
France Wagner remained in Geneva for the time being.

At the beginning of March Cosima (with the consent of her
husband) arrived in Geneva for a visit of three weeks while
Buelow was away on a concert tour. Important decisions were
now made. Since the King, though still longing for his friend's
return, could not make up his mind to clear the way by dismissing
the persons indicated by Wagner, the latter decided to give up the
idea of Munich altogether and find a quiet harbourage somewhere
in Switzerland where he could work undisturbed. Cosima was
also to take permanent refuge here as soon as possible.

It was only on the last day of her visit and after having scoured
the whole of German Switzerland and practically given up all
hope (she had to be back in Munich on the first of April) that they
at last succeeded in finding what they were looking for in Triebschen near Lucerne. The house was unassuming from the outside,
but it lay on slightly rising ground on a tongue of land jutting
out into the Lake of Lucerne. Set in the midst of the fresh green
of young poplars it was truly a little natural gem, a haven of
peace and domestic happiness. No royal decree could have
provided a more glorious spot for the completion of Wagner's
work than this " Isle of the Blest " (as Nietzsche later called it)
remote from the world and surrounded by all the wonders that
Nature scatters here with such a lavish hand. Wagner went
enthusiastically to work to put the somewhat neglected house in
order, after which it was furnished with the usual extravagant
luxury, once more with the help of his Penzing dressmaker.

The King was naturally much distressed over this turn of
events. He implored his friend in vain to select one of the royal
hunting lodges or castles as residence. But Wagner stood firm.
He now longed for nothing but a final tranquillity of scene and

of spirit to go on with his work. The witches' cauldron at
Munich was not going to have power over him a second time.
Only the separation from his companion as a result of his residence
in Switzerland lay like a deep shadow over the new-found Asyl.
He therefore addressed himself to Buelow.

"Now my good Hans, a friendly word to you ! (he wrote on 8th
April 1866) I have taken a beautifully situated and spacious country
house for a year. I took it solely with the idea that you would occupy
it with me as long as possible. For only if you agree to this can I bear
to remain cut off from my comfortable circumstances. If you don't
comply with my wish, nothing would have any meaning for me and
I would fall into a restive state which would be fatal to my projects
for all time. Therefore listen, old man ! !

"My house has three floors. The lowest one with drawing-room,
etc., belongs to you and your family, the middle one to me, and the
top one to the children and servants. In this way we can live together
without disturbing one another in the least. My income, especially
since the death of my wife, is quite sufficient to keep a large family
supplied with all that is necessary with ease and dignity. You and your
wife and children and servants are therefore most cordially and warmly
invited to share this country place with me and to take my humble
hospitality as it comes. If you agree to my request, *you will be doing
the greatest, and in fact a unique, service towards my well-being and the
successful development of my work, and of my future activities.* You can
regulate things just as you like ; go back and forth just as it suits your
convenience—only from this spring on (and as long as in any way
possible) regard my house as your own, my household as your household, and as the domestic base of any future operations.

"Hans ! you *will* do as I ask ? Of course ! For you know that I
love you, and that—apart from my intoxicatingly wonderful relation
to this young King, nothing—nothing binds me to life so much as
you and yours. That—you know ! You have proved yourself loyalty
itself ; I should think so indeed ! Shouldn't we be one of the world's
wonders ? Johannistag ! Johannistag ! Hans Sachs—Hans Buelow !
So let's live together to our heart's content ! Farewell, and be infinitely
kind ; *alors, sire, vous faites bien.*"

This time, too, Buelow acceded to his friend's request. As he
was still detained in Munich he sent Cosima and the children on
to Triebschen, where they arrived on 12th May. In the meantime
Wagner awaited his beloved in an agony of longing. An ardent
love letter which he had written to Cosima in Munich failed to
reach her before her departure, and falling into Buelow's hands
was opened by him in the belief that it might contain a com-

munication which he ought to telegraph her at once. This letter
revealed to him the whole bitter truth! The stupendous lie of
the last two years suddenly stared him relentlessly in the face.

In addition, the Munich opposition, roused by the King's
surreptitious and impulsive visit to Triebschen in honour of
Wagner's birthday, raised another storm, and as Wagner was no
longer within reach, they poured out all the vials of their wrath
on his disciples and adherents, and on Buelow in particular, whose
family affairs (after Cosima's recent journey to Wagner) afforded
welcome points of attack and were dilated upon in public in the
most shocking manner. Therefore the only course open to the
doubly deceived man was to hand in his resignation in Munich
and then betake himself to Triebschen to get full information on
the matter, and above all to silence evil tongues.

" After ten years of a marriage that can hardly have been a bed of
roses for him (wrote Cornelius) Buelow now sees himself forced to go
to Lucerne and put the final decisive question to Cosima : do you wish
to belong to Wagner or me ? This is what hindered and stifled his
confidence in me, for it might have brought up for discussion questions
which he hardly dared put to himself. Now he sees the newspapers
discussing in the most scurrilous manner what he did not venture to
discuss with his friends. The only time he let anything slip was when
he remarked that Liszt had been very angry with his daughter for
going to Wagner. Well, to-day is the anxious day of decision at
Lucerne. I know what the answer will be. Cosima will stay with
Wagner, for so it must be so that her destiny may be fulfilled. And
Wagner's also."

And Cornelius proved to be right. Buelow consented to a
separation from Cosima. He made the great sacrifice as a friend
of the Master's art.

" What do you mean (asked Wagner) when you continually call
me ' Honoured Master ' ? I have so often appealed to your heart, and
yet you now say that the friend sacrifices himself to the Master ? May
I truly only lay claim to the friend's sacrifice in the quality of ' the
Master ' ? Am I to go on creating—or am I finished ? That's the
decision that hangs over my head. I too have made great sacrifices—
believe me, supreme sacrifices on the altar of friendship, so as to be
able to go on creating. Now it is inexorably marked out that this is
only further possible through a friend's sacrifice."

And for Buelow, faced by this bitter alternative of renouncing
his wife and giving Wagner the companion who was indispensable for the fulfilment of his artistic mission, there was no

hesitation. With true nobility of soul he unselfishly sacrificed his own happiness to the higher aim. But he stipulated that out of consideration for himself and the world's opinion Cosima should not remarry until a year had elapsed, and the intervening period should be spent with her father in Rome. But she and Wagner would not make this sacrifice for him—the only thing that could have rendered Buelow's future position in the service of the Wagnerian cause morally tenable. They were determined to shoulder all the consequences of their action courageously before the world, and " the friend " had to be sacrificed to their union. After Buelow had spent more than two months in Triebschen solely for the purpose of counteracting the Munich gossip, he left his family with Wagner and went off alone to Basle for the winter, having already previously tendered his resignation in Munich. He no longer had any hope, but he still felt there might be a way to avoid a scandal. He therefore sought to disguise the real situation even from his closest friends. Cosima often went to Basle to discuss various matters with him.

" Cosima in fact is actually in Basle at the moment (wrote Wagner to Mathilde Maier on 15th December 1866) and will only be back during the course of the week. On the whole she seems to be feeling fairly well, but her health is a curious matter, one is never quite free from worry about it. For the past nine years she has always seemed at the brink of an abyss and ready at any moment to make the plunge. Naturally such natures cannot be gauged by ordinary laws. They are a law unto themselves ! " ·

When the scandal broke out in the Munich Press, Buelow tried in vain to protect his wife's honour. On 30th May the *Volksbote* published a notice to the effect that

" Yesterday Wagner was sued here for notes amounting to no less than 26,000 *gulden*. Meanwhile ' Mme. Hans,' known to the public since last December by the significant name of ' Carrier Pigeon,' is with her ' friend ' (or what ?) in Lucerne, and she was also there during the visit of an exalted person."

Whereupon Buelow challenged Zander, the editor, to a duel. But as Zander refused to accept the challenge and also declined to retract the statement, Buelow inserted the following rather unfortunate declaration in the *Muenchener Neueste Nachrichten* on 1st June 1866 :

" The undersigned begs to inform that portion of the worthy public who have remarked the caresses with which a local paper (with all due respect—the *Volksbote*) has tried for some time past (but especially with increased ardour since 26th May of this year) to suffocate the writer and his family, that the editor of this ' organ ' stated to my duly qualified representative that in publishing the aforesaid compliments he wished only to stand up for his ' national ' principles.

" Without denying his authorship, he yet courageously and magnanimously declined to offer the satisfaction that is usual in such cases in civilized society. Only two alternatives remained open to the recipient of these favours if he wished to avoid the reproach of moral insolvency : he might follow the example of the director of the Royal Bavarian Court Theatre, Herr von Dingelstadt,[1] or seek redress by law. Neither of these methods appealed to the taste of the undersigned and tastes (as everyone knows) are not a subject for argument. The writer is therefore content to commend the ' national ' services of the editor of the *Volksbote* to the public recognition of his fellow citizens, since he, the ' foreigner,' is unfortunately not in a position either to reward them or to rate them understandingly at their full value.

" G. Hans von Buelow."

This mixture of irony and sham bravado was of course doomed to fall perfectly flat. Triebschen therefore resolved to take an extremely hazardous step, since it was feared that the current rumours might have a disastrous effect on the King's relations with Wagner. The gossip did indeed make a very painful impression on the monarch. " I cannot and will not believe (he said) that Wagner's relations with Frau von Buelow exceed the bounds of friendship. That would be horrible." All the same he sent for Wagner's manservant and questioned him minutely ; but the latter refused to give his master away. Then on 6th June 1866 Wagner demanded from the King a public *amende honorable* for Buelow.

" Depart from your royal silence at least in this one instance (he wrote). In a letter to my friend, Hans von Buelow (which you will give him permission to publish), give expression to your great satisfaction and at the same time to your royal indignation at the base treatment meted out to him and his wife by some newspapers in your capital. And in the event that you come to recognize that it is impossible for Buelow to remain longer in Munich, then through your royal attitude towards him and his wife (who has also proved herself such a devoted friend to you) give both at least the satisfaction they require in such an unheard-of situation so that they may not appear to have been dismissed ignominiously from the enjoyment of your hospitality.

" My King ! I implore the most magnanimous fulfilment of this

---

[1] Dingelstadt thrashed the editor of the comic paper *Jocus*.

plea, which I ask at the same time in the name of friendship. Since I must assume that my kind friend stands too far above the common degradations of life, to which we others are subjected, to be able to judge how to express yourself most effectively in the requested letter, I therefore beg to enclose (as a suggestion) a draft which I myself have prepared."

Cosima, who immediately hurried to Munich, seconded this request next day with the following appeal :

" For the first and last time, I plead to you for us. I fall on my knees before my King to plead in humility and distress for this letter to my husband, so that we may not leave in shame and ignominy the country in which we intended, and I think I might also say have done, nothing but good. My dear exalted Friend, if you make this public statement, then all will be well, then we can remain here, then we can build upon the ruins again, bravely and full of encouragement, as though nothing had happened. Otherwise we must go hence, reviled and abandoned, and rob Him of the only friends who could offer Him no more than their own existence, with repute and fame, and who will now have to build these up again elsewhere in order to be able to offer Him an abode.

" My most august friend ! you who came into our lives like a divine apparition, O do not allow us, *the innocent ones*, to be driven out. Your royal word alone can restore our tarnished honour. It can do so absolutely ; everything will vanish before it. . . . Do write my husband the royal letter ! If this is possible, then I shall persuade my husband that we should return home. Otherwise, how could we remain in a city where they could treat us as criminals. *How could my husband carry on his work in a city in which his wife's honour has been besmirched ?* My royal Lord ! I have three children, *to whom it is my duty to transmit their father's honourable name unstained.*[1] For the sake of these children, that they may not one day revile my love for the Friend, I implore you, my most exalted friend, to write this letter.

" If the letter is possible, I will cheerfully bear all earthly trials in return for such happiness. If it is impossible, then I will take leave of my kind friend, kiss his royal hand in humility and gratitude, implore God's blessing on his august head, and go away with my noble and perhaps mortally wounded husband to some place where the weary and innocent may find rest and respect."

This appeal, so skilfully worded to play on the King's sympathies, did not fail in its effect. Firmly convinced of the flimsiness of the rumours, he made the desired declaration without any hesitancy. His letter to Buelow—a precise copy of Wagner's draft—read as follows :

---

[1] Wagner was the father of her third child (Isolde) !

" After having induced you to give up your post in Berlin a year and a half ago in return for the very slight advantages that I was able to offer you at the time, through my desire to have you work side by side with the Master Richard Wagner in Munich towards the realization of the latter's noble artistic aims, which do such honour to the German spirit, nothing could be more painful to me than to see that by the hopes I placed in you I have already brought persecutions upon you, and then calumnies and insults to your honour, which have been particularly hateful in the very recent past, on the part of certain public journals in Munich ; and which I can well understand have made you very indignant.

" Since I have come to know your most disinterested and honourable attitude, and the Munich public your incomparable artistic achievements ; since furthermore *I have had the opportunity of becoming thoroughly acquainted with the noble and high-minded character of your esteemed wife,* who with the most sympathetic solicitude comforted and supported her father's friend, her husband's ideal, it rests with me to get to the bottom of those inexplicable criminal public calumnies so that having arrived at a clear understanding of the shameful proceedings I may bring the offenders to justice with the most pitiless severity.

" Should this assurance not suffice to render your sufferings—if not forgettable—at least bearable, in consideration of the high aims that are at stake, and should I be unable to persuade you (as I sincerely hope to do) to hold out, to retain your post for the present, I unfortunately have no other recourse (apart from securing justice for you) than to give special expression to that recognition to which I desire to bear witness to-day through this letter, and through the sincerest expression of my genuine respect for you and your honoured wife. A thousand hearty greetings from a loyal friend to the dear inmates of cosy Triebschen."

Even in the face of the King's letter, which Buelow immediately released to the Munich Press, the *Volksbote* refused to retract a single word of its former statements ! One can well imagine in what a painful situation the wilfully deluded King would be placed if the rumours he had stigmatized as slanders should prove to be true after all ! Cosima had ventured to play a dangerous game. She had won a passing victory which was to change all too soon into a defeat fraught with heavy consequences.

The Munich scandalmongers unexpectedly found a welcome witness for the prosecution in the person of Malwine Schnorr, Wagner's much-lauded Isolde. She had moved to Munich in March 1866, where she drew a pension of 2,000 *gulden* from the King. She had been an intimate friend of Cosima's ever since the " Tristan " days, when their common admiration for the

Master had quickly brought the two together. But when she learned by accident of Cosima's true relation to Wagner she was seized by wild jealousy as she herself had had serious designs on him since the death of her husband. In order to destroy her rival she now threatened all sorts of painful revelations. Details of this hitherto unsuspected romance are revealed in two of Wagner's letters, one addressed to his friend and fellow revolutionary, August Röckel, and the other to the unfortunate Malwine herself.

"I'm in for another hair-raising adventure of the kind that can only happen to me! (he wrote Röckel on 22nd November). Frau Schnorr is at the point of going completely out of her mind and doing no end of mischief. Just listen to this!

"It seems this unfortunate woman recently went quite dotty after the death of her husband, at least so we heard in Munich. She threw out mysterious hints when writing to me about his death, which at once gave me the idea that my friend's widow expected me to marry her, particularly as I recalled a certain look of hers when I was in Dresden for the funeral. This is why I was very reserved towards her and in my letters to her. As I had no dealings with any of the King's secretaries after my departure, Frau von Buelow (who still kept in touch with them) managed to put through the pension of 2,000 *gulden* which the King had promised me he would grant her. Since then she has shown herself so sympathetic and friendly to our friend that the latter counted her among the very few in whom she could frankly confide in every way.

"After Buelow's family had come to live with me for the winter she still continued to be a devoted friend to us all. Then I learned that a certain Fräulein Isidore von Reutter of Dresden, a voice pupil of hers, over whose Amazonian figure and other somewhat grotesque peculiarities she often poked fun in a good-natured way with Frau von Buelow, had followed her to Munich.

"This person who (as Frau Schnorr herself told me) was not in very good odour with her parents on account of her lying proclivities and other bad characteristics, finally managed to install herself in her teacher's home. If we had reason to remark the strange, somewhat provincial familiarity with which Frau Schnorr wrote of the very difficult and delicate relations with the King as well as my own strictly family affairs, it would seem that these two women also discussed these matters by the hour between themselves in an exceedingly free and easy manner.

"Reutter, a low-down, ignorant person, heard all sorts of things from Frau Schnorr about me and the King as well as about Frau von Buelow, etc., out of which she proceeded in her way to weave the most fantastic and shameless intrigue. From statements and facts that had all originated with us (for example, regarding certain powers

possessed by unusual individuals) she spun a web in testimony thereof
with the over-excitable Schnorr, which to begin with was slanted to the
critical mental quirk of this woman, who for instance writes letters to
her dead husband every night and receives answers from him in her
dreams. Just because I had once spoken to my friends with consideration and respect of an extraordinary woman who had fascinated me as
a fortune-teller and set me thinking, she was firmly convinced that if
she presented herself as a medium I would readily fall under her spell.

" As regards Frau von Buelow, she knew that during her last stay
in Munich when Frau Schnorr was constantly with her, she was
suffering acutely and for several days was anxiously awaiting an
important letter from me (which we heard later had been lying all the
time with my Munich servants), from which she concluded that Frau
von Buelow was thrusting herself on me, etc. In short, when things
got this far, she represented herself to poor Schnorr as being visited
by the spirit of the latter's dead husband (who for secret reasons was
unable to appear to his widow) in order to reveal to the latter in this
way the messages and wishes which he deemed necessary for the
salvation of his soul.

" On 2nd November I received a letter from Frau Schnorr in which
she informed me that she must see me in order to communicate to me
the revelations made to her by her heaven-appointed guardian angel
in the person of Isidore von Reutter, and demand that these supernatural orders be executed with all possible speed. Without waiting
for an answer, a few days later she announced by telegram her arrival
in Lindau.

" My first impulse was to take to flight immediately so as to keep
out of the way of this lunatic, but Frau von Buelow, who feels called
upon to sacrifice herself in the noblest way to ensure my undisturbed
quiet for the completion of my ' Meistersinger,' persuaded me to stay
and promised to divert the storm from me in her solicitous way. And
so the two of them (Schnorr and Reutter) arrived here on Saturday a
week ago ; were received by Cosima and left a voluminous document
for my perusal before the desired interview ! This represented Reutter's
notes regarding her supernatural visitations and the conversations held
on these occasions with the spirit of Schnorr. Passing through several
phases to a crescendo, the spirit's directions finally amounted candidly
to this : Isidore von Reutter was ordained to be the wife of the King
of Bavaria, and I was to arrange the matter since I could do anything
with the King, even to making him fall in love with Isidore von
Reutter ! The first thing was for me to arrange immediately a meeting
between Fräulein von Reutter and the King. Otherwise the instructions contained absolutely nothing, but what this person had heard
from Frau Schnorr was already on foot, as far as I am concerned.
Prince Hohenlohe had also been recommended by mistake by the
spirit, the parties being ignorant of my change of sentiment towards him.

" So I went down to the women thinking to meet a crazy visionary of the silliest kind. But the first glimpse of poor Schnorr warned me to take the utmost precaution. I realized at once from her looks and manner that she was on the verge of complete insanity. I therefore adopted a mild and conciliatory attitude, agreeing in substance, but in fact pointing out that I was already doing everything advised by the spirit ! During dinner I studied Isidore von Reutter and soon came to the conclusion that I had to do with a perfectly stupid vulgar *intrigante*. Frau Schnorr declared that she wished to stay till I was in a fit condition (for she thought me looking ill) to hear the most terrible, but at the same time comforting, of her communications. What she meant by the word comfort I realized by an indescribably insane amorous look she gave me. Next day Frau von Buelow called on the two ladies at the hotel and delivered a letter from me to Schnorr, in which I informed her that she must get rid of Isidore von Reutter at once if I were to have anything more to do with her. At all events my house was closed to this impostor from that moment on.

" This unhappy woman now vented all her fury on Frau von Buelow, whom she warned not to come between me and herself unless she wished to be crushed. Then she came to see me by herself, but exhibited the most imperturbable gentleness, treating me entirely as a misguided and deluded person whom it was her mission to save. Dinner provided an interruption. After dinner, excusing myself for half an hour, I came to the conclusion that I am not in the world to be the plaything of any kind of lunatic. I wrote a few lines saying that I was unable to associate with her any longer on these terms, sent it to her by the servant, and left the house.

" The fresh air restored my sense of balance and gave me strength to be patient. I was ashamed of myself and turned to go home when I met Frau Schnorr on the way, who considered my return had been directed by a higher power ; and now walked about with me for an hour while she told me all the details of her husband's death, which naturally moved me very deeply, although several times I was upset and impelled to be cautious by stray comments and evil constructions made obviously with shamefully calculated intent. With the cunning tactics peculiar to the insane she had realized from my whole demeanour that she couldn't possibly make any overtures to me at that moment. Indeed she perhaps saw that she must give up this idea altogether ; for she had already complained to Frau von Buelow of a total lack of responsiveness on my part. In short, she now resolved to set me at rest once for all on this point by telling me that her husband's spirit did not wish her to marry again.

" When we reached home she gave me an illegible note the deceased had written me on his deathbed. She saw how deeply affected I was by this, let matters go at that, and departed in order to look after her friend who (as she said) was in the throes of the greatest anguish.

Next day I received a tender letter from her in which she expressed herself as satisfied with the results of the day before and voiced the conviction that the scales would soon fall from my eyes, that I would recognize my true heaven-sent friend, and would hasten to her (in Munich) whom I had now repulsed because a false friend had come between us, in order to beg from her all the communications that I now disdained. She threatened to crush Frau von Buelow. The latter wrote her kindly and affectionately to Munich, but added my remark that after perusing Schnorr's letter—which she had left with me—I had decided to have nothing to do with her for six months and to answer no further communications from her. Now the crazy lunatic gave vent to furious imprecations. Once more she threatened to pursue Frau von Buelow to the bitter end. This impelled me to write her again, setting forth definitely the consequences of her folly."

The letter to Frau Schnorr to which he referred read as follows :

"Dear widow of my deceased friend! Most esteemed fellow-artist ! These you are to me, dear Malwine, and on these two titles is based our intimate friendship which in a profoundly affecting moment of our artistic collaboration led to the adoption of the brotherly and sisterly *Du* (Thou).

"You recently made some communications to me about my deceased friend and his death, which deeply moved me, and again showed very definitely and in a supreme degree the link there is between us. Since then it has become clear to me through the letter you left for me here that you regarded these communications and their effect on me not as the motive of your visit but as a means to an end. From the same letter I also saw this motive was to destroy my confidence in Cosima. You had no cause to do this before, but discovered one recently when Fräulein Isidore von Reutter convinced you that she had been appointed by God to be the guardian angel, and even the wife, of the King of Bavaria. The way to achieve this destiny required first of all that you should replace Frau von Buelow, that is, win my confidence so as to be empowered to correspond personally with the King of Bavaria. I once delegated this task to our friend for the simple reason that I no longer could have any intercourse with the individuals of the King's Cabinet, whereas she was still able to maintain her relations with them for a long time. By this means it was possible for her to relieve my pressing anxiety about my friends when I could not address myself to the King directly, and so she succeeded, for instance, in obtaining a gratuity for Heinrich Porges and a pension of 2,000 *gulden* for you, and that under exceptionally difficult circumstances. Furthermore, at a time when I deemed it highly imperative for me to keep silence, she was able to satisfy the King's urgent demands for news of me and the state of my health.

"This position, of which Fräulein von Reutter—through her lack

of education—hasn't the faintest conception, she now desires to fill in
order (to speak plainly) to exploit it to further her marriage with the
Bavarian King. According to documents thoughtlessly left in my
hands, I'm to induce the King to fall in love with Fräulein von
Reutter. Since I protested against this, I'm threatened with pressure
which will force me to obey. The nature of this pressure I have
discovered from your recent communications to Frau von Buelow.
You propose to accuse her of having illicit relations with me and to
denounce her first of all to her husband. I myself am at the mercy of
your discretion since it's your idea at the moment to admonish me as
a ' Tannhäuser and miserable sinner.'

" Hereupon, and after taking due cognisance of this whole business,
I first decided simply to avoid all contact with you ; that is to say, to
keep unsullied my former sentiments towards you and the memory of
the deceased *so basely tarnished* by this affair. But finding, however,
that this might give rise to misunderstandings, I have recourse to this
one and final communication to you.

" Accordingly I call to you once more ! *Rid yourself at once of this
impostor!* As long as you associate with this lady I can—as I already
told you very definitely here—have no further intercourse with you.
If you fail to do this you must take the consequences of your own
folly. Herr von Buelow will give you the rebuke you merit and you'll
have to swallow it. And now you have the treachery and insolence to
repulse a noble, self-sacrificing friend of whom you know nothing
but what she herself has innocently confided to you, or what you have
gathered from gossiping tongues. I for my part shall only think of
you as one who traded on my tenderest and most sacred feelings with
an intention which I must regard as reprehensible even towards
yourself, if I didn't make allowances for your illness and at the same
time realize that you, too, are deceived.

" I regard Isidore von Reutter, however, as a criminal and first and
foremost towards you. With respect to her behaviour towards Frau
von Buelow and myself, I recognize her, however, as such a fitting tool
for the intrigues of my well-known enemies that I don't hesitate to
treat her straightaway and solely as such. It would be a very bad sign
of my inability to learn by experience if I should overlook the fact
that a scandal would be highly welcome to our enemies, and particularly now when it's a question of who's to come out on top—and
a scandal launched through the instrumentality of such an apparently
intimate friend of ours, as your attitude towards us must already make
you seem to the world of Munich.

" If you are therefore moved to stage any such mad demonstration
as you fairly openly threaten to do, then our enemies and those of the
King will have attained their ultimate aim. A new scandal will only
expose the King to libellous vexations and unpleasantnesses in the
very entourage that he himself brought to Munich. His relations with

JUDITH GAUTIER IN 1875

PHOTOGRAPH OF THE PORTRAIT BY C. WILLICH, COMMISSIONED BY WESENDONC:
AS A PRESENT FOR HIS WIFE.   THIS HAS NEVER BEFORE BEEN REPRODUCEL

me will be made impossible,' and the results of it all, for us as for him, will be easy to calculate. If you are then so crazy, in your presumptuous belief that you are impelled by God, as to proceed to destroy in this way the peace so hardly won, then understand that in future I can only view you too as a tool of my enemies, and am definitely decided to act accordingly.

" For *you* there is only one way to avoid this disgraceful attitude towards me : recognize your own effrontery, your absolutely depraved presumption, humble yourself to be what you are and what you can only be. Further, cast off at once the temptress whom—should you refuse—I can from now on only treat in the most rigorous way. Do this and my whole heart is with you. Moreover, this is the last communication from your old friend."

In another letter to Röckel he described the measures to be taken against the Munich conspirators.

" Cosima left last Monday to join her husband at Basle (he wrote). Buelow, who knows Isidore von Reutter's father, is writing the latter to persuade him to fetch his daughter from Munich. Besides, both are consulting the lawyer Gotthelf to tell him our conjectures and if necessary authorize him to put the matter in the hands of the police. Gotthelf has also been sent a copy of Reutter's scandalous vision (the original of which was left with me) in which she is exhorted to marry the King.

" You know enough now, old chap, to understand what I'm asking of you. Go and see Frau Schnorr and try to save what little sense she has left. Refer to my last letter to her in which I warned her of the serious measures I propose to take in my own defence if she stirs up a scandal and doesn't get rid of Reutter at once.

" Judging by her latest announcements, she seems determined to go to the craziest lengths in order to shake off her rival (as she believes). So you have a job on your hands. Therefore see Gotthelf without delay. It looks to me as if on the one hand it were a case for the doctor, and on the other for the police. See what a pretty mess I'm in ! And all the time I'm supposed to be—composing ! So see what sort of a philanthropist you can be. Let me know the cost of the excursion ! I really don't know a soul but you in whom I can really confide ! "

It will be seen that Wagner left no stone unturned to render these dangerous women in Munich innocuous. But Frau Schnorr was by no means mad, as Wagner maintained. She was simply crazy with jealousy, and her passion, under the influence of her cunning friend, drove her to employ the romantic methods that he described. That these failed was due to the fact that her story found no credence in the one quarter that mattered, that is to say, with the King. For the time being, therefore, Malwine had to deny herself revenge.

But when Cosima returned to Munich the following winter Frau Schnorr's hatred of her favoured rival flamed up again and she launched into insults which caused Wagner to write to the King's Cabinet Secretariat on 18th November 1867 and demand that she be turned out of Munich. When this was not done he repeated his demand on 30th November, threatening that he would not set foot in the town again until the offender was removed. This time his request was granted, and Frau Schnorr was told to leave Munich or run the risk of losing her pension. She then moved to Hamburg.

King Ludwig's visit to Triebschen and the political events of the year 1866 finally brought about the fall of Wagner's enemies in the Bavarian Cabinet. Munich now became habitable again for him and his adherents, in particular Buelow. But it took a long struggle—painful for all concerned—before the latter could be persuaded to go back to the " Munich Inferno." To begin with, Wagner pictured to his friend the King the bitter suffering imposed on his friends, the Buelows, in Munich. In so doing he again was silent on the real reason, the break up of their marriage !

" Buelow managed to break away from his distasteful but still absorbing activities in Basle and to triumph sufficiently over his ill health to spend a few days with his family in Triebschen in order to recuperate (he wrote his royal friend). It broke my heart to see him. He is absolutely unrecognizable. He suffers from daily attacks of fever that are not amenable to treatment. In sheer desperation he tried through uninterrupted activity, even in the most restricted sphere, to hold his own against his illness. Yet I can see that he will soon have to give up the struggle. And he has every reason to do so.

" He looks back on a frustrated life and career. He sees his achievements—the more extraordinary they were—rewarded with the complete triumph of his enemies and—because this is not sufficient for his humiliation—he must again see his honour, in the honour of his wife, dragged through the mire. If he asks himself why this misery must come upon him, then the answer must be : because of his loyalty and friendship for me, and this in turn because of the love of the most noble friend for a person who cannot even look to this love to safeguard him from the insults and derision that are meted out to him.

" This cannot fail to have ill effects on the delicate health of his wife. Even if a superhuman, steadfast faith supports her intellectually, her health is disintegrating. She is unable to sleep, now on the eve of her confinement[1], and her husband is unable to care for her at home and must therefore delegate this task to his—in this respect—more fortunate friend."

Wagner therefore demanded from the King as essential for Buelow's return to Munich :

(a) A distinguished order from the King.

(b) Buelow's appointment as director of the projected Academy of Music.

(c) Buelow's appointment as Court conductor in " extraordinary service," with the necessary authority in the theatre.

Lastly he requested the King to send a duly delegated official to Buelow in Basle or Triebschen for the purpose of completing the negotiations with him. The King agreed to everything and entrusted arrangements to his Court Secretary Düfflip. First of all the latter had an interview with Wagner in Triebschen which resulted in complete agreement, but the outcome of which later met with a blunt rejection on the part of Buelow. In fact, Buelow's characterization of the offer as beneath the dignity " of a Prussian nobleman " created a very unpleasant incident.

" Buelow is ruined in health, broken in spirit (Wagner wrote the King). May those who have brought this upon him be called to account ! One can't argue with him. He's coming to see me on Sunday. I'm still hoping to save him, and us. In these distressing circumstances, treat the victimized friend as your royal heart dictates ! Only be good enough to remember that here you have to do with shattered, hypersensitive intellectual and emotional forces and not with unwillingness and insubordination."

" Buelow is causing me unheard-of trouble (he continued on 20th February 1867). It was extremely indulgent and gracious of you not to let yourself be misled by his crazy behaviour. For me it was not so easy, and I had already made up my mind to break with him completely—which naturally would have had serious consequences. He arrived here at last on Sunday the 17th to smooth matters over with his wife, who naturally was no less exasperated by the ' Prussian nobleman.' He arrived just on the day when she gave birth to a fine daughter. The mother—our poor, unselfish friend—is now (I hope) out of danger. The poor, unhappy Hans also seems to have calmed down somewhat. He has been too long without the great and always clarifying and illuminating influence of his wife. A great misfortune has befallen your loyal subjects. One cannot shut one's eyes to this

[1] Wagner's second daughter Eva.

fact. And if we get over it, that will be saying a great deal. All at once Buelow is filled with a positive abhorrence of Munich, and if *we* surmount it, then the miracle will really only be due to our love for the most marvellous Lord of our life. I still hope that your wishes may be fulfilled. If we fail in this, then much will be ruined."

Wagner was in Munich from the 9th to the 18th March—the first time since his banishment. The visit was disappointing in so far that the King only received him in audience twice during the entire period, and he had to recognize anew that he was unable to work in the continuous excitement and tension of the Munich atmosphere. Nevertheless after Buelow had at last accepted the proffered post and had come to Munich for the final negotiations, Semper's projected festival theatre seemed to be an assured fact as well as the school of music, the model performances of " Lohengrin " and " Tannhäuser," and the première of " Meistersinger."

But Wagner had scarcely arrived in Triebschen when he received an alarming letter from Röckel telling him of new difficulties that had arisen, this time on the part of Düfflip, who was still nursing a grievance over his bout with Buelow in Basle and the " Prussian nobleman " incident. Wagner therefore left for Munich at once and requested an audience with the King. Düfflip apologized; the decree necessary for Buelow's recall was immediately signed by the King, and Wagner went personally to Basle to deliver it to Buelow and obtain the latter's definite promise to take over the Munich post on 15th April. That this was by no means a simple matter is shown by Wagner's complaint to Mathilde Maier on 17th November 1867.

" Munich and the situation there, as such, are no longer capable of agitating me to any extent, but the effect is still much the same owing to Buelow's unfortunate character. Everything is not yet as it can, and will, be. I would have patience enough myself if I didn't have to put up with Buelow's angry tirades over the situation and his taunts that we have again persuaded him to his ruin ; which of course is sheer tommy-rot. So it's all up with my patience in every direction."

Buelow returned to Munich the middle of April 1867 as special Court conductor " in extraordinary service," and Director Designate of the Academy of Music. The award at the same time of the Grand Cross of the Order of St. Michael, first class, served as *amende honorable*.

This turn of affairs now cried out for a settlement of the Wagner-Buelow marital tangle. In order not to stir up things again and attract notice, Cosima had no other alternative at first than to agree to a separation from Wagner, not only because of the King but also in order not to jeopardize the position they had regained after such bitter struggles. " Cosima is in perfect accord with your wishes and arrangements (Wagner wrote Buelow on 21st March 1867). She will come and help you move to Munich as, and when, you wish."

On 16th April came the parting in Triebschen. While *en route* Cosima sent the following eloquent message to her lonely friend :

> *Es ist bestimmt in Gottes Rath*
> *Dass man vom Liebsten, das man hat*
> *Muss scheiden.*
>
> *Meisterin.*[1]

" I have never been so sad in my whole life as I am now ! (wrote Wagner in Cosima's Brown Book on the receipt of this parting greeting). How easy it is to say it, and how inexpressible it is ! I walked home and collapsed with fatigue. A short, leaden sleep that often brings out a cold brought out all the misery of my life, as it were from the profoundest depths of my soul. I long for a severe illness and death. I've reached the end of my tether. I can't take anything more. O, if there could only be an end to it all—an end ! To-day she left me ! What this parting means ! What's the good of seeing one another again ! The parting remains. It is misery ! "

In Munich the Buelows took a large flat in the Arcostrasse, in which two rooms were reserved for Wagner's use. He often had to be in Munich in connection with the model performances planned for his works and had already definitely given up his house in the Briennerstrasse when he removed to Triebschen. His letter to Buelow of 10th September 1867 shows his spiritual attitude to his young friend and the basis on which they had apparently agreed as the only possible *modus vivendi* for the three— an arrangement in which Buelow sacrificed his own wife to his friend, since she was indispensable to him for his creative work.

" Everything that has to do with you touches and moves me, from the very beginning down to these sad days in which the essence of our relationship in life is to be tested in the deadliest earnest. Our Munich relationship was based on the expectation that art would clarify the situation. That which divided us was to hold us together, that which

[1] " It is certainly God's decree that we must part from the one we love most."

we sacrificed was to enrich us. You often moved me deeply and sincerely when we were at the very highest pitch of our task. Then everything was clear and comprehensible to you also. Now we have lost this *rapport*. What enthusiasm alone illumined for us in a flash should now come to us in a quiet clear light—confidently and distinctly —and a sensible plan of action be drawn up for the essentially necessary. . . . Do you believe in friendship and a master's love ? If I can only still bring real joy to you ! Let's hope so ! "

The children accompanied Cosima to Munich. Only the baby Eva (just two months old) remained behind with Wagner, under Vrenli's care.

" The most glorious of all is Evechen (he wrote), who has made my lonely house wonderfully cheerful and pleasant during her first year of life."

" How often (wrote Vrenli) he used to come up to the top floor to pay little Evechen a visit. He also had her brought down to him every morning after breakfast, dressed in a pink satin frock. Then he would play over some little thing for her, and laugh heartily when the child beat time to the music."

When Wagner was away from home, as was frequently the case during the rehearsals for the Munich première of " Meistersinger " (this first fruit of his secluded life in Triebschen) all his letters to the faithful Vrenli contained expressions of touching anxiety about the child's welfare.

When in Munich he always stopped with the Buelows, and Cosima again surrounded him (as during the " Tristan " period) with an atmosphere of loving care and tried to shield him from annoyances and interruptions. Many people, especially his old friends, took pique at this " tutelage," which led to some unpleasant incidents. It was also the cause of a little tiff with his favourite niece, Franziska Ritter, who had come to Munich for the " Meistersinger," but was unable to see her uncle because Cosima refused to admit her. In the following hitherto unpublished letter Wagner sought to come to Cosima's defence.

" Your letter, which after all was only meant to tell me how pitiable I appear to all those who truly love me and from whom I am impenetrably cut off, showed me again how thoughtlessly and stupidly people judge things which they know only by hearsay (he wrote her on 10th July 1868).

" I was sorry to hear in what way Buelow's and my wish to bring you to Munich had been dashed. In looking into the matter carefully

I can only see that acting upon the letter of an extremely officious person (young Michalowitsch) your husband despatched an incredible letter to Buelow, whereupon the latter had no other recourse than silence. Unfortunately Liszt also told me when he last came to see me in the autumn that Sascha was one of those on whom friendly favours do not sit lightly. The arrival of you both in Munich was now doubly welcome to me. Why didn't you let me know the time you were coming to see me? I expected this of you. It's difficult to find me in by chance on such days. Now I see what the reason was. It pleases my friends to pity me as a prisoner. I advise those who wish to maintain this attitude to get in touch with Frau Schnorr.

" And now to have to answer *you* on such a matter makes me very sorry indeed. I am very fond of you. I wouldn't have bothered to write anyone else. I was looking forward to seeing you and straightening out your misunderstanding with Buelow. But I learn on the contrary that it must be surpassingly sweet to nurse a powerful hatred, no matter how silly it may be!

" So now I have nothing further to say to you except to warn you once more not to be influenced by gossip and silly criticism if we are to go on being friends. For it isn't only that I've had my fill of nonsense but I can't, simply can't, take it any more under any circumstances. My patience is no longer up to it. How foolishly you spoilt the poor ' Meistersinger ' for yourself this time! You childish person! Good-bye and be good."

The day of the " Meistersinger " première (21st June 1868) was the supreme climax of Wagner's artistic career to date in so far as pure externals were concerned. During the performance he occupied a seat in the Royal box alongside the King, and when the enthusiasm of the public became ever more fervent and insistent, he acknowledged the ovation from this privileged position, in response to a sign from the King. This little incident, which was contrary to all Court etiquette, caused a terrific sensation. The King undoubtedly wished to afford the composer this public satisfaction for the ignominious treatment accorded him in the preceding years. But it proved a fatal kindness. For next day when the jubilant Wagner returned to Triebschen the Munich Press played the full stream of its sarcasm on the new work that was unique in the history of art. The waves of hatred and envy surged forth again and burst at the same time over the devoted pilot of the Wagnerian bark : Hans von Buelow. The newspapers openly cast in his teeth that he owed his influential Munich post to " his complaisance as a husband " and that

" the political machinations of the Wagner clique had their mouthpiece in Buelow's wife during Wagner's absence."

These rumours also found their way to the King. With his faith still unshaken he nevertheless considered it his duty to send Cosima the following warning.

" As a true friend, I felt obliged two years ago to communicate to you the contents of Frau Schnorr's letter in which she had the impertinence to throw out the most shameless slanders against you and our friend. As a true friend, I feel that I cannot now conceal from you that I have learned from a most reliable source that a man whom Wagner always looked upon as a faithful and upright friend has been spreading the same contemptible slanders against you and our friend. This man is Röckel. You will appreciate how hard it was for me to tell you this, but feeling towards you as I do, I should always have had to reproach myself if I hadn't informed you of it. I beg you to beware of this person and warn our friend against him, too.

" O this contemptible calumny ! You can imagine how it pains the faithful Parsifal to see his loyal friends perpetually exposed to treachery and malice. O humanity ! The false friends ! The world takes pleasure in sullying the radiant and dragging the noble in the dust. But fear not, there are still wonderful hearts that respond to the sublime, the marvellous. How true are Schiller's words ! Do not fear your enemies —they will prove powerless, their weapons will break on the firm, steadfast trust of the King, your friend.

" Accept my kindest regards and rest assured that my love for you and our friend is boundless. It is impervious to calumny."

This vow of loyalty on the King's part was not without its tragic side. It came just at a moment when Fate decided against him and revealed to all the world the reality he had hitherto refused to believe. Wagner recognized from the Munich reaction that he could have nothing more to do with the " Munich Inferno " and that his only course was to flee to the solitude of Triebschen to complete his work. Yet he could only find the necessary concentration and tranquillity if his companion were permanently at his side. He was therefore firmly resolved to put an end to the self-banishment, the unendurable separation from the woman he loved, which had been his miserable lot for two years.

The fateful decision was reached during a pleasure trip to Italy which they made together. On 3rd October Cosima wrote Buelow from Faido that she had decided to link her life permanently with that of Wagner. She and the children then returned to Munich in order to persuade her husband to grant her a divorce. Buelow was willing to do so, in principle. But he stipulated that she join her stepsister Claire Charnace in the south of France, or her father in Rome. Wagner raised very vigorous objections to this. Since he could not intervene personally in the Munich negotiations he asked Countess Charnace to go there and use her influence. But this led to a sharp quarrel with Cosima, who telegraphed him that

" Wilful interference makes life unbearable. Acutely bitter over play with the peace of mind of a weary person. Greatest unpleasantness through Claire's arrival. Greatest sorrow through refusal to go to Rome."

Cosima then left Buelow's house and moved to the Mrazeks', Wagner's servants. Wagner, who in his correspondence with the King had frequently tried to prepare him by giving out discreet hints regarding the impending change, took an open stand for Buelow in his letter of 18th October.

" Necessary decisions, the motives for which do not concern the superficial world, will apparently put Buelow in the position of recognizing that his one mission in life, his only satisfaction, is the most loyal performance of the professional duties delegated to him. May this not be made difficult for him in any way ! He has had to bear a heavy, an unheard-of burden. His only recourse has been a restless activity which has really astonished the world.

" Without any reserve, I publicly declare him to be one of the most significant, indeed the most sensitive, musicians of to-day. No one can surpass him—as a real musician—in his work at the school of music, and his influence on musical education will be beneficial in the extreme. As an orchestral conductor I do not know his equal. In my opinion this testimonial that I will make before all the world should carry weight.

" I fear that Buelow will soon be all alone and he will need protection from ignominious attacks. I appeal to you, my noble friend, to accord him this protection, as the only one competent to do so ! If Buelow has the strength to continue his artistic activities it will be a fortunate thing. God grant that he may not be robbed of this last succour by being delivered over to his enemies and jealous rivals. But I know humanity and I fear the worst. If you, dearest friend, should fail to give him your powerful protection, then I too must lose all heart and probably must come to the conclusion that from now on I too will need no further protection."

At the beginning of November Wagner requested an audience with the King, fully determined to reveal to the latter the real truth of his relationship with the Buelows. But Ludwig, deeply annoyed by the whole affair and the Munich gossip, which amounted to open *lèse majesté*, refused any personal contact with him. Since Cosima was also unable to reach any definite agreement with Buelow, who on Liszt's account wished to await the latter's impending arrival, she left in all secrecy (and this time for good) for Triebschen on 16th November, taking with her Wagner's two children, Isolde and Eva. Now she was irrevocably decided to defy all the world, regardless of other duties and obligations, and dedicate herself to the life task that destiny had cut out for her. Thus the long-overdue settlement of the Buelow-Wagner domestic tangle, which had been so frequently postponed, found an unexpectedly abrupt solution. Public scandal could no longer be avoided, and the Munich muckrakers and calumniators had a field day.

The King was profoundly shaken. He was never able to overcome fully the shock of disappointment over his dearest friends, the feeling that they had wilfully deceived him for years. Owing to his abnormal tendencies he was doubly sensitive with regard to friendships, and he now felt that Wagner had basely betrayed him. Again and again he showed ill-concealed jealousy. In addition his almost morbidly developed majesty-complex was painfully affected by these public disclosures, for after all, he had pledged himself for Cosima's honour in his personal letter to Buelow. He never received Cosima again and did not cross the threshold of Wahnfried when he was in Bayreuth in 1876. But in the case of the revered Master, enthusiasm for the cause triumphed in the end in spite of personal discords, which often caused long interruptions in their relations. In times of need he continued to lend a helping hand, and always remained true to his youthful vow to be the protector of Wagnerian art. But from then on he avoided Wagner the man whenever possible.

Meanwhile the faithful Buelow had been placed in a very anomalous position through Cosima's secret flight from Munich. In the first flood of emotion on receiving her letter from northern Italy with the announcement that she had definitely left him, Buelow was prompted to expiate his friend's treachery with a revolver. But in a calmer appraisal of the situation his impulse broke down before the realization that he could not separate the man from the revered master before whom he stood defenceless.

Cosima was fully cognizant of her own guilt as far as Buelow was concerned, and suffered intensely from the realization that she was bringing such pain and sorrow upon him. But her mission to save Wagner and make it possible for him to create and complete the great works which his genius still had to give the world was mightier than any other consideration. She felt that she alone could do this, and this great duty came before any personal consideration for Buelow.

" Buelow would never have lost me (she wrote in her dairy) if Fate had not brought me into contact with *him* for whom it was my mission to live and to die. I wanted to try and combine my former existence with my new life. I believed it would be possible to fuse the most divergent emotions. But calumnies and insults showed me that I was a fool, and nothing remained for me but to make my choice—and to suffer.

" It seems cruel to me to have deserted Hans. But I then said to myself that even if I sense this cruelty, it is clear that there was a divine power within me that decreed it, and not I myself who wished and elected to do it. But I do not hold it against anyone who does not see things as I see them, and who—lacking my faith—condemns me. I will bear the contempt of the world gladly and light-heartedly. But Hans's suffering robs me of all joy. . . .

" They wish to drag us through the mire. I will suffer all these things gladly if I may only remain at his side. Let them damn me to the remotest ages, provided I have helped him, have been permitted to hold out my hand to him, and say to him—' I will follow you even unto death.' My only prayer is that when the day comes, I may die in the same hour with Richard. My greatest pride is that I have thrust everything from me to live for him alone. My greatest bliss—his happiness."

In the beginning Buelow's two children, Daniela and Blandine, remained with him in Munich. Cosima's presence at Triebschen was to be kept strictly secret. Buelow spread the official report everywhere that she was staying with her half-sister in France on account of her health. He hoped in this way to stamp out the public gossip and make it possible for him to continue his artistic activity in Munich through the winter (the fight for Wagner's works !). He was also ready to send his two daughters to her in Triebschen in the spring and then apply for a divorce. Until his departure from Munich he continued to correspond with Cosima, and even with Wagner, on perfectly friendly terms. But the spiritual turmoil within him and the intense bitterness and disgust that suddenly gripped him at moments crushed him in body and in spirit and brought him to the verge of desperation.

" I am being gradually gnawed to pieces by the rats of my past," he wrote. In a letter to Countess Charnace on 15th September 1869 telling her why he now had instituted the hated legal action with its opening of the question of fact, Buelow gave a deeply moving picture of his last years.

" Please believe me (he wrote), I have done everything that was humanly possible to avert a public scandal. For more than three years I submitted to a life of incessant torture. You can have no conception of the gnawing worries and agitations to which I have been continually subjected—finally sacrificing to them even my professional and social position. There remained for me only one more final sacrifice— that of my life. I admit that this would have been the simplest solution —to put an end to all the difficulties and to cut the Gordian knot. But I shrank from this sacrifice. Can this be held against me as a crime ? Perhaps I should not have recoiled even from that had I observed on the part of the other—*who is as sublime in his works as he is incomparably abject in his actions*—the very slightest sign of an approach towards loyalty, the most fugitive suggestion of a desire to act in a decent and honourable manner.

" I am not blaming or condemning anyone as I fear to destroy thereby the only thing that remains to me, namely, the consciousness that I have been more sinned against than sinning. But the accusation to which I have just given expression and to which a twenty-year acquaintance has provided me with proof more than enough, is necessary in order to protect another from censure, someone who in former days, dear Countess, resembled you very greatly, not only in the superiority of her intellect but also in her fair-mindedness, frankness and nobility of character. When your stepsister is free (we must perhaps wait a year till the divorce is granted), when she has publicly legalized the union with her lover, then she will be herself again and not be obliged to lie from morning till night.

" What is therefore illogical about my wish for a divorce, even if at first I was unwilling to consider a legal settlement ? When I asked her last September—which was perhaps indelicate of me—why she was in such a hurry to leave me (I had begged her in vain to await Liszt's arrival in January) Cosima saw fit to reply to me with a false oath.[1] Why she did this I only learned a few months ago through a newspaper which, without glossing over anything, reported the Maestro's happiness over the fact that his mistress (her name was written out in full !)

[1] " *Lui ayant posé une question presque indiscrète, Cosima a trouvé bon de me répondre par un faux serment.*"

had at last borne him a son who had been called Siegfried and was taken as a fortunate augury for the impending completion of his opera ! The edifice—of my cuckoldry !—was therefore crowned in the most splendid manner.

" I couldn't flee from Munich, but the hell that I went through during the last period of my activity is beyond imagination. I was constantly surrounded by a host of musicians, teachers, and students of the Academy and yet had to face a publicity that spared me nothing. After my last performance of the newly rehearsed ' Tristan ' the most widely read paper in Munich praised me for the devotion that I had brought to the work of my wife's lover. I therefore only had the choice between two situations—either to be regarded with the most insulting pity as a man ignorant of what was common knowledge, or have my disgraceful position as the minion of a king's minion contemptuously thrown in my teeth.

" At the same time, even before I had taken any steps in the matter, the papers reported that my divorce was imminent. I have made every sacrifice in order to obtain the divorce in the most decent and considerate manner possible. But I can't change the course of Prussian law. It cannot be obtained on the basis of a ' common wish.' I had no other recourse than to charge ' wilful desertion.' . . .

" It is said that time repairs many injustices, but there are limits even to this. I am too covered with contumely ever to expect a favour from time. I feel myself driven from my musical fatherland, driven from every civilized country. I will try to pass the miserable days of my future in the humble position of a piano teacher. The only satisfaction that remains to me is the consciousness that I have been punished for all my sins while still on this earth."

What had hitherto deterred Buelow from applying publicly for a divorce was that the question of fact had to be discussed. He was ready to take partial responsibility on himself on the score of " his complete unfitness for the rôle of husband." But he was not willing to see the woman to whom in spite of everything he owed so much hailed before the courts " as a guilty party." Liszt also wanted to avoid any scandal if possible, and after Cosima's flight to Wagner broke off for years all correspondence with his daughter. It was only Cosima's bold stroke in joining Wagner at Triebschen and linking her life publicly with his, with the inevitable social scandal attached to it, that forced Buelow finally to abandon any further consideration for her.

On the Lake of Lucerne, however, the sun, after so many anxious ominous days, broke triumphantly through the dark clouds. Deep peace dwelt in the souls of the two fugitives, even though at times the clamour of the outside world penetrated to their ears and many bitter tidings reached them while friends, even the King himself, angrily turned their backs on them. Tranquillity and happiness had returned to their spirits. Wagner resumed work on " Siegfried " with heightened enthusiasm after an interruption of eleven years in order to complete this audacious " Nibelungen " work in spite of everything. During the quiet winter evenings he also dictated the story of his life to his companion, a story which, though strongly under the influence of his views at that time and with the greatest consideration for Cosima's feelings, he endeavoured to put down a true record of his career for his family and friends. The French writer Judith Gautier, a friend of Cosima's, left a delightful picture of her visit to Triebschen.

" The Master led us to a pavilion situated on a hillock from which (as he said) the view was glorious. The children romped in the soft grass, laughing and shouting with joy. The view was really entrancing. A waving sea of green foliage in which the house seemed to be submerged rippled from hill to dale as far as the clear blue lake, its surface dotted here and there with white sails and reflecting in its mirror the violet hues of the great peaks. Nature was bathed in exquisite light. It was an unforgettable moment.

" Richard Wagner—his two hands resting on the rude country fence—stood erect, silent, with the earnest expression of concentration peculiar to him at moments of deep emotion. His eyes, blue as the lake and almost immobile, seemed to be sucking in the picture which created for him a whole world of ideas. This refuge, this charming hiding-place won for him by the tenderness of the woman he loved at a time when he was pursued most cruelly by the bitternesses of life, this lovely wilderness, enlivened by the laughter of children and where the blows of Fate could only reach him (as it were) over a rampart of love, it was of this that he was thinking with emotion and gratitude. He realized that I had followed his train of thought and then continued his reverie aloud. ' And yet this patch of earth, so full of memories, does not belong to me. Later on, however, I plan to buy a bit of land so that my children can come back to it and find something of the cosy nest of their childhood.' "

The zenith of happiness was reached at Triebschen on 6th June 1869 when a son was born to the Master.

" Who can fathom what that means to me (he wrote Alwine Fromann). He is so strong and beautiful that I could call him Siegfried, and in his honour, too, I completed my work. Helferich is another of

his names, because he is to become a useful helper. But now I must
first bring up the youngster. My wife's four daughters are growing up
with him, and their education and upbringing is the daily task of this
noble woman in our complete seclusion. Everything is flourishing."

Only now, " on this happiest day of his life," as he once called
it, did his life take on real purpose. He now had a son for whom
he could work, and who after his death would " look after things."

After the birth of Wagner's heir, Cosima wrote Buelow a long
detailed letter in which she set forth " her former, her present,
and her future relations " to him.

" I hear from Hans Richter that you have tendered your resignation,
and from another side that you wish to leave Germany and want to
come to an understanding with me regarding the fate of our children
and the division of our property. That gives me the courage to address
myself to you. I do this with great hesitation and with the request not
to be impatient if I approach you at an unpropitious moment. I have
never had much luck in my discussions with you. When I tried to
re-establish an honourable peace between us, you answered me
ironically. And when I demanded a definite break, you wouldn't hear
of it. To-day I beg of you to listen to me with kindly feelings,
hearkening only to the inner voice within you, without being influenced
by outside factors ; and to remember what we have both suffered
during these years.

" If you are tendering your resignation because you feel incapable
of standing up any longer against the intrigues and baseness by which
you are surrounded and deluged, then there is nothing to be said
against it. In this case I could only wish that you might take the
trouble to motivate this, point by point, so that it is clear that you
didn't perhaps accept a position just for the position's sake, but that
you wanted to serve your art and that you left with regret the service
of the King who had big projects in mind, because the pettiness and
malice of the people with whom you had to deal prevented this. But if
you leave Munich, forced by the alternative of dissembling or not
dissembling, then if you will permit me to say so, you are acting
wrongly.

" Whatever your future relations with me may be, no blame or
opprobrium can ever fall on you. Your character is known, you are
respected by everyone and any horrid clamour that may arise will be
directed against me. First of all I am a woman and therefore expected
to have regard for the moral law ; secondly I am a mother who appears
to be sacrificing her children ; and thirdly, you are an honourable man,
and I married you of my own free will and accord. When you tell me
that the opprobrium that is heaped on me naturally falls back on you—
even were it only because it grieves you—then I would reply that it
lies within your power to shield me from it. When you say that the

persecutions to which we were subjected in Munich undermined our family life to such a degree that we both were determined to separate, you will be stating the situation correctly in one of its many aspects, and even though I may not escape the severest blame we will still be spared at least disgrace.

" For my part, I would wish that you would stick it out in Munich— I admit it frankly—apart naturally from considerations of health which require an extended leave of absence—I wish it for the sake of the children, because I think it will be easier for you to put something aside for them from your salary, and even for yourself, since you aren't fitted for the life of a strolling artist, and I know of no place, either in Germany or elsewhere, where you would feel better off.

" I left Munich in November under the delusion that your position would improve with time and it would be possible for you to find a home for our children while it was my task to unfold their hearts and their intellects. Here I deluded myself, and we're now stuck fast in the wreckage, and I must bear the heavy blame of being responsible for this whole catastrophe. Let us jointly seek a way to vindicate me and if possible extricate ourselves from the tragic situation in which we find ourselves.

" In the solitude and peace of my present existence I've often thought over my past life and examined my conscience. I've never had any illusions regarding the extent of my injustice towards you. Yours consists solely in the fact that you married me. I can say that during the seven months of our separation I've only had one main anxiety and worry, and that was you. (I hope you are listening to me with sufficient tranquillity and good will to believe my words.) I've asked myself a hundred times what I could and must do, and I swear to you that it was never a selfish reason that prevented my hastening to you. The memory of our family life from the second year of our engagement always stretched out before me as proof that no matter how hard I might try, I could in no wise make you happy. None of my efforts were successful. Even when you were ill you sent me away from your bed without my knowing why, and when I was pregnant with Loulou you will remember that I didn't dare tell you, as though the pregnancy were illegitimate—and I confessed it to you in a dream.

" In the meantime, rest assured that I should never have left you if another life had not crossed my path that is so indissolubly fused with it that I don't know how they could ever be separated. You will never know how I struggled and what I have suffered, and I can never depict my consternation when it became clear that the project of a life à trois would not be practicable.

" It was not the humiliations that you heaped upon me that then goaded me to desperation. Believe me, I have already arrived at a point when I can bear suffering almost easier than happiness and where I welcome every expiation of my sin as of my joys. I had a presenti-

THE PARENTS OF
COSIMA WAGNER

At right
COUNTESS D'AGOULT

At left
FRANZ LISZT
IN 1858

PARIS (1861)   PETERSBURG (1863)

MUNICH (1865)   BAYREUTH (1873)

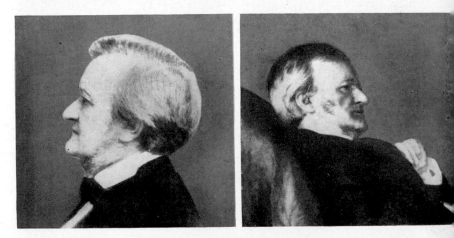

LONDON (1877)   BAYREUTH (1882)

SIX PHASES OF WAGNER

ment that things could not go on like this and that you yourself were
hastening the catastrophe. But though I had to leave you, and even
though you unfortunately had to contribute towards this separation,
nevertheless my interest in you and your fate can never change and
will always touch a chord in me. You are the only person in the world
who fills my thoughts, the only one whose great trials and anxieties I
share from afar.

" I don't believe that you can think lightly of this affection which
has never changed and will outlive all the vicissitudes and changes of
our lives. And in this sense I beg you, if you have the strength to
separate from me publicly, to let me bring up our children—and keep
in touch with me. If you find my proposal unreasonable and reject
what I have said to you, then tell me so without anger and sarcasm ;
for I have spoken to you from the depths of my heart, and it is not my
fault if my complete estrangement from the world lets feelings rise
within me which the world knows not, and cannot comprehend.

" I believe I have the right to bring up my children because I love
them and because the life I have chosen, cut off from all association
with the outside world, permits me to live for them alone. It would
perhaps be easier for me to renounce this one of my requests that
entails the greatest sacrifice if I knew a single person in your family
who could take my place. But your mother (on whom I have never
permitted myself to pass judgment because I had a duty to fulfil
towards her), your mother, I fear, would rob our little ones of all joy
and light-heartedness, for in spite of the rigidity of certain points of
view that spring from unfortunate experiences, she doesn't possess the
deep conviction and none of those qualities that it takes to make of
childhood a paradise and the germ of a noble and pure development.

" The world and your family are in the right when they advise you
against permitting me to bring up the children, for they quite justifiably
see in me only the woman who has broken the sacramental bonds of
marriage in order to follow the call of passion. But you, I believe (and
rightly so) look on me in a rather different light and know that I will
bring them up well, and that with me they will see nothing and hear
nothing which would make them unworthy of you. I will bring them
up for you so that one day they may be a comfort to you. And for
their sake I beg of you—if it is not too great a sacrifice to you—to keep
in touch with me. When you wish, I will bring them to you wherever
you may be, and I will stay with them there where you are, even in
Munich, for I fear no one, and dread no place. For when I separated
from you I separated myself from everything—except the children.
For their sake I hope you will retain the post in which you now are—
naturally under better conditions. It is your task to introduce them to
the world, your name, your talent, your character, everything enables
you to give them an honourable position. Since I am alone and an
outcast I can only bring them up to be honourable and God-fearing,

P

and you know me well enough to know that neither trials nor joys can detract me from this task.

" As far as our property is concerned, I would like to ask you to keep it entirely for the children, even as I would ask you to lay aside for them (if you don't need it) the 6,000 francs which I have from Father and Mother. Otherwise I have nothing more to say ; and still my heart is so heavy that I fear my inspiration was not a happy one and that I have to look forward to one of those bitter replies which you may feel you are justified to make, but which my heart and my conscience tell me I have not deserved."

Buelow had worked like a galley-slave all winter in Munich and had just brought his four years' work there to a close with a newly rehearsed " Tristan," the première of which had marked the opening of his Munich *étape*. He was now at the end of his tether. External circumstances having made it impossible for him in the future to act as trail-blazer for Wagner's music, the axe had been laid at the roots of his existence. Although he had gone through terrible experiences in Munich, he martyred himself for weeks on end " by weighing the pros and cons of a decision that he realized was irrevocable."

" My situation is so incredibly and uniquely horrible (he wrote) that any other way out than out of the world altogether would demand superhuman courage. If everything were only settled the best would be for some sympathetic soul to give me the required quantity of prussic acid."

But he finally roused himself from this desperate lethargy and applied to the King for his release.

" I will pass over any reference to the joylessness of my personal existence (he wrote) which has suffered a severe blow in the definite separation from my wife, since she prefers to devote her life to the higher consideration of the creator of immortal masterpieces in the service of Your Majesty."

He then filed the petition for divorce in Berlin, a step that he would gladly have made any possible sacrifice to have spared his master and father-in-law, Franz Liszt.

" That I myself will come out of it quite unscathed, even in the eyes of the evil world, is small consolation for the inevitable hue and cry against the great Master. But I can't make any more sacrifices *now* ! "

Before he went abroad, a homeless man, he poured out his heart to Cosima in a moving letter in reply to hers.

" I am grateful to you for having taken the initiative (he wrote) 17th July 1869) and I will seek no motive to regret it. I'm too unhappy through my own fault not to avoid anything that might wound you by any unjust reproach whatsoever. In this exceedingly cruel separation which you felt you were called upon to make, I recognize all my errors and I shall continue to emphasize them in the most definite way in all the unavoidable discussions on this matter with my mother and your father. I have made you a very poor and a very sorry return for all the devotion you have shown me in our past life. I have poisoned yours for you and I can only thank Providence for having given you compensation at the eleventh hour when courage to continue must already have failed you.

"But in fact, since you left me, I have lost my sole support in life and in my struggle. It was your mind, your heart, your friendship, your patience, your indulgence, your sympathy, your encouragement, your advice, and above all your presence, your countenance, your speech, all these taken together constituted the foundation of my life. The loss of this supreme treasure, whose full value I only recognized *after* its loss, has brought about my moral and artistic collapse and has made me realize that I am a bankrupt.

"Do not think that this lament (I suffer so keenly that I may permit myself to complain, though in so doing I lay the responsibility on none other than myself alone) implies any irony or insult towards you. You have preferred to devote your life and the treasures of your mind to a person who is exceptional in every respect, and far from blaming you, I *approve* of your action from every point of view, and admit that you are perfectly right. I swear that the only consoling thought that from time to time has lightened the darkness and mitigated my external sufferings was that at all events Cosima is happy.

"It has seemed to me necessary to preface my personal explanations by this sort of prelude, which in name, or rather in character, is for me an absolute profession of faith. Now (for the last time) I must ask your indulgence if the following explanation is not absolutely clear nor correctly expressed. Pardon me, but as of old I must take refuge in my busy life ('He has a lot to do, this sacristan,' Loulou once said to you in church). To-day and to-morrow orchestral rehearsals for 'Tristan' from nine till two; the Academy of Music from three to six; correspondence, calls, etc. And I am so physically weak that every two or three days I have to stay in bed a whole day doing nothing.

"It's true that I sent in my resignation a week ago. As motive, I stressed my shattered health. All the world understands that, and Dr. Rubner gave me a certificate two months ago. The intrigues, calumnies and opposition—ill-will in short—the anxieties and misunderstandings have been increasing from month to month. Since you were absent I had no counterweight (my mother as substitute? I don't need to unburden my heart to you on that subject). My moral and physical strength, my desire to continue a game that wasn't worth the candle, diminished in inverse ratio. The few satisfactions which I may be able to enter on the credit side provide no serious compensation and give me no encouragement to go on.

" My work for the King of Bavaria brings in only 4,000 *gulden* (I've never expected an increase in salary), which does not cover my expenses. Furthermore, I am now firmly convinced that I shall not in any way be serving the cause—the cause of art—by continuing my work here and standing my ground, which would ruin me completely in one or at most two years. Moreover, the very foundation of my position is rocking. As a matter of fact I can only look upon myself as a king's favourite, and the opinion that I have gained this position through my complaisance as a husband is pretty widespread ! Klindworth, though he hasn't the reputation, and even assuming that he possessed only half my ability, intelligence, and talent (which is not the case, for I consider him almost my equal), would have a much better chance of making himself useful than the present *démissionaire*. Then again, the obligatory work with the gigantic but highly fatal ' Tristan ' has literally finished me. The public performance is to take place Sunday. I assume full responsibility that it will not be a profanation, as I already wrote Wagner yesterday. But it will mark my last appearance at the head of the orchestra.

" My stay in Munich will therefore end where it began. That rounds it off in a way—more a fatal than a faulty revolution—and will make it easier for me later on to look back on all the events and sufferings (the punishment of my transgressions towards you) which fall within the four-year period (between the two performances of one and the same work) like a nightmare. Yes, without any reproach to its mighty creator, ' Tristan ' has given me the *coup de grâce*. I haven't such strong nerves as you, who have been able to endure long years of intimacy with one so congenitally bad, or ill bred, as I—and have still survived the torture !

" During the rehearsals the work sent poor Eberle [a coach enjoying Richter's protection] out of his mind. The official interpretation is that he had had too much beer—and I must assure you that I, who in all the numerous enticements offered me to throw up the sponge have lacked the necessary courage, could scarcely have resisted the temptation if someone had offered me a few drops of prussic acid. The temptation unfortunately did not present itself, and though cursing the fact, I still must recognize the terrible will to live that is stored up in my nature. But how shall I satisfy it except by leaving a city which has become a hell for me since you went away ; and by making a new start elsewhere, I still don't know how.

" This separation from you (you had no other alternative ; always remember the beginning of this letter) must be complete ! I must free myself of everything touching you and R. W., even *in thought*, as far as that is humanly possible—my past life knew only these two guiding stars (at most I could also include your father). Don't misunderstand me ! by no means do I suggest to you the fuss or unpleasantness of a divorce. But if your father wishes it, if he prefers to have your union with the life of R. Wagner receive this official affirmation, then I have no objections to make on my side. In that case, however (as you can well imagine), I have no desire, inclination or impulse to take action on my own part. I have no reason for suggesting or insisting on a divorce.

" Furthermore, I leave you our children, leave their education to you, since I consider this the best they could obtain, especially since I have no other to offer them and because I entirely agree with you that it is absolutely impossible to entrust them to my aged mother or any member of my family, if I can speak of a family. But if your great heart is willing to bring up our children free of all antipathy and all the justifiable resentment which you bear their father—then I see no reason why I shouldn't leave you my name. I would consider it petty and unworthy of the situation if I manifested a sensitiveness which might be wrongly interpreted with regard to the proposals and sacrifices which you make to me. Therefore permit me to reply definitely, simply and briefly.

" The allowance which your father (and your mother) gives you belongs to the children. Since you are taking charge of their education, your 6,000 francs must—and quite rightly so—be employed for their education. The partner of your present and future life would therefore only have to invest anything that you might be able to save on a pinch from this sum. The dowry which you brought to our unfortunate marriage—was this not the first stumbling-block for me in view of my poverty ? the first disturbing note ? the sense of duty, even love itself ?

" I cannot avoid building up the financial security of the children with the help of your money. All that *I* can guarantee them—for the time being—is the little legacy from Aunt Frege (5,000 *thalers* invested in the Frege Bank) which, with luck, may be doubled by the time they come of age. You will understand—and I beg you to do so—that I consider all our household belongings to be your personal property. When I leave here, and that will be the first of August, I hope, I shall only take a few things that are indisputably mine, such as clothes, books, music. Everything else I will leave in the flat which belongs to us until 1st October. Then you can have the Mraszeks carry out your orders either to sell or send part to Triebschen and to store and insure at the warehouse such furniture as we jointly consider the property of the children.

" When I leave Munich, and possibly Germany also, my future plans are very undecided, and for the moment I consider them very secondary. The most important and urgent thing now is to get away, and I am exceedingly anxious to take with me as little as possible of anything that might recall the past. For only by breaking with it

definitely and radically will it be possible to start a new existence.
There is only one thing, one alone, that will remain with me always,
and that is the most grateful memory of all that you have contributed to
my artistic development. I shall be eternally grateful to you for everything you have done for me in this respect.

" Permit me to set your mind at rest to some extent on the manner of
my departure from Munich. I shall remain at the Academy of Music
until the end of the semester and will also assume the loathsome job
of the examinations if my legs and my head are not too recalcitrant.
The opera is closed in July, and the beginning of August Richter will
start the ' Rheingold ' rehearsals. I have also already delegated the
next ' Meistersinger ' performance on the 27th to him. As soon as the
Conservatoire closes (August) I am going *on leave*. Düfflipp, in the
name of the King, has asked me to reconsider the matter and if possible
think over my resignation, and has offered me indefinite leave of
absence till my health is restored. As things now stand, two months
would be no use—I need at least a year for that—so I shall take my
definite departure on 1st October while accepting provisionally the
leave which the King desires to grant me. In this way I shall leave
with the least rumpus, the least fuss.

" Do not misjudge me (which R. W., I fear, will do at once) and
think I am playing a farce and that a change in my post or emoluments
could induce me to alter my point of view and bring me back to one of
the most incredible travesties of a *Heimat*. In spite of addresses by the
pupils of the Conservatoire, friendly letters from Rheinberger, Wüllner
and other touching evidences of affection on the part of some of the
members of the orchestra, I feel that I no longer have the strength to
begin over again there. I prefer a thousand times the position of piano
teacher in a small town. With people like Perfall as one's chief, one
can only do routine work in which one loses one ability after the other.
I won't enumerate all I've lost during the past year. And not a soul to
sympathize ; don't fear ! I've done complaining !

" Do you recall the fact that I was perfectly aware of what would
happen after you had left me ? Do you remember that I only wanted
to return to Munich together with you ? God knows I don't say that
to reproach you belatedly. It was impossible for you to stay here ; I
understand that, and understand it only too well. In recapitulating, I
only wish to soften in your eyes the evident brusqueness of my
decision which has been maturing more painfully day by day since your
departure. The task was beyond my strength which (morally and
physically) has seriously deteriorated for some time now. I have
plunged into activity in order to forget, which was impossible since
the illusions regarding the purport and object of this activity have
vanished one after the other. I shall therefore be leaving early in
August. I have demanded my 2,000 *Reichsthalers* from Bechstein, thanks
to which I can live quietly and without anxiety for a year. When I

have recovered my health and self-control, I shall find some kind of a new existence, but an independent one and without incidental obligations. (Nevertheless I shall never forget that any later position will be traceable to the position Wagner made for me in Munich; but I shall be able to bear this feeling of dependence to a certain degree.)

" This is a badly written letter, far from worthy of being read by the author of the one to which it is an answer. In point of fact it is actually not a reply. It is a sort of testament written by a brain and heart that are really sick, half deranged. Yet it contains nothing crazy, nothing unreasonable, and I beg you to accept it as ' an emergency product.' I beg you, furthermore, to share with me—for the last time—the sentiments by which I am animated; and by your approval and acceptance, help me to carry them out. May God protect and bless the mother of the fortunate children to whom she will continue to devote herself."

It is interesting to note Wagner's attempt to shake off any personal blame for Buelow's departure from Munich—which was so painful for the King—and gloss over the true cause of it (their domestic relations) by clever exploitation of Buelow's own chivalrously unselfish explanation.

" Herr von Buelow's departure from Munich was *not* dictated by the latest developments in his marital affairs (he wrote Düfflipp on 7th September 1869). On the contrary, I have his express written declaration to the effect that whereas only an important, independent and noble sphere of activity could have compensated him for the decisions with which he was inevitably faced, it was the realization at last that such a sphere of activity was impossible in Munich that drove him away.

" This difficult point will become clear if I explain that it was not the divorce from his wife, but the deferring for years of the definite separation from her that was the source of truly unbearable suffering for all concerned. Ever since—now nearly four years ago—the Munich daily Press began slinging mud at the marital relations of my friends (to go straight to the heart of the matter), inspired by that quarter which you yourself indicated to me as that which you now hold,[1] it couldn't be expected that these relations would remain unaffected by it. Even at that time a divorce seemed the only way of saving the husband's honour, already irreparably wounded by the vilest calumnies, and his wife therefore proposed it. What prevented this solution was the great and all-confiding faith in the King of Bavaria, common to all of us, to whose protection we again appealed, so that united—as each of us desired and considered the only tenable solution—we might devote ourselves to a great artistic work, rich in blessings and to the glory of all.

[1] The post of the King's Cabinet Secretary, then held by von Pfistermeister.

" But the experiences of the past two years have destroyed just this guarantee for us, and with it undoubtedly the sole bond which should and might have held us together at the cost of great spiritual sacrifices. I realized at once that everything had gone wrong the moment I set foot in Munich again at the end of 1867. I experienced one disappointment after the other, and I soon saw that I must forgo any wider activities and confine myself to producing my newest work (the ' Meistersinger ') for the King. The annoyances that I experienced while carrying out this undertaking, resulting from the incapacity and ill will of the theatre management, were so disastrous for me (since I felt obliged to conceal it) that I could only recover from the severe illness that overtook me on my return from Munich by firmly resolving not to have anything more to do with any artistic undertaking there. At the same time I learned through a letter from His Majesty to Frau von Buelow that this lady's honour had again been dragged into the old game. The announcement was sufficient to revive her decision to put an end to the untenable situation by obtaining a divorce from her husband.

" From that time until quite recently Frau von Buelow was unable to persuade her husband to agree to a divorce, his only reasons being high-mindedness and sincere affection. That which each of those involved suffered under these circumstances does not concern outsiders in any way. There is just this still to be said, that not long ago Frau von Buelow quite rightly advised her husband very urgently to remain in Munich ; for if anything had compromised his position there, it was the contemptible accusation, to which he was perhaps liable, of owing that position to his complaisance as a husband ; but as soon as he was divorced from his wife, there would no longer be any ground for criticism. Herr von Buelow recognized the truth of this and thanked his wife, but declared that this very position and the clearly evident impossibility of meeting the King's high expectations when his activity was subjected to such intolerable interference and was poisoned for him by constant friction, had determined him to relinquish it.

" On this point, as I said, I possess the most unequivocal documentary evidence, and I mention this expressly in submitting these explanations so as to obviate any distortion of facts and motives, or at least to prevent any such misunderstanding in the decisive quarter. The real truth of the matter and the result of it all (which you, too, must certainly admit) is that no one who is seriously committed to me can endure life in Munich for any length of time. This opinion has been brazenly insinuated to others, in the manner of a threat, by persons close to His Majesty, such as Count Holstein.[1] But you will now see from the departure of the last of my collaborators (whose request I would hereby commend for your endorsement) that we also are no longer in any doubt about it. So that's how the matter stands. Things

---

[1] Chief equerry to the King.

certainly might be totally different, but I've no intention of going into it further. I can never tell you what we, and everyone connected with me, had to put up with in Munich. But one day history will have a tale to tell."

Buelow's departure from Munich coincided with an event that threatened to lead to a serious conflict between Wagner and his royal friend. The latter had given orders for a performance of " Rheingold " contrary to Wagner's wishes and repeated requests that the attempt be abandoned for the time being. Hans Richter was booked to conduct, but no one else associated with the undertaking was in any way capable of meeting the demands of a work so totally different from the ordinary operatic fare. Which led to a catastrophe. Richter refused to conduct and Franz Betz, the Wotan, sent a desperate appeal to Wagner to take steps to prevent his work and the artists being made a laughing stock. The King, who was very embittered and irritated by the scandal which also reflected on him and had now been brought to a climax by the Buelow affair, insisted on his orders being carried out, and considered Wagner's opposition (which was inspired solely by artistic considerations) as " criminal and scandalous."

" This is an open revolt against my orders, and I cannot tolerate it ! (he wrote Düfflipp on 30th August 1869). The people at the opera have to obey my orders and not Wagner's whims. For if these abominable intrigues of Wagner's are allowed to pass, then the whole rabble would get more and more cheeky and brazen till there would be no holding them in the end ; therefore the evil must be pulled up by the roots. I have never known such insolence ! "

He followed this up next day by a telegram, in which he informed Düfflipp that

" An end must be put as soon as possible to the quite unpardonable intrigues of Wagner and confederates. I hereby give distinct orders that the performance is to take place on Sunday. Richter is to be immediately dismissed. If Wagner dares to offer any more opposition his stipend is to be revoked for good, and not another work of his is to be produced on the Munich stage. Make every possible effort to prevent his coming here. He need not learn that this is my wish, otherwise hell is loose and the business will never come off, either now or later."

In the meantime, however, Wagner had already left for Munich to try and straighten out the hopeless muddle as best he could. But in view of the attitude of the King, which was well known to

Perfall, the Intendant, he only ran up against obstacles and difficulties, and after two days returned to Triebschen without having accomplished anything. The King, who to escape the whole affair had left for his shooting box in the Bavarian Alps, wrote Pfistermeister on 2nd September that

" To bring this now detestable ' Rheingold ' affair to a climax, Richard Wagner has arrived in Munich quite against my wishes. It would serve him quite right if there is an unpleasant demonstration against him, now that the Buelow affair is *au comble. J'en ai assez.*"

But the performance had to be cancelled after all as there was neither a conductor nor a Wotan, Betz having left. However, the King ordered the work to be given as soon as possible with Munich artists. When Wagner offered to conduct the rehearsals Dülfflipp advised him against it.

" It has never been a habit of mine to cast a stone at another (he wrote him on 10th September). I much prefer to let each individual be answerable to his own conscience for his actions. However, I should regret it very deeply if you are not yet convinced that it is imperative in your own interest not to carry out such a project. If you even set foot in Munich under present conditions, then the whole Press will jump on you again in a body and we'll soon find ourselves in a far more hopeless mess than we're in at present. This is the truth, believe me, and I should be a disloyal friend if I concealed this from you."

Wagner therefore took no further action in the matter of the " Rheingold " performance, which had now become a prestige issue with the King. It was finally given on 22nd September with Franz Wüllner as conductor.

After long and painful trials[1] Wagner's private affairs were on the eve of settlement in the summer of 1870, which was very essential in the interests of his intercourse with the outside world.

" Certainly we'll come (he wrote in reply to an invitation from Frau Wille) for you must be the first to whom we pay our respects as a married couple. It has cost us much patience to attain to this state— though essential for years, it took suffering of every description to achieve it. Since I last saw you in Munich I have never left my Asyl, to which she also found her way whose mission was to prove that I *could* be helped and to disprove the theory of so many of my friends

---

[1] The town council of Horw, a little place not far from Triebschen, passed a motion, in all seriousness, that Wagner be expelled from Switzerland on the grounds of moral turpitude !

that I ' was past all hope.' She knew that I *could* be helped, and she *has* helped me. She defied every kind of opprobrium and suffered every condemnation. She has borne me a wonderfully beautiful and healthy son whom I could make bold to call Siegfried. He, like my work, is progressing and gives me a new lease on life, *life that at last has been given a purpose.* And so we managed to get along without the world from which he had entirely withdrawn."

On 18th July 1870 the Berlin courts granted Cosima a decree of divorce as follows :

> IN THE NAME OF THE KING. In the divorce suit brought by the Royal Bavarian Court Conductor (Ret.) Hans Guido von Buelow of Berlin, plaintiff, against his wife Cosima von Buelow, *née* Liszt, at present residing at Triebschen, Switzerland, defendant, the Royal Municipal Court . . . etc., has decreed : that the marriage bond existing between the parties be cancelled, the defendant declared the guilty party, and as such be required to pay the fourth part of her unencumbered estate to the plaintiff as divorce penalty and bear the cost of the proceedings.

> *Legal argument :* The parties have been married to each other since 18th August 1857 and have begotten several children of the marriage ; the husband is a member of the Evangelical, the wife of the Catholic, Church. The plaintiff claims : that his wife left him in the year 1868 while they were residing in Munich and in spite of repeated demands has not returned to him. After a fruit-less attempt on the part of the competent clergymen to re-establish their conjugal life, the defendant was ordered by mandate, dated 6th April 1870, to return to her husband within four weeks. The plaintiff claims that she did not obey this mandate and that he, therefore, after the attempts at reconciliation on the part of the clergy had proved futile, petitioned to have the marriage dissolved, the defendant declared the guilty party, and sentenced to forfeit one-fourth of her estate as divorce penalty. The defendant did not appear in court, but in reply to the attempts of the clergy at reconciliation as well as in a written reply to the charges has declared that she will never return to her husband and accepts the legal consequences of her action. This being the case, the court deems it established that the defendant has been guilty of wilful desertion of her husband.

The main obstacle to her remarriage was thus removed. After the complicated formalities in connection with the marriage licence had been complied with, the wedding took place on 25th August (the King's birthday) in the Protestant church in Lucerne. For this it was not necessary for Cosima to be received into the Protestant Church as she was born in Italy, and the civil marriage laws of that country gave her the right, even as a Roman Catholic, to remarry. On 21st August, a few days before their wedding, Wagner wrote to Cosima's mother, Countess d'Agoult, as follows:

" Please permit me to-day to grasp your hand and to press it respectfully and gratefully to my heart. I approach the mother of my Beloved, who in order to be to me that which only she could be, allowed no consideration for the world to influence her decision, but whom your own great heart, dear Madam, spared the most difficult sacrifice of all : for she did not need to break with her mother since this mother understood her and stood by her with sisterly encouragement. This was a blessing, dear Madam, in which I also beneficently shared. May I therefore hope that you will not withdraw your hand when I come to thank you for this blessing.

" When our union is publicly blessed a few days hence, it will be as though I myself were witnessing a human event that, carefully weighed in all its phases and motives, gives a powerful new impetus to the observer's often wavering faith in a noble providential ordering of human destiny. Of all the sorrows we have had to endure here, not one was tainted with egotism. If after unspeakable tortures we could no longer bear not to belong to one another, it was still only the pangs of sympathy for those we must hurt that really vexed our lives. But it was a question of saving the lives of all concerned, and from the dark flames of suffering we can already see rising resplendently the clear light of a comforting reconciliation.

" If I have come to view my life and destiny as the centre of a mælstrom of the most grievous happenings, now that the eddies have passed into a luminous calm I can look with happy exultation on the significance of this, my own destiny. As a person new born, I enter on an existence whose preciousness I can only so far consider deserved if I view it as the reward of a life exposed over a shamefully long period to insufferable torments. A seminal love force now lives in and about it, which while it envelops me inwardly, also soars up out of me to celebrate each day the noblest of nuptials.

" And so I bless the mother who bore me this unique woman, who had insight deep enough to comprehend a poor sinner like myself and who was high-minded enough to dedicate herself to me. And so I now do honour to the noble woman who, of similar mind, cherished kindly feelings towards the noble-minded one who proved a tremendous encouragement to her. May my good wishes, my gratitude, as the recompense (though small) for her great kindness, fill her with warmth towards him who sends thanks and good wishes from an overflowing heart."

Wagner did not inform the King directly of the important event, though on 28th August he sent him, through Düfflipp, the orchestral sketch of the first act of " Götterdämmerung " along with a poem " *Huldigung* " (Homage). Some tension had arisen between them again as a result of the King's order to present " Walküre " in spite of the unfortunate experiences with " Rheingold " and Wagner's protests to the contrary.

" Since this world and all it metes out to me no longer refreshes or fortifies me (he wrote Düfflipp on 21st August) I must view it as an incalculable favour of destiny that along with the noble-minded King (from whose presence I unfortunately am still banned) I have been granted the companion in my lonely life who alone is able to compensate me for all the failures and disappointments. And so I have to thank this wonderfully happy union for the spiritual care that heals all my wounds again and leads me back once more—and with renewed strength—to the highest mission of my life.

" It now gives me great pleasure to be able to inform you to-day that after the elimination of all intervening obstacles, my marriage with my magnanimous friend is to take place next Thursday, 25th August, in the local Protestant parish church. What this means to me you will be able to measure when you put at its true value the incomparable loyalty and devotion which inspired this high-minded woman to suffer patiently every condemnation and to endure every calumny because she knew that she and she alone could really be something to me.

" I now beg you to communicate the foregoing to my noble protector, the author of my freedom and every possibility of my earthly and spiritual well-being and success. Will you also convey to our most gracious sovereign that we are both deeply touched at being able to celebrate our marriage on the birthday of our gracious noble friend. Through its being possible for us to set this, for us, inexpressibly significant day for our wedding, Fate has dropped us a hallowed hint that we joyfully welcome as a lucky omen."

" I brought your letter to the King's attention the day before yesterday (Düfflipp telegraphed in reply on the 25th) and waited yesterday for His Majesty's instructions. But since none have been forthcoming, I will not wait any longer but send you my warmest congratulations for the day that after long struggles and battles and unpleasantness of every kind now at last opens up a new chapter in your life and guarantees a kinder and happier future. And so I rejoice sincerely and heartily over the event which takes place this day in Triebschen."

But the King finally roused himself to telegraph his congratulations.

" For the time being, accept herewith my warmest thanks for the heavenly gift that fills me with the greatest joy. I do not need to assure you that I am more than ever with you and the friend in spirit on this so portentous day ! Letter follows soon."

Yet the letter announced in this message, which was so cool and formal in comparison with his usual effusions, did not materialize until six months later ! Cosima noted in her diary :

" Our wedding took place at eight o'clock. May I be worthy to bear Richard's name ! My prayer concentrated on two things : Richard's welfare, that I might always further it ; and Hans's happiness, that he may be granted to know a happy life—far from me."

The following wedding announcement communicated the event to their more intimate friends : " We have the honour to announce herewith our marriage in the Protestant Church at Lucerne on 25th August of this year. Richard Wagner—Cosima Wagner, *née* Liszt." The baptism of little Siegfried on 4th September, for which event the Willes came over from Zürich, rounded off the intimate family ceremonies. A fervent echo of these happy days was reflected in the deeply moving " Siegfried Idyll," especially composed for Cosima's birthday, and in which Wagner did graceful homage to the mother of his son through its performance in Triebschen on that day. Rarely have a husband's love and a father's pride been sung in more inspired tones ! When the score was subsequently published Wagner added a dedicatory poem to Cosima which admits the reader into this little enchanted kingdom.

It was Thy noble, sacrificial willing
That found the birth site for my work's outflow ;
In consecrated peace, all clamour stilling,
Where it has flourished, mightily to grow.
The ancient realm of heroes by a thrilling
Magic become a homeland that we know,
Then midst my tunes a cry of joy withal !
A son is born ! Him Siegfried we must call !

In music showed I gratitude unending
For him and Thee (what sweeter eulogy ?),
The joyful hearth all inspiration lending
That deeds of love here grew to melody.
Those who towards Siegfried warmth and kindness spending
Proved themselves faithful so to us to be,
To these shall now by Thy high grace be proffered
The sonant joy our quiet home has offered.

(Translation by Olga Erbsloh Muller.)

The two lived solely for each other in Triebschen, practically cut off from the outside world. Through Cosima's presence Wagner found the strength to resume work on the " Ring" cycle. About the time of Siegfried's birth the third act of " Siegfried " (this jubilant love song) was completed and work on " Götterdämmerung " begun immediately. Hans von Buelow's words to Klindworth : " If Wagner ever writes *another* note, then Cosima alone is to thank for it ! " were all too true. Without the intrepid act of this woman, the " Ring " would never have been completed. The painful sacrifices and spiritual suffering that she endured for the sake of her recognized mission—her diary furnishes deeply moving evidence of this—were not in vain and gave the world an immortal masterpiece. Wagner was quite right when he called out joyously one morning : " Cosima, your name should be Helferich Wagner, for you have helped me in very truth ! "

The tranquil and peaceful creative work in Triebschen was only interrupted now and then by short excursions in the neighbourhood. They also visited old friends in Zürich and Mariafeld. At first Wagner avoided meeting Mathilde Wesendonck. Cosima had written her of their marriage, and as a symbolic gift Mathilde had sent her a little bunch of edelweiss on her wedding day. Now after the old friendship with the Willes had been resumed, Cosima on one of her visits to the Willes in Mariafeld went to call on Frau Wesendonck.

" In spite of all my persuasion, Richard refused to accompany me (she noted in her diary). Mathilde's poem, *Aufruf an das deutsche Volk,* greatly displeased him. He also claimed she had behaved very unkindly towards him in the recent past. For the first time in eleven years I crossed the threshold of the rooms in which I had acted as a sort of mediator and confidential friend. I found my friendly hostess was now a brunette, while four years ago in Munich she was still a blonde. That confused me. I was pleased with her friendly manner, looked at the pictures, and on the way home mused on the strange dreamlike quality of life. Eleven years ago when I tried to persuade her to take a more generous attitude towards Richard if anyone had told me that I myself would be involved with Richard in his great destiny, I might have believed it ; but it would still have frightened me dreadfully."

In February 1871 Wagner himself accepted an invitation from the Wesendoncks and he and Cosima were guests for a day in a home that had once meant everything to him.

" I am glad that I succeeded in this (Cosima again confided to her diary). Frau Wesendonck was visibly pleased to see Richard again and find him happy. Her black hair disturbed Richard a little, but he got over it and she was amiable and friendly. Next day we visited the Willes, where the children feel much happier than in the brilliance and glamour of the Green Hill, with all the beautiful toys. But when we got home, we said : ' We no longer belong out in the world of men. We are only happy when we are alone by ourselves,' whereupon Richard said : ' Here is my world ! ' "

Even though it is quite understandable that Wagner, wholly under Cosima's spell, wished to discount the importance of all other women in his life in order to present her as the culmination, his longed-for redemptress, nevertheless this cannot excuse his ugly thrusts at Mathilde both in his autobiography and in Cosima's diary. What can one say to such statements as " in order not to give rise to any soft-hearted, tender error I have returned her letters to Frau Wesendonck and had mine burned, because I do not wish anything to be on hand that might lead to the assumption that there had been anything serious between us " (!) or : " As pleasant as I found this sympathetic acquaintance, who desired to take care of me, and was in a position to do so, I was always on the point of breaking away," or " Minna's fight with Mathilde, the way each one of them tried to annoy the other, and angered and irritated each other—and I—I hadn't a thought for either one of them " (!). As a matter of fact, after the meeting in Venice Wagner's feeling for Mathilde cooled more and more and the rejection of his Penzing appeal for help led to a temporary rupture in their relationship. After her heart had turned once more to her husband the enchantment that emanated from " the Master " also gradually paled in the case of Mathilde, who was shocked to learn of Wagner's numerous liaisons. Although she had written him in 1863 that " till now my tears have protected the Asyl from other tenants, but I very much doubt that I shall be able to achieve anything *more* in the immediate future," four years later (1867) she was able to bring herself to offer it to Johannes Brahms ! And in 1873 she even sent Brahms her little cycle of poems " Mignon " (dedicated to Wagner) so that he might set them to music. One sees that the desire of the authoress to launch her own creations finally got the upper hand even with Mathilde Wesendonck, and silenced the voice of her heart.[1]

The following autumn Cosima and Buelow exchanged some letters of very great importance. She had requested his permission to allow their children to join the Protestant Church, as she herself intended to do. In his heart of hearts Buelow was opposed to the idea, but as he did not want to create any cleavage between the mother and the children he finally gave his consent, to a certain extent from pedagogic motives. His reply, written from Rome where he had gone to celebrate Liszt's sixtieth birthday, contained the following comforting words for Cosima, whose heart was continually tormented by pricks of conscience.

" I have hoped and prayed for a long time that she who was once the unhappy companion of a second-rater is now the *happy* comrade of the greatest poet and artist of the century. May Heaven grant her a cloudless present as recompense for the unhappy past. . . .

" Of course I had to endure the bitterest of sorrows, yet in the most devilish hours of my life I still derived a certain comfort from the conviction that the great mission allotted you by Providence, which you had to fulfil at the side of His Majesty, the greatest genius of our century, was a necessity. And it would have been impossible for you to have fulfilled this mission without personally experiencing an earthly passion. Perhaps all the stupidities for which I must blame myself in my relationship with you, and which called forth and facilitated this passion, also bore the character of a ' predestined mission ' and therefore indirectly served the goal of your own."

Then followed a confession that seemed strange, coming from Buelow.

" In the children's evening prayers, include a name (I leave the choice to you), the name of some saint—one of the purest of saints—and at your convenience let me know the one you have chosen. This name is to indicate a person who, without being aware of it, has given me new life as father, man, and artist ; who along with peace of mind has restored for me the glow and passion of life and of struggle ; in short has given me myself again, and in a new and improved edition.

" May this confession remove from your heart the last trace of retrospective bitterness and remorse. You fulfil the difficult and varied duties that always fall to you in such a truly devout and loyal manner that you should no longer suffer from such things. Please bless the angel who ' led to Rome.' "

A letter to his old friend Carl Bechstein cleared up the mystery.

[1] Her poetic and dramatic works were always brought out in expensive editions, but attracted little notice.

" Yesterday Princess Wittgenstein asked me if it were not possible for me to reconcile myself with Wagner again. I protested vigorously against this word. I have never quarrelled with him. Why therefore the necessity of a reconciliation ? Frau von Schleinitz doesn't seem to have profited greatly from association with geniuses if she thinks differently.

" But there's another point to be considered. I very much fear that it will be absolutely impossible, physically or morally, for me to live anywhere else than in Italy and among Italians. Furthermore, for two years I must play the part of the wandering virtuoso ; that is irrevocable. After the tour, I'm going to London for the spring season. In July and August (not yet positive and a deep secret) back to Munich for the ' Tristan ' rehearsals. The first of September to America for at least eight months.

" Each of my three children must be able to receive at least 10,000 *Reichsthalers* from me during my lifetime. Under one condition —in strict confidence between ourselves, dear friend—I could, and might, have to decide to accept a post in Germany or Russia, that is, if the seventeen years' old star of my life can be persuaded to serve as my constant companion. Then I must have a position to offer her, and by taking this Italian to Germany with me, I might be able to forgo my new and real country. However, it is impossible to make any prognostications in this respect. First the father-as-pianist rôle must be played to the end, and the already frequently mentioned star be two years older."

This " star " was the Countess Julie Masetti, a tender fancy that soon vanished like a dream.

Buelow turned a second time to his old comrade in a delicate private matter. Before leaving for America he made his will and wrote Cosima of it, on account of the children. In this he left a legacy to a Russian, Sophie Alexejewnia de Poltovatzki, in the event of his death.

" May I venture to trouble you with a delicate and very confidential matter (he wrote). This concerns the transfer of a sum equivalent to 5,000 francs (4,000 *Reichsmarks*) to a foreign country as a remembrance to someone who was ready to love me, but whom I was forced to renounce through the doubly bad luck of last winter, it being quite immaterial whether this renunciation prevented new qualms of conscience or not. I've no one in the world to whom I might turn to execute this posthumous caprice. If you were disposed to do me this friendly service (whereby I would naturally request that you do it personally, that is, write in my name) I would be very greatly indebted to you and ask you to let me know by a simple yes so that I can include this legacy among others, with the notation : ' for Frau Richard Wagner, for a purpose known to her alone.' "

But even in the Triebschen "Paradise," as Wagner called it later to Vrenli in a mood of melancholy retrospect, there arose an archangel Michael who drove the dwellers from its sweet tranquillity into the turmoil of a hostile world. Wagner's artistic mission imperatively demanded its rights ; that which had been created and completed in this quiet undisturbed atmosphere now had to be touched to life. Bayreuth must arise and this called for the sacrifice of Triebschen. On 22nd April 1872 Wagner, with heavy heart, left this cosy nest with all its blissful memories, to prepare the new and final home at Bayreuth. Cosima and the children followed him a few days later.

" Last Saturday was the day of the sad and deeply moving farewell to Triebschen (wrote Nietzsche). Triebschen is now no more. We walked about as if among ruins—emotion was all about us, in the air, in the clouds. The dog refused to eat, the servants were always in sobs when one spoke to them. We packed up the manuscripts, letters and books—*Ach!* it was heart-breaking."

Two energetic unselfish women assisted Wagner in the realization of his Bayreuth project and remained his friends throughout the rest of his life. One was the wife of the Comptroller of the Royal Household in Berlin, Countess Marie von Schleinitz, who as a young girl had heard Wagner conduct a concert in Breslau in 1863 and thereupon became an admirer of his art. Together with Carl Taussig she drew up the subscription plan (Patronatscheine) for guaranteeing the expenses of the Bayreuth Festival and initiated a lively propaganda in its interest. At Court in Berlin she worked tirelessly in the Master's interests, and Emperor Wilhelm's visit to Bayreuth in 1876 was largely due to her persistent efforts and intercession. In Vienna a similar rôle was played by Countess Marie Dönhoff, who was also soon numbered among the Bayreuth faithful.

On 22nd May 1872 (Wagner's fifty-ninth birthday) the cornerstone of the Festival Theatre was laid in a solemn ceremony attended by the friends and admirers of this bold reformer of German art, who had flocked to the lovely Franconian town from all directions. The ceremony was consecrated by a perfect performance of Beethoven's Ninth Symphony, in which Wagner's niece, Johanna Wagner, was the contralto soloist, and Lilli Lehmann, daughter of his old friend Marie Löw, the soprano. Lehmann proved a true friend and unselfishly devoted artist who was always happy to place her art at his disposition at subsequent festivals. Wagner completed the musical sketches of " Götterdämmerung " on 22nd July 1872.

" I regard the completion of this work (wrote Cosima in great delight) for which I have lived and suffered, as the supreme blessing God has bestowed on me, and the achieved goal of my new life."

On 31st October 1872 Cosima, with the consent of her father, was received into the Protestant Church in Bayreuth in order to resolve any dissonances between Wagner and herself.

" It was a deeply impressive ceremony (she wrote in her diary), my whole soul was thrilled, and the Dean spoke from the depths of his heart. Richard was greatly moved. When we embraced, it seemed to me that only now had our union been effected, only now were we made one in Christ. It meant almost more to me to go to Communion with Richard than to the marriage altar."

There was still a great deal of excitement and worry attached to the construction of the Festival Theatre. Funds came in very slowly, and Wagner's appeal to the German nation met with no response. The intrepid undertaking often threatened to collapse at the last moment. Finally, here as so often in the past, the King of Bavaria proved the saviour. After the preliminary rehearsals in the summer of 1875 the Bayreuth Festival of 1876 put the crowning touch to Wagner's life work in the performance of the " Ring " cycle, the first to be given strictly in accordance with his intentions and an achievement effected solely by his own efforts and determination. Practically all his old friends and well-wishers (Liszt, Nietzsche, the Wesendoncks, Willes, Mathilde Maier, etc.) were present. The King attended the general rehearsals, the first meeting between the two friends since the memorable " Meistersinger " performance in Munich eight years before ! But this strange character who already fled from contact with his fellow men could not bring himself to cross the threshold of Wahnfried and sent his aide-de-camp with his excuses.

" I wish to avoid anything even remotely related with an ovation on the part of the people (he wrote). I hope I will be spared banquets, audiences, visits of strangers. I detest all this kind of thing from the depths of my being. I'm coming simply to gain inspiration from your great work, to refresh myself heart and soul ; not to be gaped at by the inquisitive and offer myself up as an ovation sacrifice."

He was not present at the actual festival performances, which were attended by Emperor Wilhelm I and other notable guests from all over the world. He only came to Bayreuth again for the third cycle, and then fled back to his mountains as soon as it was over. But his old enthusiasm for Wagner's work, the dream of his youth, was reawakened.

" O you understand how to shatter the foundations, to melt— through your triumphant light—the icy crust that had begun to gather round heart and mind as the result of so many sad experiences. Seduced largely by historical studies, I chased other ideals for a time, sacrificed to other gods. But I now feel it more clearly than ever ! It was impossible for anything on this earth to divert me from my fountain- head."

Outwardly the festivals were a great success. Thanks to Wagner's indomitable energy and fanatical faith in his work, the Festival Theatre was now a material fact in the little Franconian capital on the " red Main," a temple of German art waiting for its worshippers. But these worshippers failed to appear ! Once more the Master, as so often in his chequered career, though victor in the difficult battles for his goal, now stood powerless in face of the lack of comprehension and the hostile derision of the broad masses of the people. From the very outset a deficit of alarming proportions prevented the repetition of the festival every summer, as originally planned. But Wagner did not lose courage ; he sacrificed the well-earned rest of his old age and went forth again to battle with unabated energy. He conducted concerts in various German cities, and in London, in order to reduce the burden of debt. Buelow also unselfishly placed himself in the service of Bayreuth, though he was prevented from taking any personal part by untoward fate. He contributed 40,000 *Marks* to the festival fund as the fruit of his piano concerts.

But when all efforts proved vain and there was no possibility of continuing the festivals for the time being, Wagner turned again to his creative work and sank himself in his " Parsifal." And yet he would hardly have been equal to the wearing struggles and the excitements that consumed his vitality had he not had his companion beside him to assist and care for him, and that home of his own which he had so hardly won and in which the happy group of growing children cheered him and fortified his spirit over and over again. Here no noise of the hostile outer world was allowed to enter. Cosima shielded him relentlessly from every discordant element. Her cleverness and self-denial even went so far that she silently suffered a last sudden flaming of passion for a pretty young woman because she knew that the creative artist needs unusual means to excite his imagination. She even associated with this young woman as a friend.

Among the Festival guests in 1876 was the French authoress Judith Gautier (daughter of Théophile Gautier), who had already been a guest at Triebschen on several occasions when she was married to the writer, Catulle Mendes. Even at that time the beautiful, charming Parisian, then scarcely twenty years of age, was completely fascinated by Wagner's strong personality.

" He surprised me at the threshold of his study, the Holy of Holies, which I did not dare enter, as I stood looking at the piano and the sheets of manuscript strewn about everywhere, with the ink still wet upon them (she wrote in her *Memoirs*). The sight of these little material instruments of the creative genius who to me was something more than human, moved me deeply. Suddenly—I caught my breath ! —I heard his laugh quite close to me, the laugh of the man who seemed to me—as I surveyed the centuries—to stand alongside Homer, Æschylus, and Shakespeare, the man I ranked with the very greatest. ' Are you really so enthusiastic ? ' he asked. ' You mustn't overdo it ; it's bad for the health ! ' He spoke in a jesting tone, but the tender look in his eyes showed me clearly enough what was hidden beneath his laughter."

Judith's account leaves no doubt that even then she felt his charm very strongly. But he too was not unmoved by the scarcely concealed passion of the young woman. As always when he was bubbling over with happiness, he suddenly developed great acrobatic agility—just as once in the Biebrich days during some frolicsome bantering with Fredericke Meyer and to the no little terror of the other guests, he suddenly stood on his head on the railing of the balcony ! Now, while walking with Judith in the grounds of Triebschen he scrambled up a high tree, and another time climbed up the façade of the house by means of the ledges and cornices to the balcony on the first storey. " If you look at him so admiringly," said Cosima to the fascinated Judith, " then there's no telling what he may do ! " This pride in his muscular agility and strength was unquestionably due to his desire to be admired not only as a genius but as a man, in spite of

his age. It is strange the charm he always had for women despite
the fact of his insignificant appearance, which was anything but
seductive. From his youth he had been a sensualist with an
unappeasable longing in his heart. And he remained one to his
old age. With him passionate experience was necessary for
artistic creation.

Judith was already divorced from Mendes when she came to the
Festival of 1876, and the episode that started in the Triebschen
days now found its consummation. Wagner often met her in
secret, and when the big evening receptions took place in
Wahnfried—which he really loathed—he would often slip away
to the house where Judith was stopping. Or he would write her
notes that glowed with passion.

" Dearest, I'm unhappy. To-night there's another reception, but
I'm not going down to it. I shall read over portions of my autobiography that I once dictated to Cosima. . . . Did I kiss you this
morning for the last time ? No ! I shall see you again ! I will ! Because
I love you. Adieu ! be kind to me."

This last passionate flame stirred up his inner being once more
and enabled him to bring forth his last creative work, the text of
" Parsifal," and transmute into music the sensual passion of the
seductress Kundry and the Flower Maidens.

" When I am in your arms, I feel inspired by you—your glowing and
yet gentle heart ! You are the blessing of my life, my *superflu enivrant*!
(*Beau français, n'est-ce pas ?*) *Mais c'est égal , vous me comprenez.*"

Of course he still loved Cosima. She alone could guarantee
him the undisturbed peace and tranquillity for his creative work.
Under her protection he completed " Meistersinger " and the
" Ring," which he had conceived before their union. But she
was not his muse. Up to 1876 he had lived from the rich seed
once sowed by the sweetly painful period in the Asyl in Mathilde's
unattainable proximity. Now to create " Parsifal " he needed new
stimulants for the senses that had become dulled in the meantime.
He found them in the brief affair with Judith Gautier and in the
external aphrodisiacs that he had formerly used in Penzing and
Munich. In earlier days the dressmaker had to make him silk
dressing-gowns and down-pillows ; he intoxicated himself with
colours and rich materials, and the touch of glimmering satin.
Now he added to all these stimulants, perfumes and voluptuous

scents. And Judith had to supply them, for was she not residing in Paris, the fountain source of all such riches ?

" My Judith, Beloved ! (By the way you can write me directly as I have arranged everything.) How I should have loved to have had a note from you. From my writing-desk, I can still see you before me on the sofa to the right, watching me (God, what eyes !) write autographs for our poor singers. O, the really extraordinary thing about it all is that you are *l'Abondance de ma pauvre vie, si bien calmée et abritée depuis que j'ai Cosima.*

" I recall your caresses as my most intoxicating and proudest experience. They were a last gift of the gods that didn't want me to succumb to grief over the false fame of the ' Nibelungen ' performances. But why should one mention the whole miserable business ? I don't weep, but in my best moments I preserve such a sweet and pleasant longing—the longing to caress you again and never to lose your divine love. . . . You are mine, *n'est-ce pas* ? In a few days I shall have finished the composition of the first act. And soon you will receive a short excerpt from it. Love me, my beautiful, suffering Abundantia ! "

" Sweet, glowing soul ! What a great creative urge I feel when I am in your arms ! Must I forget it ? No ! I dream of wandering again round the dirty streets of Paris as a fugitive, deserted by the whole world ! Suddenly I meet you, Judith ! You take me by the arm, take me home with you and cover me with kisses ! *Ah! c'est très touchant, très touchant!* O space and time ! You enemies ! I should have found you, *alors. . . . Il est longtemps de là !* "

" But let's talk business. First of all, the boxes haven't arrived yet. I will keep the silk brocade. I want to order ten yards, but perhaps there are other colours that are more to my taste—I mean, silver grey instead of chamois, and pink (*my* pink, very pale and delicate) instead of blue. You frighten me with your perfumes. They'll make me do all kinds of silly things. In general I prefer sachet powder as the material absorbs it better. Never mind about the money ; above all with the bath perfumes—the amber, for instance. My bathroom is located just underneath my study and I like it when the fragrance mounts up to me from there. Don't scold me for it. I'm old enough to permit myself these *enfantillages* ! I have my three ' Parsifal ' years before me— and nothing should tear me away from the pleasant quiet of my busy seclusion."

" Come, dear beloved soul ! Everything is so tragic—everything that is *real*. But you will always love me, and I should be lost without your love, even with the best will in the world. A thousand kisses."

" Everything has arrived safely, the slippers and the Milk of Iris. First rate ! But I need a lot, a half bottle for a bath ; and I bathe every day. Please bear this in mind. Rimmel's Rose de Bengale is better than the White Rose. I'll continue with that; please send me a large quantity—as I use a lot."

"I want some satin. That's the only sort of silk I like because the light plays so softly on its folds. For my sofa I need a very lovely cover in a striking pattern which I shall call Judith! Try and see if you can find some of that material they call ' Lampas,' or something like that. A background of yellow satin, as pale as possible, covered with a network of flowers—roses. I need all that for the lovely morning hours when I am occupying myself with ' Parsifal '! Good-bye, my dearest, my *dolcissima amica.*"

And thus the sweet memories of Judith's embraces and the exotic sensual atmosphere generated by Rimmel's sweet perfumes, the iridescent satins, silk dressing-gowns, and soft gay-coloured slippers were the midwives of the fascinating harmonies that Wagner drew forth from his genius in his " Parsifal." Judith came to Bayreuth again for the " Parsifal " rehearsals in 1881 just when Wagner was busy with the orchestration of the Flower Maiden scene. " She's in the seventh heaven of bliss! " wrote Liszt to the Princess Wittgenstein.

In the autumn of 1881 Wagner had his last conflict with Buelow, this time over the children. The latter had grown up in Wahnfried and as they had had no contact with Buelow they looked upon Wagner as their father, and he now wanted to adopt them formally so that they would all bear the same name and all discord would be banished from their lives. But Buelow strenuously objected. A short time before Liszt had brought Daniela, the eldest daughter, to see her father in Berlin and the latter, deeply touched, wrote Cosima that he " thanked her on his knees."

" What an adorable child ! (he said). What a soul you have developed here ! This twenty-seventh day of April has exalted me. I thank Providence that this inexpressible joy has been reserved for me, this happiness whose sweetness is so great that all the unhappiness, all the regrets, all the reproaches that are mixed in with it cannot disturb it.

" Tell me, magnanimous noble woman, what my responsibilities are towards this beloved creature who captured my soul completely the very first moment ! I would like to erect a chapel on the spot where your father brought her to me. Thank you ! Thank you ! I have to thank you for an incomparable happiness—as painful as it may be. A thousand blessings on you, you great, good woman. Daniela's deportment is admirable in every respect. She is worthy of her mother."

The thought was unbearable to him that this child whom he had just found again should now drop his name. On the other hand, Wagner made the justifiable point that Isolde had no right to the name of Buelow, and under such circumstances he was obliged to disavow his own child before the world. As so often in the past, Cosima stood between the two men and tried to act as mediator and adjust the differences.

Wagner finally consented to her meeting Buelow in Nuremberg for a personal discussion. On this occasion the two old comrades met for the first time in twelve years. Buelow had arrived from Berlin with Daniela. Cosima was shocked at his appearance. Her diary gives the following account of the meeting :

" Lusch (Daniela) at the station—poor dear child ! Sad reports of her father's health. She left me at two o'clock. Poor little orphan ! Who could—who would want to be gay ! Hans with me from four to half-past six. I tried to calm his violent emotional excesses and to overcome his injustice towards Daniela. Hopeless task ! He asked me to stay till the following morning as he hadn't presented the matter to me as he had wished. I consented. The three of us were together in the evening. Woeful gaiety ! A strange night. Richard's telegram sounded more than sad. ' *Was koenntest Du wehren, elendes Weib!* ' A second interview. Hans said he couldn't tell if white was black, or black white. He no longer has any guiding star ; a nervous twitching overcomes him. We said good-bye ! I fetched Daniela and wanted to speak to him again, but he didn't wish it. Return journey accompanied by tears and gratitude.

" Arrival in port. Richard happy to have us back again. Everything was sad that I had to report, and yet a homey feeling came over us and we could discuss things without agitation. But one thing is clear to us, and that is that I can only be with him and the children, and that all other intercourse with strangers and even with friends is a trial and an injustice !

" It was as though a new life began for me after this meeting. I entered the house disconsolate, and yet with peace in my heart, made happy only through his happiness and with the knowledge of an inexpiable sin in my heart. The one is to be enjoyed, the other never to be forgotten—and here may God help me ! "

This time Buelow did not give in. If his attitude towards Cosima was altogether conciliatory and if he viewed her action as foreordained, nevertheless in his heart of hearts he nursed an undying rancour against the *man* Wagner that broke out from time to time and could not be quieted.

*   *   *   *

In the summer of 1882 the Festival Theatre reopened its doors. During the six long years that it had taken Wagner to recoup the losses from 1876 he had been obliged to abandon his artistic plans. Now he was to bring his swan song, " Parsifal," to life, a work that he wanted to restrict exclusively to Bayreuth in the future. To his great regret the King could not bring himself to be present. Sixteen performances of " Parsifal " were given at this second festival, and the season was also successful financially, so that they could count on a repetition the following year. At the last performance of " Parsifal " Wagner quite unexpectedly took over the baton during the third act and conducted the opera from the conclusion of the Transformation music to the end, giving the work an unthought-of fire and pathos. It proved to be his artistic farewell to the world.

To recover from the exertions of the summer he left for Venice in the autumn of 1882 with the entire family. They found comfortable quarters for the winter in the Palazzo Vendramini on the Grand Canal, one of the most beautiful buildings in the city, and here in the bosom of his family, with frequent surprise visits from friends and disciples (Liszt spent Christmas with them) he passed the last days of his life in peace, without cares or worries. It was the last respite of the tireless fighter. On 13th February 1883 the weary heart, steeled though it was by life's battles, now gave out. Seized by a heart spasm he passed into the " realm of night " in the arms of his faithful comrade.

Cosima refused to leave him. Unable to comprehend the incomprehensible, she knelt for twenty-four hours beside the body, remote from the world, in quiet communion with the dead. He should not be all alone that first night in the realm of death. She would watch over him until they tore his mortal frame from her. She would gaze into the beloved countenance as long as she could still partake of it. It seemed as though she were determined to follow him of her own free will.

Yet even in this most tragic hour of her life the idea of her high mission triumphed at last in this strong-willed woman. If throughout two decades she had loyally fulfilled that mission to the living master, now his legacy was waiting the far-sighted, clear-headed custodian. It remained for her to hand down his work to the world, to secure the crown of his achievement, to guarantee Bayreuth. As Buelow telegraphed his one-time companion on hearing of Wagner's death : " *Sœur, il faut vivre !* " this knowledge had also penetrated her own consciousness during the last long night. She ordered her daughters to cut off her long hair, which reached almost to the ground, and which Richard had so loved. This she laid beside him in the coffin as a last love offering.

The Master's mortal remains were taken to Bayreuth by special train and homage was done to it all along the route. And here he was laid to rest in the garden of his home Wahnfried. At the same hour, far away in another country, a woman whom Fate had once delegated to fill an important rôle in the life of the departed artist, dedicated to his memory these lines of pensive remembrance.

On the Funeral of Richard Wagner in Wahnfried

A cry of grief goes through the world,
Tidings of bitter sorrow
Go through the heart of all mankind
That waits a dark to-morrow.
From deepest depths swells up her woe
Like the sea's tides unbounded.
Stricken in her most glorious son,
With a death-wound she is wounded.
Lay silently the wreaths and offerings down.
Here stand we full of tears but not alone ;
Greatest of the departed, all mankind
Kneels at your bier to consecrate the stone.

When death almost without a pang had reft
From us in icy kiss that godlike head,
A tremor passes through her very blood,
She weeps—her own, her genius is dead.
Yet we have naught but bitter tears to offer
You who so often freed us from earth's pain,
For at that moment when we saw you dying
The darkness fell, we dare not hope again.
Abandoned now, forsaken stands the temple
Which you devoted to a theme sublime.
High priest, you wrought for timeless generations,
Alas ! to us can bring you back no time.

Then do not scorn us, who remain but mortal,
That deep despair would now our hearts subdue,
That all our hoping, striving—all our loving,
Is but a single breath that mourns for you.
Often and willingly you spoke of dying,
Calming the beating heart to stillness soon ;
I well remember how I heard you speaking
Of peace in death as of a precious boon.
Longing for death is in the love of Tristan,
Longing for death Amfortas's tortures all,
And Kundry too, receives upon her forehead
The death-devoted kiss from Parsifal.

Your life on earth was one long day of labour,
The evening came at last and night brought rest.
Peace of the grave surrounds your head in honour,
Now it is finished—we may call you blest.

(Translation by Olga Erbsloh Muller.)

Chapter VII

EROS AND THE WOMEN IN WAGNER'S LIFE
AND WORK

Not goods, nor gold,
Nor splendour of gods ;
Not house, nor land,
Nor masterful pomp ;
Not troublous covenants'
Treacherous bands,
Not custom's dissembling
Rigorous law ;
Blissful in joy and grief,
Grant us—nothing but love.[1]

THESE words of Brynhilde's ran like a leit-motif through
Wagner's whole career. For love was the fulcrum of his
existence ; the well-spring of his creative genius. And still he
was no favourite of Venus, no darling of the fair sex like Goethe
or Franz Liszt, who even at an advanced age found infatuated
women ready to throw themselves at their feet. For Wagner's
appearance as well as his personality lacked the outward charm of
a Don Juan. The cavalier graces, the lovable cajolery, the graceful
dallying, all the expedients of a Lothario at home in distinguished
drawing-rooms, were denied this honest son of a petty Saxon
official, with his innate strain of melancholy.

Strongly sensual by nature, Wagner who (as he tells us in
Mein Leben) derived sensual pleasure—when only a little lad—
from the mere touch of a woman's hand or articles of his sisters'
clothing, learned all love's secrets at an early age. As a youth he
gave himself over to reckless dissipation ; like his " Tannhäuser "
later on, love for him meant only " sensual gratification." As

[1] Passage from Brynhilde's final oration which Wagner rejected when he wrote
the music to " Götterdämmerung."

usually happens in such cases (especially when thrown constantly in the company of close feminine relatives as in Wagner's father-less house) the stirrings of gradually awakening spiritual emotions along with the physical satisfaction of his sexual desires were transmuted into a Platonic adoration of the beloved.

This emotional cleavage was only resolved when these two nether poles of the sexual instinct were combined in the person of mistress and wife through the ennobling of what was initially a purely sensual amour.

In later years this elementary sexual instinct in Wagner departed more and more from its natural orbit. Owing partly to his tragic marriage, sensual indulgence itself gave way more and more to the *yearning* for that indulgence. His unheroic effeminate nature, so prone to self-pity, revelled in all the torments of disappointed love. His spasmodic, feverish desire for love, the cry of a famished person, now became merged in the yearning for redemption. Here Love and Death were intermingled. This theme of redemption also runs like a scarlet thread through his works. In the Wagnerian heroes, Love is not a bond uniting the living, a striving towards earthly union; but a means of redemption. They achieve redemption by abstaining from sensuality—a redemption through " pure " love. Where sen-suality is encountered it is no healthy sensuality but lust, a voluptuous orgy (Tannhäuser, Kundry) that can only be redeemed by chaste virginity, purity and renunciation (Elizabeth, Parsifal) or else something contrary to nature (self-mutilation—Klingsor). This naturally gives the concept of " death " an entirely new significance. Here it is not termination but culmination. For the lovers can only become united through the instrumentality of death. And that they die disunited heightens the tragedy of their fate. Wagner overcame the terrors of death by lauding it, not as a dreaded annihilation but as the longed-for beatific redemption.

His creative work derived less from an over-abundance of energy than from the torments, bitternesses and promises of his emotional life. These tempests unlocked, as if by magic, the richest treasures of his genius. Catastrophes that would unques-tionably have destroyed a different type of person, actually drew forth the best that was in him as he voluptuously drained the cup

of bitterness to the dregs and intoxicated himself thereon to the
point of frenzy. For him creative work was a healing process that,
cleansing as a thunderstorm, relieved the cramping tension of
his spirit. Art had to compensate him for life's privations. " If
we could really live, art would be unnecessary," he once wrote.
" Art begins precisely where life leaves off."

His own art therefore led logically to renunciation, to escape
from the world. At the end of his creative achievement stands
the ascetic " Parsifal." How different it was with Beethoven ! As
the finale of his far less happy life, Beethoven placed the life-
affirming " Ode to Joy " ! With him, too, love often swelled to an
ecstatic climax, lashing his senses powerfully, without leaving
any appreciable traces in his music. Indeed, Beethoven—wholly
sunk in his artistic mission—sometimes felt that Eros was
actually a hindrance to the fulfilment of his art. What to the
erotic Wagner was the *conditio sine qua non* of all creative art was
to Beethoven a disturbing factor. Wagner could only draw from
the deepest sources of his art when a grievous passion devoured
him, inflamed him. The more his erotic reactions faded with the
years, the greater became his need to resort to artificial stimulants,
and inclined as he was to erotomania, to turn more and more
to narcotics to excite his blunted senses. His study was furnished
with sophisticated elegance. Heady perfumes, glaring lights and
colours (daylight being entirely excluded), the brilliant shimmer
of the heaviest silks, soft furs and rich satins, the mere touch of
which excited him violently, were the principal stage properties.
Wagner's ever-increasing craving for such things seems almost
as though he were afraid his inner fires were dying out.

In no other artist do we find a more intimate connection
between his works and his erotic life. Even his earliest youthful
efforts were closely allied with his personal experiences. When
his unhappy youthful infatuation for the Pachta sisters became
known, it explained at once the much-disputed genesis of the
text of " Die Hochzeit," saddled by the ponderous Wagner
philologians with the most extraordinary scientific hypotheses.
Here also the God of Love had inspired the pen of the budding
poet.

As regards the contributing influence of his personal experience
on the structure of the " Liebesverbot," he himself tells us in

Mein Leben that " love-sickness for Minna led him to intensify the ' extravagant situation ' of his drama." Other eloquent proofs of this are the glorification of a sister's love in " Rienzi," written shortly after the death of his favourite sister, Rosalie, and the scarcely noted circumstance that in the first sketch of the " Flying Dutchman " the redemptress was called Minna, not Senta. In Pierre Dietsch's " Le Vaisseau Fantôme," a French opera based on Wagner's sketch, the name Minna was retained. On the other hand, the great extent to which his own spiritual dichotomy and the conflict of the artistic genius with the every-day world round him contributed to the shaping of " Tannhäuser " and " Lohengrin " is, of course, well known. The " Ring " cycle then brings the supreme love song in the redemptive triumph of this elemental force over all earthly powers. But it is precisely the development of this monumental work that shows most clearly how his creative genius was affected by outward influences.

In the midst of his work the Master broke off and turned to a new composition. Naturally there were other contributory reasons for this, but the basic cause was a deep spiritual one arising from his emotional life. Mathilde Wesendonck had entered his life. And when the Master, whose acquaintance with the works of Schopenhauer had made him out of tune with his original revolutionary, optimistic conception of the work, was about to write the music for the exultant jubilant love scene of the third act of " Siegfried," his inspiration failed him. The elements whipped up within him by the blissful yet painful experience with Mathilde claimed their rights, the sunny hero had to retire and the tempest within him resolved itself in the febrile ardours of *Tristan,* bringing him relief. " I have *you* to thank with all my soul and to all eternity that I wrote ' Tristan,' " he himself confessed later in a letter to Mathilde. And to his friend Liszt, ignorant of the Asyl incidents, he wrote : " No more about intimate events in my quite recent past. But you will learn of the *most* intimate when you once hear ' Tristan.' "

In view of these and many other personal admissions on his part, it seems all the more strange that attempts were made by Bayreuth, for Cosima's sake, to minimize, and in fact directly to negate Mathilde Wesendonck's influence on his work. But for

R

this he himself is chiefly to blame, for as his autobiography and other things prove, he promulgated this thesis out of love for Cosima. We have to thank Wagner's love for Mathilde not only for "Tristan" but for "Meistersinger," and to a certain extent even for "Parsifal." He only arrived at complete renunciation of his beloved after they had met in Venice, the first encounter after their separation, when his Muse reminded him of an early sketch for an opera ("Meistersinger") which he had given her. This renunciation revealed to him all at once the full secret of the Hans Sachs drama. His own painful resignation was transmuted and found relief in that of Sachs. On the way back to Vienna, Mathilde's suggestion took more and more concrete form. He could even hear the music.

"Only now am I completely resigned (he wrote her). Steel your heart against Sachs. You are going to fall in love with him! It is really a wonderful work. The old sketch offered little or nothing. Ah, yes! one must have been in Paradise to see what there is in a thing like this."

Through this mood he came to appreciate the full meaning of compassion and he tried to explain it in detail to Mathilde, writing her that the third act of " Parsifal " would some day make it fully clear to her. This work as well as the projected Buddhistic drama " Die Sieger " had their roots in the fruitful Asyl period. And his prophetic words to Mathilde that, " it is quite clear to me that I shall never create anything new again. That one peak period of fertility germinated in me such a plenitude of seed buds that now I've only to reach into my stock and it's then a simple matter to cultivate the flower," were literally fulfilled.

If one should ask which of the three women (Minna, Mathilde, Cosima) who played a decisive rôle in his life had the most profound effect on the creative artist, the answer can only be Mathilde Wesendonck. As his Muse, she possessed the secret power of setting into vibration all the strings of his magic lyre and of evoking the supreme revelations of his genius. This was perhaps less due to her personality and its effect on the Master than to the dispensations of Fate which turned their love to tragedy, forced them to sorrowful resignation and thereby (given his temperament) induced in him a spiritual mood that offered the most favourable soil possible for the unfolding of his genius.

He unquestionably loved Mathilde as he loved no other woman before or after. Even years later he wrote : " She is and remains my first and only love ! I feel that more and more definitely. It was the zenith of my life." When she crossed his path he was also at the height of his powers and creative fertility, whereas he was over fifty when Cosima became his wife. Whether Mathilde with her gentle pensive nature would also have been able to fill the rôle of wife ; whether she, who was destined to be his Muse, would also have proved an energetic crusader such as he later required for the realization of his creations, is justly open to doubt.

Minna, his first wife, possessed these qualities to a far greater degree than Mathilde, though on the other hand she altogether lacked the latter's merits and advantages. In any case when she was at his side there was no question of any such thing. Fate had meted out to her the most thankless task of all the women in his life. At the time of their marriage she was a popular actress, and he a poor devil of a *Kapellmeister* out of a job. She felt herself far superior to him in every way, and later when he had long outdistanced her and had unfolded the wings of his genius, she failed to revise her point of view, which is usually the after-effect of such a first impression. She lived through the leanest years with him, destitute and hungry. Then after a short spell of unalloyed happiness she saw what had been so laboriously achieved suddenly dashed to ruins through (as she considered) sheer wantonness on the part of her husband. And later when the sun of good fortune burst forth in glory over Richard's head, she found herself cast off, a lonely, sick, embittered old woman.

If in Minna he possessed the faithful, self-sacrificing partner who tenderly cared for and looked after him, without however being capable of appreciating his artistic genius—and in Mathilde he found the artist's stimulating Muse—it was the evening of his life that brought him, in Cosima, the woman who combined both these characteristics. A talent akin to his own enabled her to keep pace with his genius in any direction, while a fine business head, an intrepid and fanatical energy that pressed forward steadily and ruthlessly towards their common goal, directing all her actions to a chosen end, indifferent to her family and the judgment of the world, made her an invaluable collaborator and helper to the Master. In addition it was given her to gratify his ardent wish for a son and heir and provide the long and vainly sought home for the rudderless, storm-tossed artist whose yearning for affection found satisfaction in her austere, almost masculine nature. And just as Cosima achieved the sheerly impossible after Wagner's death and with iron will and determination put the crown of victorious achievement on his life work by saving Bayreuth for the world (a deed that can never be too highly praised), so also during his lifetime she was the mistress of Wahnfried, the all-guiding and determining force. Wagner's self-centred nature, so ill fitted for intercourse with the world, required some such powerful advocate for his cause. If Cosima in her ambitious zeal and blind adoration of the Master fostered some of his weaknesses, and by establishing a sort of princely court in Bayreuth, conjured up that cult of his person which Nietzsche (even in 1876) found so distressing, these are but passing shadows which cannot tarnish her picture as a whole.

Minna, Mathilde, Cosima! these three centres of Wagner's love life! The one he married; the one who was his " immortal lover "; and the one who married him—each had her special mission in his life, each entered his career at the vital moment for her particular task. To which of them should fall the crown? A difficult, idle question. Each in her own way rendered imperishable service to man and artist, and all three have equal claim to the gratitude and esteem of later generations. Therefore let us drop at last all petty rivalry and jealousy and by recognizing that had it not been for these three women we would scarcely be the possessors to-day of the Wagner art work in its present greatness and scope, let us bow in homage to this brilliant feminine constellation :

Mathilde

Minna   Cosima

THE BURRELL COLLECTION

THE name of Burrell first came to the attention of the public in 1898 when there appeared in London a large and sumptuous privately printed work (limited to 100 copies) containing facsimiles and beautiful reproductions of a series of hitherto completely unknown documents from the early days of Richard Wagner's career. This important treasure-trove of Wagneriana, which soon became a collector's item, was intended as the first of a magnificent twelve-volume edition along the same lines. The author was the Honourable Mrs. Burrell, a devoted Wagnerian, who after Wagner's death in 1883 made it the sole aim and object of her life to collect all the available material anywhere in the world touching the career of her idol, and spared no expense in tracking down every new clue that would lead her to the desired goal.

And she not only had the wherewithal to carry out her ambition but—which was far more important—luck was with her! She learned that in 1870 Wagner had eighteen copies of his autobiography privately printed in Basle by the printer Bonfantini, and she succeeded in purchasing a copy of this rare treasure from the widow of the printer who had surreptitiously struck off another copy for himself. In this way it was possible for her to follow up all the clues mentioned by Wagner in his autobiography without having to fear that anyone would interfere or encroach on her preserves, since the work at that time was inaccessible to the public. It was not published until 1911!

The most valuable information that Mrs. Burrell derived from this source was the discovery of the then wholly unknown fact (1890) that Wagner's first wife Minna, at the time of her marriage, already had an illegitimate nine-year-old daughter, Nathalie, whom she always represented as her younger sister. Nathalie had lived for years in the Wagner household, and Minna in her

will designated " her sister Nathalie " her residuary legatee.
If Mrs. Burrell were now successful in locating the whereabouts
of Nathalie and could obtain her undoubtedly copious collection
of Wagner memorials, it would be nothing short of a fantastic
stroke of luck. And the improbable came about.

After a tireless search, Nathalie was traced to an almshouse in
Leisnig near Chemnitz, where she was living in reduced circumstances. And Mrs. Burrell was able to win her confidence gradually and acquire little by little Minna's entire legacy of
correspondence and personal Wagner memorials, which were
still in Nathalie's possession.

This collection contained numerous original works of Wagner,
such as his early tragedy " Leubald," several overtures, drafts
and sketches for the operas " Die Feen," " Liebesverbot,"
" Rienzi," " Tannhäuser," etc., besides a number of hitherto
unknown photographs of the highest interest, and about 150
letters of Wagner to Minna, which Nathalie had very cunningly
held back when she returned Wagner his letters after Minna's
death. Comprising the most ardent love letters from the early
days of their acquaintance, this part of the collection provides the
most illuminating and eloquent documentary proof of the shocking
and touching tragedy of Richard Wagner's first marriage, the
full significance of which is yet to be generally recognized. Mrs.
Burrell also succeeded in persuading Nathalie (then sixty years
old) to write her personal reminiscences of the twenty-six years
she spent in the Wagner household in Paris, Dresden and
Zürich. This fills two thick volumes and from a critical point of
view naturally represents a fund of important biographical
material.

These treasures acquired from Nathalie form the basis of the
Burrell Collection. In addition it comprises the complete correspondence with Wagner's Paris friend, the painter E. B. Kietz,
the great Dresden tenor Tichatschek, the printer Bonfantini in
Basle, the publishers Volz and Batz, and a large number of
miscellaneous letters of the very highest interest. It was the
intention of Mrs. Burrell to edit this material herself, and she was
in the midst of the work when her death occurred. Her husband
then issued the first volume, as a memorial to her in a certain
sense, but did not continue the project. From then on this

valuable and interesting material was pigeonholed in the Burrell family archives.

In 1911 I tried in vain to obtain access to these documents in connection with the first edition of the present work in which I attempted, for the first time, to do full justice at long last to Wagner's first wife, who had always been neglected, or passed over in silence by the official Wagner historians. But the then owner, the daughter of Mrs. Burrell, after hesitating for a long time, finally refused her permission since, like so many autograph collectors, she nursed the idea that the autographs would lose their value on publication. She died soon after this, and during the years of the first world war, we in Germany lost all trace of the collection. But strange to say, the English heirs also do not seem to have been aware of the value and importance of the documents that had fallen into their hands. These were simply deposited in a bank, chiefly in clothes-baskets and boxes, and nobody bothered about them any longer. In this way a portion of the collection was lost, and no trace has ever been found up to the present time.

In the spring of 1929 chance again brought the collection to public attention. In looking over the collection in the bank an American journalist, Philip Hurn, came across a package of Wagner documents and then began to follow up the matter in earnest. Most of the collection finally came to light and a detailed catalogue was made in which the 518 documents and other items were listed. The owners then resolved to offer the collection for sale *en bloc* at a price of $500,000, but beforehand decided to publish the priceless documents for the benefit of Wagnerian research. They thereupon wrote to me asking if I would be willing to edit this entire material and assume charge of the publication which was to be issued simultaneously in Germany, France and England in a two-volume edition. The contract was signed with me and the publishing house of Erich Reiss in Berlin in the autumn of 1929. However, since it was impossible for me to go to London for a period of several months in order to sort out and edit the material, and since furthermore the valuable documents could not be shipped abroad, it was agreed to forward me photostatic copies at regular intervals.

The first volume of the projected work was to be devoted

exclusively to the marriage tragedy of Richard and Minna Wagner (with the publication of the 150 original letters in their entirety), while the second—which was still more important for Wagner research—was to comprise (besides the shorter collections of correspondence) the still unknown drafts, prose sketches and original editions of " Leubald," " Die Feen," " Liebesverbot," " Rienzi," " Tannhäuser " and several hitherto unknown youthful compositions.

At first everything went according to schedule and the photostatic copies and facsimiles reached me regularly. Suddenly everything stopped, and after numerous inquiries it was learned that Wahnfried had persuaded the Burrell heirs to refrain from the publication of these documents which was very unwelcome to Bayreuth. Therefore the publication of the Burrell Collection, which had been announced for the autumn of 1930, fell through. The collection was subsequently sold to Mrs. Mary Curtis Bok of Philadelphia, who at first refused to place it at the disposition of Wagner scholars.

The collection has now at last been issued under the editorship of Mr. John Burk of Boston. It contains nothing really new to Wagner research, nor anything that would invalidate previous assumptions and deductions. Nevertheless, indisputable documentary evidence is now at hand, unfortunately not in the German original but in English translation which, as every Wagner expert knows, is sometimes very disturbing and misleading in spite of the greatest care on the part of the translator. I consider the book in its present form simply a collection of documents that is of the highest value for the Wagner student, but one that can offer little to the general reader who is not already informed regarding the events of Wagner's life. Very true, the editor has endeavoured to explain the various *étapes* of Wagner's life and link the different items together through running comments and explanations. But the uninitiated reader will not get much out of it. Episodes such as the Laussot affair in Bordeaux and the Wesendonck tragedy in Zürich must be told in their entirety in order to be comprehensible and cannot be grasped through the medium of scattered and isolated correspondence.

One must not forget that the newly published letters to Minna,

even though they are among the most interesting, still only represent a third of the entire correspondence ; and after all at least
two-thirds are necessary for a complete understanding. The
chronological arrangement of the material is also, in my opinion,
a far from happy one and would have been more comprehensible
and effective if it had been arranged in two groups. As it now
stands the Minna tragedy is continually interrupted by extraneous
matter such as the correspondence with Tichatschek, Kietz,
Heine, etc., and therefore all the more difficult to understand. It
would also have been much more effective if the letters, contained
in Appendix A, had been inserted in their proper chronological
place in the body of the book.

The previously deleted portions of the Uhlig correspondence
forming Appendix B and based on copies of the Uhlig letters sold
to Mrs. Burrell by Uhlig's daughter, are already known in
Germany. I published these letters in 1913 in my *Collected
Wagner Correspondence*.

Appendix C contains twenty-five letters not in the original
Burrell Collection which are addressed to Kummer, Esser and
others. The greater portion of this correspondence has already
been published in Germany.

Unfortunately this very admirable edition, containing eleven
illustrations (of which Otterstedt's painting of Minna dating from
the year 1836 is the most interesting), has omitted the photographic
reproductions that would be of most value to Wagner scholars,
namely Wagner's youthful works, the sketches and prose drafts.
It is earnestly hoped that this part of the material will soon be
made generally available, and in the German original.

Appendix II

THREE points in which the author's interpretation of certain facts in Wagner's life differ materially from that of Ernest Newman in his biography of Wagner.

A. Wagner's Mother and Ludwig Geyer

Wagner's father, the Leipzig Police Actuary Carl Friedrich Wagner, married Johanna Rosina Paetz of Weissenfels on 2nd June 1798. Nine children were born of this union : four boys and five girls. The eldest son was Albert, the youngest Richard. Father Wagner, in spite of his dull business duties, had a very keen artistic streak in his nature, which took the form of a particular passion for the theatre. He even took part in amateur theatricals at times and wanted his children to go on the stage, which shocked his scholarly brother Adolph. They nearly all inherited a goodly amount of their father's talent in this direction.

One of the family's most intimate friends was young Ludwig Geyer (born in Eisenach, 23rd January 1779) who had been obliged by the unexpected death of his father to break off his law studies and support himself and his family by his unusual talents as a portrait painter. It was on Wagner's advice that he took up acting professionally and he never had cause to regret his decision. He lost his father in the first half of 1799 and made the acquaintance of the Wagners when he settled in Leipzig shortly afterwards. He joined the Magdeburg troupe in 1805, was in Stettin in 1806, and from then until 1809 was in Breslau, at which date he returned to Leipzig and took up his residence with the Wagners. He became a member of the Seconda troupe in Leipzig in the autumn of 1909 and remained with it until his death in 1821.

In the meantime living conditions in Leipzig had become very difficult after Saxony's fatal pact with the French conqueror. Carl Friedrich Wagner, however (who was the only member of the Council with a sound knowledge of French), found himself promoted to Chief of Police for Public Safety, and did great

266

service for his fellow townsmen and his native city in those troublous days. During the anxious hours of the Battle of Leipzig, which ended with the capture of the city by the Allied Armies, the flight of Napoleon and the longed-for liberation from foreign rule, he never left his post of duty.

Then on 22nd November 1813 he fell a victim to the hospital fever which was raging in Leipzig as the result of the many dead and wounded. For the family this was almost a fatal blow. Johanna Wagner saw herself plunged into the bitterest need with her flock of little children. Albert, the eldest, had just turned fourteen and was a student at the Fuersten School in Meissen, while the youngest (Richard) was only a baby of six months. But good friends came generously to her assistance. Besides her brother-in-law Adolph, Ludwig Geyer (who had long had the status of a member of the family) also stepped into the breach and assumed the responsibility of the children's education, proving himself a true friend in every way. He took Rosalie, Luise and Julius to Dresden with him, where he was playing that winter with the Seconda Company, and sent their mother regular detailed reports of their progress and well-being in cordial, friendly letters.

The complete correspondence between Johanna Wagner and Geyer, which is in the possession of the Avenarius family, was published by Ludwig Avenarius in 1912 (*Avenarianische Chronik*, P. R. Reisland, Leipzig). It consists of seven letters. The first, written while Carl Friedrich Wagner was still alive, is dated 6th June 1813; the second, Dresden, 22nd December 1813; the third, Dresden, 29th December 1813; the fourth, Dresden, 1st January 1814; the fifth, Dresden, 14th January 1814; the sixth, Dresden, 28th January 1814; and the seventh, Dresden, 11th February 1814. Mrs. Burrell published four of the letters in the original German in her book (1898), they having been shown her by Caecilie Avenarius who allowed her to copy them. One (that of 14th January 1814) is now listed in the Burrell Collection (Exhibit 15).

" Friend! (Geyer wrote on 22nd December 1813) Many thanks for your kind letter, which pulled me out of a very dispirited mood and set me up again since I found you more composed, having forcibly resigned yourself to Fate, which will surely treat you very kindly.

Intercourse with dear friends, their heartfelt participation in one's joys and sorrows, their sincere constancy, is indeed one of the greatest happinesses of life and you are in enjoyment of the same while I, buried like a badger, torn from all my dear ones, scan my room in my loneliness and at most slip over to Hartwig's now and again to see what my foster daughter (Rosalie) is up to. She is her teacher's darling and the latter looks after her with such really tender care as to merit sincere respect. This week I have both hands full with the presents for Christmas Eve. Feldkummer (Julius), whose clothes are still in good order, will receive a waistcoat and a cap—on our departure I will only equip him for the summer; Rosalie is to get a red scarf, a sewing basket, a cake, apples, nuts, and an enormous Christmas tree from me and a black frock from Mme Hartwig—the same for Luise. I am looking forward to the festivity with no little pleasure. You do the same at home and light a beautiful tree for the Cossack (Richard). I would love to have a little scuffle with the youngster on my sofa."

A week later Geyer once more assured his friend of his interest and assistance.

"Dearest friend : I once more cordially hold out my hand to you. Let us seek the purer metal in us, not the dross. I am now more susceptible to everything good, how otherwise could I then bind myself so staunchly to you and your dear ones ? Let us bind our friendship's bond ever closer over the sarcophagus of 1813; the summons to do so is great and noble. And so I exterminate all jealousy that might still cling to me ! You do the same and let us face each other staunch and true. Wishing you all happiness. Geyer."

"You surely know without further assurance how crushed I am over dear Albert's illness and the suffering it has brought upon you (he wrote on 1st January 1914). But God will not let his hand fall so heavily upon us and things will surely take a turn for the best. To my peace of mind I heard from local doctors that here more have recovered from these bad fevers than have succumbed to them. Should (which God forbid !) it sadly come about that Albert is also torn from us, then turn over the whole house to good Jettchen and come right away to us. Here you will also be surrounded by your friends and children, and perhaps you will find comfort and peace of mind sooner, since you will have put all reminders behind you. But I trust firmly in God and hope that you may not need this sad comfort, but can visit us more at ease in mind and more strengthened in spirit.

"Only keep up your good spirits, and no matter how hard Fate may hit you, don't give way too much to grief; remember that you still have great responsibilities in the world since you are a mother and your children need your care. Please hearken to the pleas of your most devoted friend, who in this case would himself not have suffi-

cient fortitude to bear this hardest of blows. Let me hear from you
very soon again and accept my warmest wishes for everything that
can bring you joy and peace of mind. I am staunchly and steadfastly
yours, Geyer.

"The children are well. May Albert and Richard also soon be
likewise."

"Beloved friend (he wrote on 14th January). From the bottom of
my heart I thank Heaven for Albert's recovery and for your renewed
peace of mind attendant on this joyous prospect. You poor dear!
Heaven has certainly marked you out for suffering; but it has also
lent you the strength to endure it, and the joy of knowing that your
prayers for Albert's life have been granted must be truly comforting
and morally inspiring. I really honestly lived through the whole
harrowing experience with you. . . . Your kind solicitude for me and
my health merits my hearty thanks, but thank God! I am well, as are
all of us here who are dear to you. . . . You will be very pleased with
me when I tell you that I haven't any more debts except the rest of the
tailor's bill. I can now also draw a free breath. Everything is also
paid up for the children. They are all well. The Cossack's wildness
cannot be otherwise than divine; for the first window that he smashes
he shall have a silver medal. May God have you in His keeping. To
all friends and to my Albert, greetings and a kiss from your ever
devoted friend, Geyer."

"There is really something wanting when I fail to receive a letter
from you every week (he wrote on 28th January). Then I always torture
myself with a thousand fancies. I imagine that you are ill or angry or
indifferent towards me, and that is also always a little weakness of
yours—at least a mental disorder, since you never let your heart argue
wholesomely in my favour, but there is always a little malady in reserve
that breaks out at the slightest provocation. But that will also pass in
time! You have promised me to be very good and to have full
confidence in me in the future, and I hope my good and very dear
friend will keep her word. I now seem different to you in many ways,
perhaps; but I swear to God that I'm a better man and hope still to
be able to prove it to you in time to come. Providence really means well
with us. He has given me the beautiful vocation of being your friend,
and in holding persistently to this course I now also find myself repaid
in my art and am making significant progress therein. When Art has
become so fond of me, will you, who with it represent the joy of my
life, cease to be my friend? Yet my demands on both are indeed too
great for me ever to flatter myself that I shall attain my desires!"

"As little pleasure as you may find in Dresden under the present sad
conditions (read the next letter), yet you must still be good and think

that it will be a great joy to us, particularly to me, to see you once again and to embrace you after the many trials you have gone through. Therefore, don't let anything dissuade you from taking this little trip, but do come—you really owe yourself this little recreation for the sake of your health. I have a lot of things to talk over with you, and I can hardly wait for the time when I can have a real heart to heart talk with you on the cosy sofa. May you be as happy as I wish from the very bottom of my heart. The children are well and send love to their mother, whom I also beg with all my heart to be always the same towards me. I am eternally yours, Geyer.''

All these letters in the original were placed at my disposal in 1911. The second letter, of which Newman assumes that the closing portion was withheld from Mrs. Burrell because it contained something incriminating regarding the relations between the two, is not complete even in the original. The letter ends with the following sentence : '' Albert asked me to-day for a cash advance for the Rector ; to-morrow I am sending him 6 *thalers*. Please ask Albert, who in the meantime will have received my letter to Koenig in Meissen, to notify the latter. *Schreiben Sie mir doch, wie Sie es auch den Weihnachtsgeschenken fuer die Lehrer ge* . . . (i.e. But please write me also about the Christmas presents for the teachers. . . .) Here apparently in opening the letter a small piece of it was inadvertently torn off and has now been lost. It could only have been three or four lines at the most. In view of the general tone of the letter and that of all the preceding ones, it is impossible to believe that the few missing lines could have contained anything that would cast a slur on their relationship. They could only have been the usual closing words of a letter. In order to provide a foundation artificially for his very doubtful Geyer Theory, Newman is here assuming something that does not exist. To claim, furthermore, that letters have been destroyed or suppressed is going very far indeed. The first letter is from June 1813 when Johanna's husband was still alive, and he is frequently mentioned in the letter in a thoroughly friendly sense. After Carl Friedrich's death on 22nd November 1813 the correspondence took a more active form, since Geyer was helping the widow of his old friend with advice and material aid and had assumed charge of the children. The letters followed one on the other with only the briefest of periods between (a fortnight at most) so that it is altogether improbable that in between these published letters others were exchanged which Newman now assumes were later on destroyed !

Johanna accepted the invitation of her friend to come to Dresden, and it was during this visit that the two decided to marry. Intimacy between them also began at this time, since Caecilie was born on 26th February 1815, while the official marriage, after the regular posting of the banns (which requires four weeks), did not take place until 28th August in Leipzig. However, it is completely beside the mark to endeavour to draw from this correspondence any conclusions regarding the existence of an earlier liaison between the two writers. *No man writes in this way to a woman with whom he has had a liaison for years—with one who has borne him a child while her own husband was living !* Individual sentences divorced from the context such as Geyer's " and so I exterminate all jealousy that might still cling to me. You do the same and let us face each other staunch and true," as well as Wagner's reference to " our father Geyer " in his letter to Caecilie prove absolutely nothing. Wagner had never known his real father as he was only six months old at the time of his death. Geyer was " father " to him in all respects, just as when he first entered school he was registered as Richard Geyer. If he had really considered himself Geyer's very own son he would not have begun his autobiography with the sentence " My father was Carl Friedrich Wagner," especially as Geyer's paternity, for artistic reasons, would have been far more sympathetic to him.

Wagner, who naturally felt more drawn to Geyer than to his own father, once expressed the suspicion that he was Geyer's child, and official Wagner literature, accepting blindly every statement of the Master's, finally took the fact for granted. Others, corrupted by Nietzsche's malicious comment that a " vulture (Geier) is almost an eagle," gaily seized on the statement to dispose of Wagner once for all as the child of a Jew. Both attitudes are as erroneous as they are unfounded. On what was Wagner's suspicion based ? Apart from the emotional factor, perhaps, of preferring to be the child of a general genius like Geyer rather than of a simple police official, it had no other foundation than the above letters. After reading them he wrote his stepsister Caecilie : " At the same time, through these letters to Mother, I was able to gain a deep insight into the relations of the two in difficult times. I believe I can now see it all very clearly, even though I feel it is extremely difficult to express how I view these relations. It seems to me as though our father Geyer, through his self-sacrificing devotion to the whole family, believed he was thereby atoning for a guilt."

Anyone who reads Geyer's letters with an open mind will gain the impression that Wagner's suspicion was erroneous and that his assumption had no real foundation in fact. What could have possibly induced the two, after the husband's death, to practise such dissimulation in intimate letters which were never intended for the eyes of outsiders ? No ! just these very letters prove clearly and irrefutably that the relations between Geyer and Johanna Wagner were pure and without stain and that Wagner's suspicion is untenable. Furthermore, one need only compare the striking facial resemblance between Richard and his brother Albert (who was fourteen years older) and between Richard and his uncle Adolph. As far as this point goes it can be said that all Johanna's children had the characteristic Wagner chin and nose which they inherited not from their father but their mother (which shows clearly in the familiar picture of her taken in her old age). Far more decisive is Richard's resemblance to his uncle Adolph, while there is no resemblance whatever to Ludwig Geyer.

The fact reported by Dr. Willi Schuh in the *Neue Züricher Zeitung* of 16th July 1933 that Johanna Wagner visited Geyer in Teplitz in July 1813 and took little Richard with her also offers no conclusive evidence for the Geyer Theory, as claimed by Newman. Geyer wrote Johanna on 6th June 1813 : " Since you usually take a trip every summer, do persuade your dear little husband (*das liebe Männchen*) to make an excursion to Teplitz— it would be really wonderful if you would give me this surprise. I am looking forward confidently to this joyous hour." Since Carl Friedrich was detained in Leipzig by his professional duties, why is it so astonishing that Johanna went to Teplitz alone and took the baby with her, whom Geyer had not yet seen ? To consider the Geyer question definitely settled beyond all further doubt by this *one* fact alone seems to me more than rash and premature. One must consider all the pros and cons of the case, and here it seems to me that at least 95 per cent. of the argument is against the so-called Geyer Theory. Even those who wish to maintain this theory for racial reasons must experience a severe disappointment, for according to minute official investigations it has been proved that Geyer's ancestors from the sixteenth century on were cantors or town musicians of the Protestant Faith. Therefore all phases of the Geyer Theory must be definitely abandoned as unsustainable. For Richard was unquestionably the true child of Carl Friedrich Wagner.

B. Hans von Buelow

It has long been a subject of controversy whether Hans von Buelow was aware of the true relation existing between Cosima and Wagner, or if not, when he actually discovered it. In this whole question the tragedy lay less in the shipwreck of a marriage than in the break-up of an old and devoted friendship. For the Buelow marriage, from the very beginning, was more a *mariage de raison* than a love match, and the erotic factor was probably always a secondary issue. Buelow's harsh judgment of the *man* Wagner later on did not spring from the fact that Wagner had taken Cosima away from him. This was a situation to which he soon accommodated himself emotionally and one for which he was ready to make any sacrifice in order to effect Cosima's wishes as unobtrusively as possible and obviate any public scandal. But his attitude towards Wagner was due solely to the betrayal of his friendship. It cut him to the quick that Wagner had consistently concealed the truth from him and abused his blind confidence. Then, when it came to full clarity between the three protagonists of the drama, and Buelow, just to save the situation for the *artist* Wagner (Wagner's relations with the King), let himself be persuaded into a course of action which, with his very strong sense of honour, almost passed the bounds of the possible, Wagner only thought selfishly of himself and sacrificed Buelow without a scruple.

Cosima's third daughter Isolde, who was born 10th April 1865 in Munich, was unquestionably Wagner's child. Exactly nine months previously (29th June 1864) Cosima arrived at Wagner's in Starnberg, while Buelow did not join her until 7th July. During this week intimacy had begun between Wagner and Cosima, and when Buelow arrived in a fairly critical physical

s

condition he suspected nothing and learned nothing of the actual situation. Personal details such as these do not concern the general public, but in this instance the individuals themselves dragged them into the public forum.

In May 1914 Isolde brought suit against her mother for recognition as Wagner's child so that she might receive her share of his legacy in terms of equality with his other two children, Eva and Siegfried. In my capacity as Wagner scholar I was summoned to serve at this trial. It was very disgraceful to see long-forgotten intimate family matters flaunted openly before the public. Isolde, who was referred to as Isolde von Buelow in all official papers, submitted documents deriving from Richard Wagner in which he declared her to be *his* child. She stated further that in the family circle and official Wagner literature (Glasenapp) she had always been recognized as Wagner's daughter. Cosima also did not deny this. She even issued a statement through her lawyer that in the period from 12th June to 12th October 1864 she had had sexual intercourse only with Wagner. The court, however, confronted this evidence with the deposition of Wagner's former housekeeper in Starnberg, Frau Anne Mrazek, to the effect that in the summer of 1864 in Starnberg, Buelow had occupied the same bedroom with his wife, which nullified Cosima's statement from a legal point of view. In addition Isolde (whom Buelow had publicly acknowledged as his child, even after he learned the truth about his wife and Wagner, and whom he also included in his will on an equal status with his two elder legitimate children, Daniela and Blandine) had come into her share of the inheritance as Buelow's daughter at the time of his death (1894). In this way she openly acknowledged herself to be Buelow's daughter, and therefore could not claim a share in Wagner's legacy as *his* daughter. Although no one questioned the fact that Isolde was really Wagner's child, the court rejected the case on legal grounds. The outbreak of the war and Isolde's death then fortunately prevented any further litigation.

Now when did Buelow learn the truth about the shipwreck of his marriage? At the time of Isolde's birth, at all events, he was ignorant of it and considered her *his* child. Wagner was her godfather! After the "Tristan" première Cosima went to Pest for

several weeks with her husband, and on 20th August 1865
Wagner wrote in the Brown Book : " Tell poor Hans quite
frankly that I can no longer live without you. This continual
coming and going—this coming and then having to go away
again. This placing yourself at the disposal of others is horrible !
May God give sight to the blind ! " It is thoroughly credible
that Buelow, who blindly trusted his wife and especially his
friend and Master, and who gladly let Cosima look after the
latter's womanless home, particularly as he himself was frequently
absent from Munich on concert tours, suspected nothing and
contemptuously ignored the malevolent gossip that was soon
rife in Munich. Even in 1868 King Ludwig himself still believed
in the complete innocence of this friendship, although even he
was not ignorant of the Munich gossip (owing to the numerous
denunciations he continuously received). Furthermore, he had
met Cosima at Wagner's in Triebschen on 22nd May 1866. Not
only Peter Cornelius's letter, in which he stated that Buelow
learned the truth through a letter which arrived for Cosima after
her departure for Triebschen, is conclusive evidence that Buelow
first learned the truth in May 1866, but Buelow's eldest daughter,
Daniela von Thode, expressly corroborated this fact to me, as
did also Buelow's second wife, Marie von Buelow, who must
have learned it from Buelow himself.

C. MALWINE VON SCHNORR

My version of the Schnorr episode corresponds exactly with
the pertinent documents which—supplemented still further in
the meantime by numerous others—are contained in the correspondence between Wagner and King Ludwig II (Vol. 5,
Supplement, pages 17-50). In his attack on my interpretation of
this incident, Ernest Newman (in his Wagner Biography,
Vol. 4, pages 15-16) bases his point of view on Garrigues's book,
Ein Ideales Saengerpaar (1937). This tendentious account has been
completely disproved by the aforesaid documents, which confirm
the correctness of *my* account of the episode in every particular.

INDEX